# The Crest of the Innovation Management Research Wave

Edited by

**Marcus Tynnhammar**
ISPIM, United Kingdom

Series in Innovation Studies

VERNON PRESS

www.vernonpress.com

*In the Americas:*
Vernon Press
1000 N West Street,
Suite 1200, Wilmington,
Delaware 19801
United States

*In the rest of the world:*
Vernon Press
C/Sancti Espiritu 17,
Malaga, 29006
Spain

Series in Innovation Studies

Library of Congress Control Number: 2019950933

ISBN: 978-1-62273-860-1

Cover design by Vernon Press. Cover image designed by starline/Freepik.

# Table of contents

# List of Figures

# List of Tables

# Preface

The ISPIM Dissertation Award was launched in 2011 to recognise the prolific contribution that PhD dissertations make to the field of Innovation Management each year. The 2019 ISPIM Dissertation Award casts its spotlight beyond the top three awardees to a much greater number of top submissions on a broad range of topics through this publication illustrating the crest of the wave in innovation management research. This is following on last years book catching different themes in research.

Due to catching a broader spectrum this year, the book is divided into chapters, and the chapters cover a wide variety of topics within Innovation Management. Research. The first chapters are, as a common trend within the field, on Open Innovation and collaboration. The following chapters cover both firm-level research and process research. Digitalization is still a strong topic in Innovation Management. As seen towards the end of the book, several chapters cover digitalization of the production system in the form of the fourth industrial revolution.

The ISPIM Dissertation Award is growing every year and manages to catch a wide variety of topics within and related to Innovation Management. There is a trend of several European based submissions, but every year we manage to get submissions from several continents. Everyone is then invited to our main conference, which was held in Florence in 2019, in Europe. The top three finalists have already been selected before the event, but the winner is not known until the conference takes place.

The publication provides both a showcase of what the latest generation of scholars are contributing to the innovation management body of knowledge as well as the insight into what they find significant and what might become important for the field as a whole over time. This year the book has a wider base and the selection made gives a good insight into the upcoming field and interesting empirical areas to research.

As soon as the previous year's award ends, a new process to find next year's finalists starts. If you have or know someone that has finished a PhD in Innovation Management in 2019, please submit for The ISPIM Dissertation Award 2020!

Chapter 1

# Knowing the Ropes in Open Innovation: Understanding Tensions through a Paradox Lens

Ioana Stefan

*KTH Royal Institute of Technology in Stockholm, Sweden*

**Abstract:** Open innovation processes may be challenged by tensions between co-creating and capturing value, often dubbed as paradox. Potential negative outcomes thereof, e.g. misappropriation of ideas, are still not fully avertable and may lead to lost jobs and hampered economic and technological growth. This chapter sets out to provide a deeper understanding of this phenomenon and related tensions. The chapter comprises five papers based on quantitative, qualitative and conceptual studies. The findings reveal: (1) characteristics of tensions, (2) factors that create tensions and (3) possible solutions and pitfalls to managing said tensions. Key findings also relate to dual-role factors that lead to either pitfalls or solutions, depending on their intensity. The findings contribute to theory on open innovation, appropriability and organizational paradox, and have important implications for practitioners and policy makers.

**Keywords:** paradox theory; paradox lens; tensions; value co-creation; value capture; openness; appropriability; virtuous cycles; vicious cycles; misappropriation.

## 1.1. Introduction

It is increasingly difficult for companies to innovate in isolation, and one way to solve this problem is to open up the innovation process. Open innovation (OI) has many benefits, such as sharing costs and risks with external partners in innovation. Yet there are also challenges, some of which remain unresolved. One such challenge relates to the tensions that emerge between co-creating and capturing value in OI settings (Laursen and Salter, 2014). Such tensions were initially highlighted by Nobel Prize laureate Kenneth Arrow through a "fundamental paradox" (Arrow, 1962, p.615). One of the most severe negative effects of such tensions is misappropriation of intellectual property (IP) and failure to appropriate rents. Smaller firms are more often victims of such issues, as can be observed in the case of misappropriation in the collaboration between a start-up and a large digital library (Lohr, 2010).

Indeed, smaller, young companies often struggle with limited resources and have low bargaining power in the face of partners that are large, established firms (Hallen et al., 2014). Yet it is not only smaller companies that are challenged by risks of misappropriation when opening up the innovation process. At a European Commission conference (EC, 2012), delegates of several large multinational companies, including Alstom, DuPont and Michelin, disclosed their own experience of various cases in which proprietary trade secrets had been misappropriated by partners. The delegates also highlighted possible consequences of misappropriation: lost jobs (a company whose IP has been misappropriated may, for instance, struggle to continue employing all its staff), diminished revenues (not profiting enough or at all from the co-created IP reduces profits), and overall shrinking innovation and economic growth (EC, 2012). Issues related to misappropriation of IP or risks thereof also raise questions concerning ethics and fairness in practice. It is thus crucial to understand how such tensions emerge between partners in OI and how they can be managed effectively or alleviated, so that negative effects in the form of misappropriation may be avoided. Nevertheless, neither researchers nor practitioners or policy makers have clear answers concerning these challenges.

In research, this "fundamental paradox" (Arrow, 1962, p.615) has been widely investigated, yet evidence is dispersed across various fields of study and under different labels. This scattering generates a rather fuzzy understanding of the paradox. Moreover, a comprehensive and in-depth grasp of the inner workings of this paradox is still missing in extant research. Recent studies point out that contemporary settings in which innovation processes tend to be more open pose increasingly complex challenges to participating stakeholders (Laursen and Salter, 2014) and that tensions between co-creating and capturing value have not yet been reconciled (Lorenz and Veer, 2019).

One way to gain a deeper understanding of this intricate phenomenon would be to apply a lens that might capture its complexities. Organizational management theorists propose the use of paradox as a lens to investigate complex phenomena (e.g. Schad et al., 2016). Researchers often value 'good' theories that are focused and narrow, yet this may also lead to a failure to completely grasp more intricate phenomena. A possible solution would be to apply a paradox lens to such phenomena (Poole and Van de Ven, 1989; Schad et al., 2016; Smith and Lewis, 2011). Therefore, this chapter also employs a paradox lens to investigate tensions between value co-creation and value capture in the context of OI.

The overall purpose of this chapter is to gain a deeper understanding of tensions between value co-creation and value capture by (1) delineating the nature of tensions, (2) pinpointing factors that create tensions, (3) identifying potential solutions and pitfalls to managing such tensions. The purpose is further specified in the following research questions:

*Q1: What characterizes the tensions between co-creating and capturing value?*

*Q2: What factors create tensions between value co-creation and value capture?*

*Q3: What are possible solutions and pitfalls to managing tensions between value co-creation and value capture?*

The purpose is achieved by combining five studies, labeled P1 to P5.

## 1.2. Background

In order to explain the theoretical background of this chapter, first, the paradox lens is presented, by introducing paradox theory. Second, the overlapping yet slightly nuanced perspectives on tensions that are used in the five studies are highlighted in the following subsection.

### Organizational paradox

Paradox in organizational studies points out contradictory yet interrelated elements that require simultaneous balance (Lewis, 2000; Schad et al., 2016; Smith and Lewis, 2011). Paradox theory emerged as a part of organizational management studies some three decades ago (Schad et al., 2016). Using paradox as a lens has been deemed helpful in understanding complex phenomena (Poole and Van de Ven, 1989; Schad et al., 2016). Tensions often arise between interdependent and contradictory elements. A recent definition of tensions, suggested by Putnam et al. (2016), proposes that tensions are:

> "Stress, anxiety, discomfort, or tightness in making choices, responding to, and moving forward in organizational situations." (p. 68)

This definition of tensions is adopted in this chapter and appended papers. Contradictory yet interlinked elements are usually illustrated in paradox theory by *pairs of poles*. According to Smith and Lewis (2011), tensions between poles may remain in a latent or dormant state, not being experienced by actors.

However, specific factors may trigger tensions to become salient—at this stage, actors perceive the tensions (Smith and Lewis, 2011). Such factors that create salient tensions are contextual and could be classified into the main categories of plurality, scarcity, change and increased globalization and competition (Smith and Lewis, 2011).

When tensions between pairs of poles are managed in practice, it sometimes appears simpler to 'choose' (or favor) one of the poles instead of attempting to balance both at the same time (Smith and Lewis, 2011; also see Lüscher and Lewis, 2008). If one pole is favored, Smith and Lewis (2011) point to an imbalance where so-called *vicious cycles* could emerge. However, if the poles are successfully balanced, *virtuous cycles* would appear (Smith and Lewis, 2011). In their study, Smith and Lewis (2011) propose a dynamic equilibrium model for paradoxical tensions: this model depicts the aforementioned contextual factors that turn latent tensions into salient ones, and also the potential virtuous and vicious cycles that may emerge as the act of balancing the paradox poles succeeds or fails, respectively. This model is used in the present chapter to inspire a framework with the main poles value co-creation and value capture. The model by Smith and Lewis (2011) is further employed as a way to structure the chapter purpose and research questions. The chapter framework is shown below in Figure 1.1.

**Figure 1.1**: Analysis model.

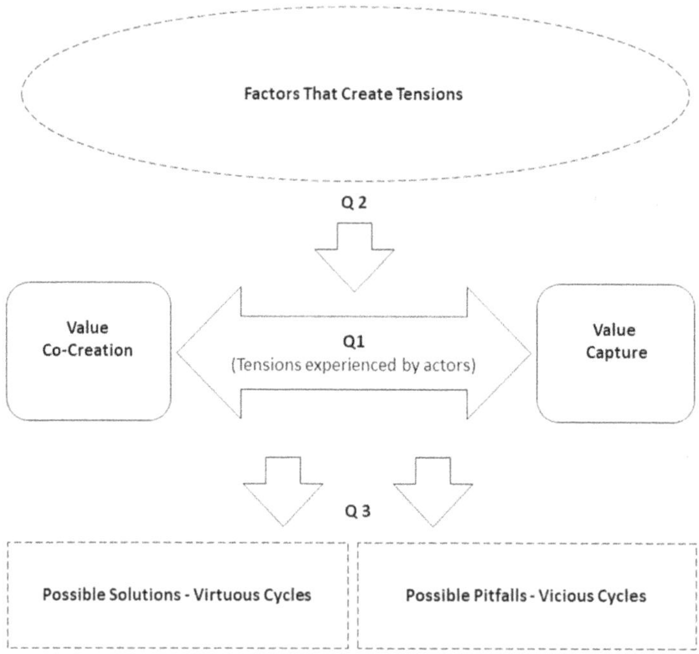

## Different perspectives on tensions

In 1962 Kenneth Arrow suggested a paradox that occurs when a seller wishes to commercialize an invention to a potential buyer. In the nearly six decades following Arrow's (1962) seminal study, numerous streams of literature in different fields of study have investigated this paradox of disclosure from slightly distinct perspectives. During this time, innovation management has evolved and several new trends have emerged, one of these being open innovation (Frishammar et al., 2019). Such trends as open innovation add a series of mechanisms and possibilities that are crucial for an improved understanding of innovation and innovation management, particularly in manufacturing firms (Frishammar et al., 2019). Specifically, the trend to open up the innovation process highlights risks of unintended knowledge spillovers (Frishammar et al., 2015; 2019).

The tensions related to the paradox of disclosure are not clearly defined in extant research, and the sources of such tensions may vary. For instance, some scholars suggest that conflicting mechanisms and strategies may be required for value co-creation and value capture. Khalid and Larimo (2012) emphasize that value creation relates to sharing mechanisms, while Veer et al. (2016) suggest that value capture demands appropriation mechanisms. Furthermore, it may be required that limited resources be distributed between value co-creation and value capture (Capaldo and Petruzzelli, 2011; Mizik and Jacobson, 2003). Another source of tensions could be that value co-creation and appropriation might happen at different levels: value co-creation may at times happen at an interorganizational level, whereas value capture happens at the organizational level (Capaldo and Petruzzelli, 2011; Ritala et al., 2013). A further example of a source for tensions could be the sharing of resources between partners in an interorganizational innovation collaboration: appropriating value entails only dividing those resources that are pooled between partners, yet there are risks that nonpooled resources may be drawn in as well (Lavie, 2006). These examples of tensions between creating and capturing value could overlap, making it difficult to distinguish between them or to categorize them.

Moreover, prior studies take slightly different perspectives on this paradox. Examples of such perspectives include tensions between: co-creating and capturing value (Lavie, 2006; Capaldo and Petruzelli, 2011; Laursen and Salter, 2014), appropriability and openness (Laursen and Salter, 2014), disclosure and appropriation (e.g. Gans et al., 2017), and more. These dyads represent somewhat different yet partly overlapping viewpoints on this paradox. For instance, Laursen and Salter (2014) investigate tensions between value creation and capture yet do so by analyzing constructs of openness and appropriability.

The studies in this chapter combine the three above-mentioned perspectives on tensions, with the value co-creation/capture perspective being the overarching of the three.

## 1.3. Research design

This dissertation builds on five studies, which employ qualitative, quantitative and conceptual methods. The five studies include: three empirical studies, one systematic literature review and one discussion paper. The quantitative studies uncovered certain patterns that were unexpected or difficult to explain. Therefore, the remaining three studies employ qualitative and conceptual methods, thus allowing a deeper understanding of the investigated tensions. Figure 1.2 shows the five studies' methods and perspectives on tensions. In the following, the key methodological aspects and findings of the five studies are summarized.

Studies P1 and P2 use quantitative methods and are based on an Open Innovation Survey of 415 manufacturing firms from three European countries: Finland, Italy and Sweden. These two studies take the appropriability-openness perspective on tensions between co-creating and capturing value.

**Figure 1.2**: Studies included in the doctoral thesis.

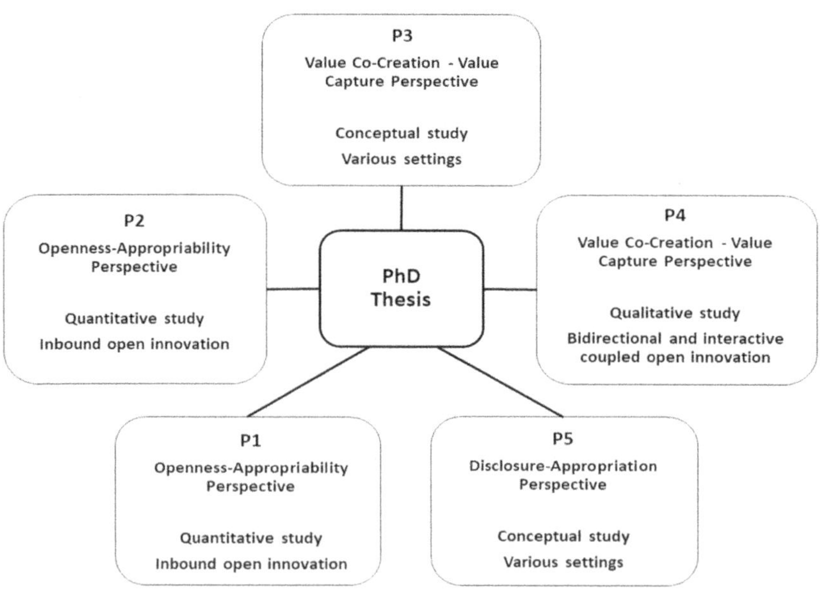


The first study, P1, analyzed the moderating effects of partner location (national or international) on the relationship between appropriability and openness. Due to high costs and the territorial nature of formal appropriability mechanisms (e.g. patents), some negative effects of such mechanisms on openness were expected, particularly in international collaborations. However, the regression output did not yield significant negative effects. A persistent pattern in the results of P1 is that firms collaborating mainly with international partners tend to rely on formal appropriability mechanisms, while companies working mainly with local partners are more prone to using informal mechanisms – regardless the type of partner.

The second study, P2, used multiple linear regression to investigate the effects of appropriability and openness on performance across different stages of the innovation process. For this study, the survey was complemented with patent data. Among the difficult-to-explain patterns in the results are the contrasting effects of formal (negative) and contractual (positive) mechanisms on performance in early innovation phases.

The third study, P3, is a systematic literature review that provides a synthesis of factors affecting tensions between value co-creation and value capture. This study reviews 143 articles and follows the three stages for conducting a systematic literature review suggested by Watson et al. (2018): Searching, Screening, and Extraction/Synthesis. P3 uses the dynamic equilibrium model by Smith and Lewis (2011) to structure the results of the reviewed articles. The findings reveal three categories of factors in accordance with the model by Smith and Lewis (2011), i.e. factors that create tensions, factors that lead to virtuous cycles and factors that spur vicious cycles. A fourth category of dual-role factors, which may lead to either virtuous or vicious cycles, depending on factors' intensity, further emerges from the literature review.

The fourth study, P4, also takes a value co-creation/capture perspective but this time linked with a qualitative approach. P4 combines a case study design with a grounded theory analysis and includes data from six case companies and seven expert informants – a total of 21 informants based in EU countries and the USA. Results identify configurations of factors that create tensions in bidirectional coupled or interactive coupled OI processes, as well as possible solutions and pitfalls to managing such tensions. Furthermore, P4 pinpoints several recurring challenges, even after initial solutions to alleviate tensions are enforced.

The fifth study, P5, is conceptual in nature and focuses on formulating propositions concerning the contradictory and interdependent nature of disclosing knowledge and appropriating value in OI. The propositions also address the potentially dilemmatic, dialectical or paradoxical nature of such tensions. Key contingency factors are linked to the extent of reliance on external resources, to the nature and modularity of knowledge to be revealed about a new product, process or service, and to the availability and strength of appropriability mechanisms.

## 1.4. Conclusion

This chapter set out to investigate the paradox of disclosure proposed by Arrow (1962), thereby gaining a deeper understanding of this intricate phenomenon and related tensions in OI settings. This is achieved by applying a paradox theory lens. Three perspectives on the tensions surrounding this paradox are included in this analysis. While the overarching perspective is that of tensions between value co-creation and value capture, two other perspectives are investigated, namely those of appropriability-openness and disclosure-appropriation. In order to improve the understanding of said tensions, this chapter pinpoints (1) characteristics of tensions, (2) factors that create tensions and (3) possible solutions and pitfalls to managing such tensions. Figure 1.3 represents the enhanced analysis model of this chapter and illustrates some examples of the key findings. Such examples are also highlighted below.

First, the characteristics of value co-creation/capture tensions depend greatly on the degree of interrelatedness and contradiction between these two poles of the paradox. Particularly crucial features are the dependence on external resources versus the availability of internal resources required to develop an invention, the overlap between the innovation solution and its characteristics—further contingent on the degree of knowledge codification (O'Dwyer and O'Flynn, 2005)—and the availability of appropriability mechanisms.

Second, the factors that create tensions can be classified in terms of plurality, scarcity, change and a fourth category of compound factors. Plurality factors include unaligned or conflicting goals between innovation partners (Kasch and Dowling, 2008). Scarcity factors emphasize a lack of resources, e.g. awareness about intellectual property protection issues (Rayna and Striukova, 2010). Change factors are linked to the unclear delineation between types of knowledge (Oxley and Sampson, 2004). Compound factors concern, for instance, combinations of unaligned, conflicting goals and technological change, such as radical innovation in coopetition (Ritala and Hurmelinna-Laukkanen, 2009); compound factors may further include, e.g. collaborating with partners such as suppliers in earlier innovation phases.

Third, potential solutions and pitfalls to alleviate value co-creation/capture tensions mirror the virtuous and vicious cycles suggested by Smith and Lewis (2011). Uneven emphasis on one of the two paradox poles—e.g. excessive external search (Laursen and Salter, 2006)—might induce vicious cycles. Further examples of factors that might lead to vicious cycles include high-intensity trust, or uncertainty about IP in early innovation phases. Achieving a balance between the two paradox poles results in virtuous cycles. For example, balancing the amount of knowledge disclosed with that of knowledge that is kept within organizational boundaries, also called selective revealing (see Henkel, 2006), would lead to virtuous cycles. Further examples encompass the use of contracts, or raising staff IP awareness.

**Figure 1.3:** Analysis model including examples of key results.

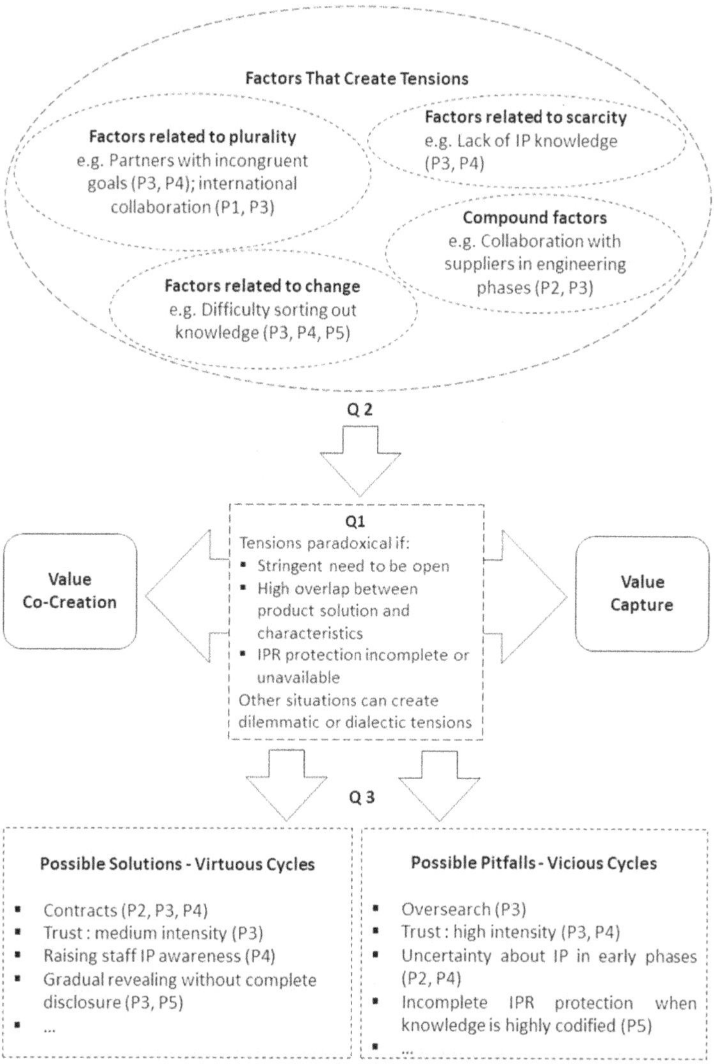

Additionally, in terms of solutions and pitfalls, this chapter highlights a new category of factors with a dual role. These factors could generate vicious or virtuous cycles, depending on their intensity. Examples of dual-role factors include appropriability mechanisms such as patents (Dosi et al., 2006) or the notion of time (Miranda and Kavan, 2005).

In essence, this chapter advances the understanding and reconciliation of value co-creation/capture tensions, thereby addressing recent studies' calls for further research (Laursen and Salter, 2014; Lorenz and Veer, 2019) and tackling compelling managerial challenges (Lohr, 2010; EC, 2012). Theoretical and practical implications of the chapter findings and future research avenues are presented in the following.

## 5. Implications and future research

### Theoretical implications

By employing a paradox lens, this chapter synthesizes factors that create tensions between value co-creation and value capture in OI and highlights possible solutions and pitfalls to managing said tensions. Moreover, this chapter contributes with an in-depth discussion on the nature of such tensions, drawing on paradox theory. By combining OI theory with a paradox theory lens, this dissertation thus bridges the fields of innovation and organizational management and has theoretical implications pertaining to both.

A first theoretical implication for innovation management, specifically OI theory, is the need for improved constructs of openness and appropriability. In terms of openness, findings show that tensions with specific types of innovation partners are also contingent upon other contextual factors. This implies that well-established openness dimensions such as depth of collaboration may require further fine-tuning. The findings also indicate that there may be a disclosure dimension of openness, in line with recent studies, e.g. Foege et al. (2019). Thus, future openness constructs might include details about the nature and amount of knowledge revealed to partners and explore the potential dichotomy (in terms of revealing) between a product's solution and its characteristics. For appropriability, future studies could benefit from using more fine-grained constructs that include items such as awareness of employees about IP protection and disclosure, or specifics on the characteristics of contractual agreements, e.g. complexity and length. Such characteristics emerge as obstacles to co-creating and capturing value in innovation collaboration and therefore require increased attention in future research. These suggestions to expand appropriability constructs build on previous studies, e.g. Hurmelinna-Laukkanen (2011).

Another implication also concerning the OI field of study is that tensions unfold in inbound and outbound OI—as was shown in previous studies—as well as in bidirectional and interactive coupled OI. This implies that future investigations of such tensions could go beyond unidirectional perspectives, i.e. inbound versus outbound.

A distinctive contribution related to organizational management, particularly to paradox theory, is the uncovering of a novel category of factors with dual roles, factors that lead to either solutions or to pitfalls, depending on their intensity. While this category is highly relevant in the context of studying tensions between value co-creation and value capture, it is yet unclear whether it might also apply to a more general dynamic equilibrium model (Smith and Lewis, 2011) that could be employed in studying other types of tensions. Whichever the case may be, for the specific context of value co-creation/capture tensions, this category of dual-role factors is valid and likely to increase the intricacy of this paradox.

Another theoretical implication related to paradox theory concerns the concept of *time*. Based on the findings of this chapter, time may have less of a role in delineating paradox in general and more of a role in determining how paradoxical tensions are managed. This implication resonates with earlier studies that proposed temporal separation as a way to work with paradox (Poole and Van de Ven, 1989).

### Practical implications

One practical implication that concerns both policy makers and practitioners relates to reduced awareness about IP protection and disclosure. This lack of awareness concerns smaller and larger firms alike. To tackle this challenge, policy makers and organizations might consider organizing and/or participating in IP workshops and similar events. These would raise awareness about IP protection and disclosure and thus aid in managing tensions in OI.

Another managerial implication is that evaluating partners' reputation prior to collaboration, or involving neutral partners such as OI intermediaries could be beneficial in alleviating tensions. This would provide an initial perspective on the likelihood of opportunistic behavior exhibited by potential future partners in OI collaboration.

Since tensions between co-creating and capturing value are complex and require specialized skills, managers might consider creating cross-functional teams designated to deal with OI partnerships, instead of relying on individual departments to handle such collaborations. Such cross-functional teams would ideally combine knowledge of IP management and IP protection (legal issues) as well as specific technological and purchasing skills and competences.

Moreover, managers need to be particularly aware of time-sensitive OI projects. The time pressure in such projects, combined with the usual uncertainty about IP outcomes in innovation collaboration, or with uncertainty about IP novelty, could lead to failure in protecting said IP in due time. Consequently, it would be difficult if not impossible to profit from the newly co-created IP.

A further managerial implication is that despite the need for caution and pre-evaluation of partners (see the above example of checking partner reputation), fear of misappropriation might also hamper successful OI collaboration for all stakeholders involved. In order to overcome this hurdle, managers are advised to increase transparency such as by simplifying complex contractual agreements, while also clearly delineating between information that should be disclosed and information that should remain within organizational boundaries.

Finally, a managerial and policy-related implication of this chapter pertains to the high costs and resources, as well as the long time required for enforcing formal IP protection. A question that arises, particularly for policy makers, is, therefore: How might firms with limited resources protect their IP while revealing it in OI, in the context of costly formal IP procedures that take a long time to enforce? This is especially challenging when the knowledge embedded in an invention is highly codified. In such scenarios, it may also be difficult to enforce other, more strategic appropriability mechanisms such as secrecy or gradual/selective revealing.

## Limitations and future research

This chapter is not without limitations, yet such limitations open up avenues for further research. One limitation concerns the focus on interorganizational innovation collaboration, which restricts the analysis at the collective level (Smith and Lewis, 2011). Future research might benefit from investigating similar tensions at micro or individual level, as it would be of value to gain a better understanding of how managers personally perceive and cope with tensions to co-create and capture value.

Another limitation is, for instance, that the propositions suggested in the fifth study have not been tested empirically. These propositions relate to, e.g. the extent of overlap between a new invention's solution and its characteristics, or to the availability and territorial nature of formal appropriability mechanisms. As such, the contingencies suggested in these propositions could unravel new implications for disclosing and protecting IP in OI.

While this chapter investigated the distinction between the dilemmatic, dialectical and paradoxical nature of tensions, as per paradox theory (Smith and Lewis, 2011), the delineations of value co-creation/capture tensions according to these categories is still not fully understood. Therefore, future research applying a paradox lens would benefit from further clarifying the distinctions between dilemmatic, dialectical and paradoxical types of tensions related to the paradox of disclosure in OI.

Finally, this chapter focused on salient tensions to co-create and capture value, i.e. tensions that are experienced by actors. In order to further improve the grasp on said tensions, future studies could benefit from investigating their latent nature. While latent tensions would be more difficult to study and measure, as they are not perceived by actors, advancing our understanding about latent value co-creation/capture tensions might illuminate the very roots of the paradox of disclosure.

## References

Arrow, K. (1962), "Economic welfare and the allocation of resources for invention", in H.M. Groves (Ed.), *The Rate and Direction of Inventive Activity: Economic and Social Factors,* Princeton University Press, Princeton, NJ, pp. 609-626.

Capaldo, A. and Petruzzelli, A.M. (2011), "In search of alliance-level relational capabilities: Balancing innovation value creation and appropriability in R&D alliances", *Scandinavian Journal of Management,* Vol. 27 No. 3, pp. 273-286.

Dosi, G., Marengo, L. and Pasquali, C. (2006), "How much should society fuel the greed of innovators?: On the relations between appropriability, opportunities and rates of innovation", *Research Policy,* Vol. 35, pp. 1110-1121.

European Commission (EC) (2012). *Trade secrets: Supporting innovation, protecting know-how* [online]. https://ec.europa.eu/docsroom/documents/14902/attachments/2/translations/en/renditions/pdf_(Accessed 9 May 2019).

Foege, J. N., Lauritzen, G. D., Tietze, F., and Salge, T. O. (2019), "Reconceptualizing the paradox of openness: How solvers navigate sharing-protecting tensions in crowdsourcing", *Research Policy,* Vol. 48 No. 6, pp. 1323-1339.

Frishammar, J., Ericsson, K. and Patel, P.C. (2015), "The dark side of knowledge transfer: Exploring knowledge leakage in joint R&D projects", *Technovation,* Vol. 41, pp. 75-88.

Frishammar, J., Richtnér, A., Brattström, A., Magnusson, M. and Björk, J. (2019), "Opportunities and challenges in the new innovation landscape: Implications for innovation auditing and innovation management", *European Management Journal*, Vol. 37 No. 2, pp. 151-164.

Gans, J.S., Murray, F.E. and Stern, S. (2017), "Contracting over the disclosure of scientific knowledge: Intellectual property and academic publication", *Research Policy*, Vol. 46 No. 4, pp. 820-835.

Hallen, B., Katila, R. and Rosenberger, J. (2014), "How do social defenses work? A resource-dependence lens on technology ventures, venture capital investors, and corporate relations", *Academy of Management Journal*, Vol. *75*, pp. 1078-1101.

Henkel, J. (2006), "Selective revealing in open innovation processes: The case of embedded Linux", *Research Policy*, Vol. 35 No. 7, pp. 953-969.

Hurmelinna-Laukkanen, P. (2011), "Enabling collaborative innovation–knowledge protection for knowledge sharing", *European Journal of Innovation Management*, Vol. 14 No. 3, pp. 303-321.

Kasch, S. and Dowling, M. (2008), "Commercialization strategies of young biotechnology firms: An empirical analysis of the US industry", *Research Policy*, Vol. 37 No. 10, pp. 1765-1777.

Khalid, S. and Larimo, J. (2012), "Affects of alliance entrepreneurship on common vision, alliance capability and alliance performance", *International Business Review*, Vol. 21 No. 5, pp. 891-905.

Laursen, K. and Salter, A. (2006), "Open for innovation: The role of openness in explaining innovation performance among UK manufacturing firms", *Strategic Management Journal*, Vol. 27 No. 2, pp. 131–150.

Laursen, K. and Salter, A.J. (2014) "The paradox of openness: Appropriability, external search and collaboration", *Research Policy*, Vol. 43 No. 5, pp. 867-878.

Lavie, D. (2006), "The competitive advantage of interconnected firms: An extension of the resource-based view", *Academy of Management Review*, Vol. 31 No. 3, pp. 638-658.

Lewis, M.W. (2000), "Exploring paradox: Toward a more comprehensive guide", *Academy of Management Review*, Vol. 25No. 4, pp. 760-776.

Lohr, S. (2010, July 18), "In a partnership of unequals, a start-up suffers", *The New York Times*, https://www.nytimes.com/2010/07/19/technology/19startup.html (Accessed 9 May 2019).

Lorenz, A. and Veer, T. (2019), "Once bitten, less shy? The influence of prior misappropriation experience on R&D collaboration", *Industry and Innovation*, Vol. 26 No. 1, pp. 31-56.

Lüscher, L.S. and Lewis, M.W. (2008), "Organizational change and managerial sensemaking: Working through paradox", *Academy of Management Journal*, 51(2), 221-240.

Miranda, S.M. and Kavan, C.B. (2005), "Moments of governance in IS outsourcing: Conceptualizing effects of contracts on value capture and creation", *Journal of Information Technology*, Vol. 20, pp. 152-169.

Mizik, N. and Jacobson, R. (2003), "Trading off between value creation and value appropriation: The financial implications of shifts in strategic emphasis", *Journal of Marketing*, Vol. 67, pp. 63-76.

O'Dwyer, M. and O'Flynn, E. (2005), "MNC–SME strategic alliances—A model framing knowledge value as the primary predictor of governance modal choice", *Journal of International Management*, Vol. 11, pp. 397-416.

Oxley, J.E. and Sampson, R.C. 2004. "The scope and governance of international R&D alliances", *Strategic Management Journal*, Vol. 25, pp. 723-749.

Poole, M.S. and Van de Ven, A.H. (1989), "Using paradox to build management and organization theories", *Academy of Management Review*, Vol. 14 No. 4, pp. 562-578.

Putnam, L.L., Fairhurst, G.T. and Banghart, S. (2016), "Contradictions, dialectics, and paradoxes in organizations: A constitutive approach", *Academy of Management Annals*, Vol. 10 No. 1, pp. 65-171.

Rayna, T. and Striukova, L. (2010). "Large-scale open innovation: Open source vs. patent pools". *International Journal of Technology Management*, Vol. 52, pp. 477-496.

Ritala, P., Agouridas, V., Assimakopoulos, D. and Gies, O. (2013), "Value creation and capture mechanisms in innovation ecosystems: A comparative case study", *International Journal of Technology Management*, Vol. 63 Nos. 3-4, pp. 244-267.

Ritala, P. and Hurmelinna-Laukkanen, P. (2009), "What's in it for me? Creating and appropriating value in innovation-related coopetition", *Technovation*, Vol. 29, pp. 819-828.

Schad, J., Lewis, M.W., Raisch, S. and Smith, W.K. (2016), "Paradox research in management science: Looking back to move forward", *Academy of Management Annals*, Vol. 10 No. 1, pp. 5-64.

Smith, W.K. and Lewis, M.W. (2011), "Toward a theory of paradox: A dynamic equilibrium model of organizing", *Academy of Management Review*, Vol. 36 No. 2, pp. 381-403.

Veer, T., Lorenz, A. and Blind, K. (2016), "How open is too open? The mitigating role of appropriation mechanisms in R&D cooperation settings", *R&D Management*, Vol. 46 No. S3, pp. 1113-1128.

Watson, R., Wilson, H.N., Smart, P. and Macdonald, E.K. (2018), "Harnessing difference: A capability-based framework for stakeholder engagement in environmental innovation", *Journal of Product Innovation Management*, Vol. 35 No. 2, pp. 254-279.

Chapter 2

# Managing Collaborative R&D Projects with Different Types of Knowledge Sources

Ana Paula F. Paes Leme Barbosa

*University of São Paulo, Brazil*

**Abstract:** Based on the idea that "one size does not fit all", the thesis related to this chapter explored contingencies on managing collaborative R&D projects with external sources. The external knowledge-source type is the contingency analyzed, specifically regarding science-based sources and market-based ones. Based on data from a survey with R&D managers, 53 R&D projects from multinational companies were analyzed. This study explored how project management success factors are related to project performance in projects in collaboration with market-based sources in comparison to projects with science-based ones. To optimize performance, the findings suggest that in projects developed with science-based sources, informal communication might be encouraged while higher formality, both related to communication and monitoring project progress, was positively associated to projects with market-based sources. The study also suggests that the type of performance measurement considered can be a source of divergent performance results in collaborative innovation projects.

**Keywords:** Project management; open innovation; technology collaboration; research and development; science-based sources; external knowledge-sources; partner dissimilarities; project level.

## 2.1. Introduction

Companies have been using R&D collaboration with external partners to leverage their innovation results (Hagedoorn, 2002). Through collaboration, they have access to new and complementary knowledge and technologies that are distributed over different actors (Chesbrough, 2003), such as universities, suppliers, competitors and consumers. However, what could be a great solution for efficiency and competitive gains is not that easy to achieve as the collaboration - which is generally associated to high uncertainty and risks, individually oriented projects, heterogeneous partners - can add more complexity to project management. This challenge makes us wonder how project management could be improved in this context of collaborative R&D projects.

Literature has advanced in understanding how to improve collaborative project management (vom Brocke and Lippe, 2015), providing evidence that the "one size does not fit all" approach should also be considered within the collaborative project's domain. Partner heterogeneity is a common concern identified in several prior studies in this contingent setting. For example, the literature suggests that success factors in project management are not the same for different knowledge sources involved in the project (Mora-Valentin et al., 2004). Also, projects developed with science-based knowledge sources, such as universities, in comparison with projects developed with market-based knowledge sources, such as suppliers, would be differently affected by the level of formality during project execution (Du et al., 2014). The assumption behind grouping the knowledge sources into Science-based (universities, research institutes) and Market-based (suppliers, competitors) types lies in the evidence of fundamental organizational dissimilarities between diverse types of knowledge sources, more specifically between university and industry (Bjerregaard, 2010; Estrada et al., 2016).

In addition, whereas prior research has identified management success factors for collaborative projects and advanced in discussing a contingent view for managing such projects, the literature does not yet provide an evaluation of the success based on the performance of the projects and the practices used in setting up and executing these projects. Moreover, most of the studies in collaborative setting use performance measures that are not directly related to R&D project performance, such as financial performance that is influenced by other functions, for example, marketing and sales.

Looking for an improvement in project management execution in collaborative projects, this research addresses not only the identification of practices that foster performance in collaborative R&D projects, but also the comparison of these practices by types of knowledge (science-based or market-based partners). The following research question guided this study:

*Do project management success factors differ in collaborative R&D projects, depending on the knowledge source involved in the project?*

Besides adding more fine-grained knowledge to the Project Management literature (and more specific collaborative R&D project management), this study has a very practical implication in helping to identify project management success factors which are suitable for each type of knowledge source and consequently, to improve collaborative project performance.

## 2.2. Background

The R&D Collaboration field has been studied through different lenses, the most connected to it being the following ones: (i) Product Development literature, (ii)

Strategic Alliance, (iii) Knowledge based-view, (iv) Network Theory, with increasing attention given to this last area and to (v) Open Innovation. This is a result of a co-citation analysis using software VOS (van Eck et al., 2010), applied to 577 papers in the R&D Collaboration topic in Business and Management in the Web of Science database considering a 10 year period (2006 – 2016) for the initial exploration of the field. The network resulting from the VOS software is provided in Figure 2.1.

**Figure 2.1**: Co-citation map from 10 years of *Collaboration* + *R&D* research.

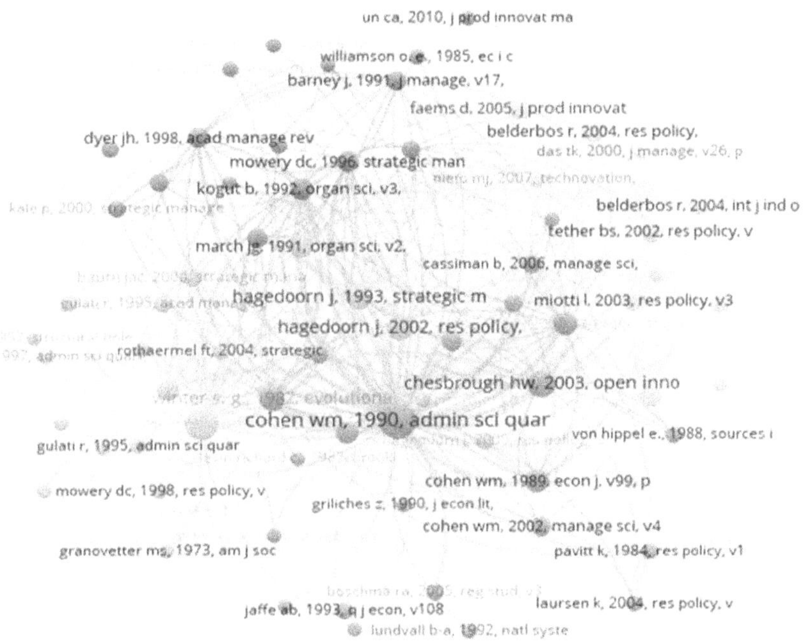


Another representation of the network map was created considering keyword co-occurrence without limiting a specific time period, as demonstrated in Figure 2.2.

Figure 2.2 demonstrates that 'performance' has central participation in studies related to R&D collaboration and articulated with 'knowledge'. It integrates several themes, especially with Product Development literature, Strategic Alliance literature, and Network Theory.

**Figure 2.2:** Co-occurrence network based on All Key works (VOS).

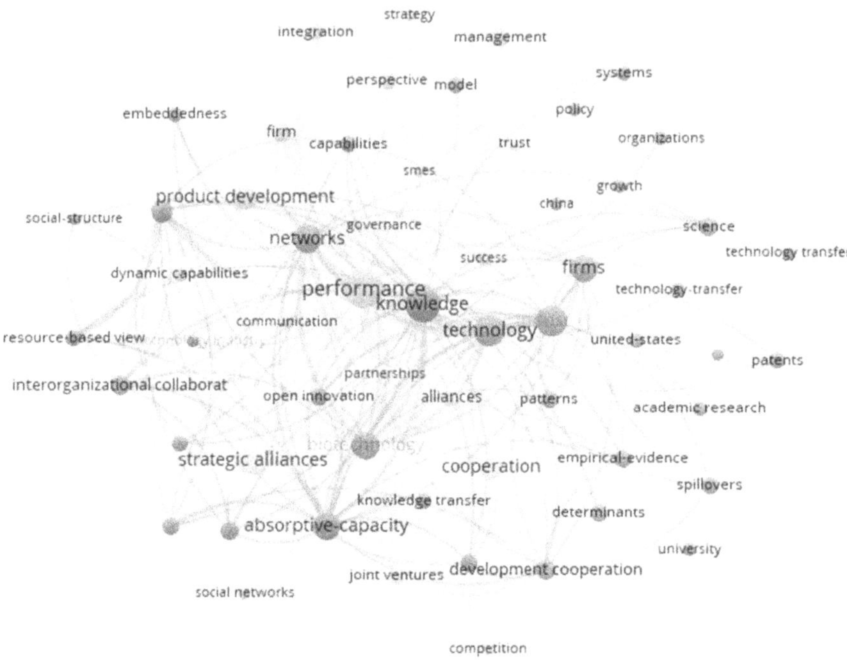


Reviewing the abstracts of these data, there was also noticed the emergence of papers concerned with the heterogeneity of partners issued in more recent publications, which reinforced the perception that this theme has recently been receiving more attention. Moreover, there was a realization that the Project management literature does not have a strong relationship with R&D Collaboration studies, which was understood as an opportunity to bring a consolidated research stream to contribute to solving challenges in R&D Collaboration.

## 2.1 Project Management in collaborative R&D projects

The literature recognizes that collaborative R&D projects with external partners face many challenges that a general project management approach does not support (Du et al., 2014; Kim and Lee, 2003; Lippe and vom Brocke, 2016; vom Brocke and Lippe, 2015) such as coordinating divergent management styles (Littler et al., 1995; vom Brocke and Lippe, 2015); aligning the budgeting process of collaborating firms (Littler et al., 1995), managing heterogeneity and dissimilarities between the parties (Barnes et al., 2006, 2002; Estrada et al., 2016; vom Brocke and Lippe, 2015), identifying and enhancing the integration of complementary aims and complementary expertise, being aware and dealing with any hidden agenda and continuity of personnel, enhancing commitment and trust between partners and maintaining corporate stability (Barnes et al., 2006, 2002), coordinating multiple and contradictory stakeholder expectations and defining the role and skill set of the project manager to be able to manage this complex setting (Mailhot et al., 2016; Ruuska and Teigland, 2009; vom Brocke and Lippe, 2015).

In general, to face the specific characteristics of collaborative projects, literature has been adapting general project management practices for the collaborative setting. For example, the traditional approach to project management states that an individual project is part of a broader strategy and direction of the organization and though, at the front end of a project, the firm needs a process to connect it to a company`s overall strategy, such as through the establishment of clear, measurable goals that can guide development and ensure the project's contribution to overall development objectives (Clark and Wheelwright, 1993, p. 2183). In the collaborative context, the same idea is applied, but in this case, the project might also be aligned to each partner objectives and strategies, which can be heterogeneous or even have hidden agendas, and so adaptation to the management system is needed. For example, to avoid organizational differences impairing coordination problems, the literature suggests that parties should devote themselves to planning activities more than they do for internal projects (Morandi, 2013).

Whilst most studies in collaborative R&D project management focus on planning activities to guarantee a shared vision, other dimensions are also being explored. The leadership, for example, has an important role in adding flexibility in terms of promoting adjustments in the project to different worldviews, facilitating communication (Mailhot et al., 2016) and solving critical innovation problems related to recombination across boundaries (Davis and Eisenhardt, 2011). Several other elements in project management are also being discussed, such as how to have effective communication in this setting (Smith, 2016), which is the level of formality to monitor the process (Du et al., 2014) and others. A good practice model developed by Barnes, Pashby and Gibbons (2006) for managing collaborative R&D projects summarizes key issues affecting the success of the collaboration, which encompasses both dimensions related to the set-up and execution phases and guides the definition of the group of variables considered in this research.

### 2.2.2 Heterogeneity of knowledge sources in collaborative projects

Behind the development of R&D projects in collaboration with external partners lies the assumption that knowledge is distributed among diverse sources (Chesbrough, 2003) and through collaboration the innovation potential of the firm can be enhanced (Faems et al., 2005). However, the way the project is managed can help capture the potential benefits of collaboration, but also can limit it. For example, a more formal project management approach is associated with better performance of projects developed with market-based sources, but not with science-based ones (Du et al., 2014). This emphasizes that "there may be several different "models" and "approaches" that the firm may develop to apply to different kind of projects" (Clark and Wheelwright, 1993, p. 2813), which is the case of collaborative project management.

Some differences in managing innovation projects with external partners are associated with inter-partner dissimilarities, which are differences in partners' organizational attributes (Parkhe, 1991). For example, universities and industries have different missions and goals, but also routines, resources and a time horizon (Estrada et al., 2016). There is a different institutional logic, which is often considered a "cultural gap". Moreover, despite some convergence being achieved due to the increasing relationship between dissimilar sources (Bjerregaard, 2010), great dissimilarities between sources are still evident.

The project management in innovation management literature recognizes that partner heterogeneity is a concern in managing collaborative projects (vom Brocke and Lippe, 2015). Several prior studies provide guidelines to overcome these challenges, for example (i) co-developing a project charter including mutually agreeing on objectives and tying-in this objectives as early as possible; (ii) conducting joint problem-solving tasks to facilitate collective competence (vom Brocke and Lippe, 2015), (iii) ensuring that parties agree on shared directions (Smith, 2016); (iv) providing training in collaborative work and intercultural awareness (Calamel et al., 2012) and many others. However, these guidelines are not evaluated in terms of their effect on performance, which can help to give evidence of their effectiveness.

## 2.3. Research design

This research empirically examined the performance`s relationship of R&D projects developed in collaboration with external partners with the Project Management Success Factors (PMSF) for collaborative projects, previously identified in the literature of collaborative R&D projects. Then, the results were compared between two samples: Projects developed with science-based sources and projects developed with market-based ones.

For that, this study used a quantitative exploratory approach, which does not seek to confirm pre-specified relationships or generalize the results. It expects to discuss the nature of the relationship between Project Management Success Factors and Project Performance in R&D projects, more specifically, to examine differences in the relationship nature by knowledge sources types. To evaluate the influence of PMSFs on Project Performance, Pearson's correlation analysis, which measures the strength and direction of the linear relationship between a pair of variables, was used. In this study, each pair includes a PMSF and a performance measure. To do this analysis, the sample was divided by knowledge source types and the correlation analysis was made after the sample division. Then, the results from each sample were compared and analysed.

### 2.3.1 Variables

*Dependent variable.* The dependent variable is the R&D project performance, which was measured through R&D outputs (patent, scientific publication and a subjective evaluation of output success) and traditional project management measures (cost, time and quality). Each variable was evaluated by a Likert-scale, which had a statement describing each value. For patent and scientific publication, a comparison with other projects of the firm was considered.

*Independent Variable.* This study classified project management success factors (Barnes et al., 2006; vom Brocke and Lippe, 2015) into the following: clearly planned issues [CPI], which refer to project set-up practices that aim to provided awareness about objectives, responsibilities, milestones, appropriation issues and strategies to solve conflicts; a mutually agreed project plan [MAPP], which refers to the level of conducting the project planning with consensus among the parties involved in the project; process monitoring [PM], which refers to the level of applying formal monitoring procedures during project execution such as review cycles with fixed time-frames; and effective communications [EC], which encompass level of formality, openness and mechanisms for knowledge integration. The presence of each success factor was measured through a six-point Likert-scale.

*Moderating variables.* Following previous literature, this study distinguished two different group types of knowledge sources in R&D projects (Du et al., 2014): (i) Science-based partners (universities and knowledge institutions – public and private); and (ii) Market-based partners (supplier firms, competitor firms, consultants). As in the database analyzed some projects used both types of sources, a third group, called "Both", was included.

*Control variables.* The following control variables were considered: project complexity (the higher the number of partners involved, the greater the complexity); previous link (first time collaborating with the partner vs. previous experience); level of uncertainty (from basic research to product improvement – the higher the "distance" from basic research the lower the uncertainty); governance mode (from lower level of integration, such as outsourcing, to higher ones, such as joint-venture).

*Sample and Data Analysis*

The database was built through an electronic survey with R&D Managers. From 335 e-mails sent, the survey received 66 answers. After excluding all observations with relevant missing data, 53 projects materialised. Being exploratory, the number of observations may not meet the ideal number for conclusive statistical analysis. With this type of research, the results contribute to a better understanding of the problem and extract new insights for future studies.

To evaluate the influence of PMSFs on Project Performance, Pearson's correlation analysis, which measured the strength and direction of the linear relationship between a pair of variables, was used. In this study, each pair includes a PMSF and a performance measure. To do this analysis, the database was divided into three samples based on the knowledge source type (science-based, market-based or both) involved in the project, and the correlation analysis was made after the database division. Then, the results from each sample were compared and analysed. A PMSF was considered critical when it is significantly correlated to the performance metric at $p < 0.01$.

As other variables may influence performance, control variables were evaluated using a Chi-square test to verify whether the frequency distribution of variables differs between the knowledge sources sample. If knowledge sources are homogeneous regarding control variables, there is evidence to believe that the significant correlations found must be due to the relationship between the knowledge sources and the PMSFs.

Of the 53 projects that are part of the sample of this study, 43% have their headquarters in Brazil. However, the sample includes companies from Europe and the USA, making up more than half of the sample, and 50% of companies from Europe are from Germany. R&D professionals from diverse fields answered the survey, most being from Pharmaceutical and Healthcare companies. For projects made with the science-based source, universities are the most frequent type of partner, and when projects were developed with both types, universities are part of almost all projects. For the market-based sources, suppliers are the most frequent.

## 2.4. Conclusion

This study explored the effect of applying project management practices identified as success factors for collaborative projects on project performance for projects carried out with external partners, but with a specific focus on verifying contingencies by type of knowledge source involved in the project. By examining correlation results, we found support for a contingent view for managing collaborative R&D project in which the knowledge source type is the moderating factor. We argue that this finding can be explained by the existence of deep dissimilarities between knowledge sources (Estrada et al., 2016).

Previous research argues that projects with science-based sources are negatively affected by increasing the level of formality in project management (Du et al., 2014). Differently, by including a list of project management success factors and different performance measures, a new discussion was opened up. More specifically, these findings led to the conclusion that the differences of the effect of project management in performance in R&D collaborative projects made with science-based and market-based sources are much greater than merely in terms of the level of formality. The type of success factors that affect each type of project (made with market-based or science-based sources) is different. It can be argued that projects made with science-based sources emphasize less bureaucratic practices, such as *Encouraging Informal Communication, Joint Problem-solving Tasks* and *Discussion of Expectations,* while projects made with market-based sources have more process-oriented factors, such as *Clearly Defining Communication Strategies* and *Formal Review Cycles with Fixed Time-frames.* Here, again, we rely on the discussion about dissimilarities between these two types of knowledge sources to explain this difference. Science-based sources have a different mission, goals, routines, resources and time horizons in relation to market-based ones (Estrada et al., 2016). Whilst the literature posits that new roles adopted by universities and also the interest of market-based sources in accessing scientific network may facilitate the collaboration process (Bjerregaard, 2010), a contingent approach in Project Management considering the most suitable approach toward the knowledge source involved in the project, would help increase success of the R&D projects.

While it is expected that communication has a positive effect on the success of cooperative agreements (Mora-Valentin et al., 2004), this research shows that the type of communication strategy used at project level should consider the type of knowledge source in order to improve performance. Prior literature suggests that some special attention to communication in projects with heterogeneous partners should be taken (vom Brocke and Lippe, 2015) and provide some guidelines, like *Having Continuous And Open Balanced Communication* to ensure that the staff understand the "big picture", *Having a Clear Communication Strategy* that includes the forms of written communication to be used, *Maintaining Strong Informal Communication*, and *Fostering Face-to-face Meetings*, especially in teams that are located in different geographical areas. However, the findings of this study suggest that the guidelines should be adapted to the type of knowledge source involved in the project and not just provide a broad guideline for heterogeneity.

In addition, planning activities are an essential step in project management. In collaborative projects with external partners, a clear and common agreed definition of objectives, responsibilities and the whole project set-up has been shown to have "a positive influence on the involvement and commitment of partners within a collaborative project" (Barnes et al., 2002). This safeguards them from misunderstandings during the project evolution due to the misalignment of partners' objectives and the low commitment of partners, especially in projects that involve partners from different backgrounds (Morandi, 2013). These findings support this view, showing that *Clear Planning* and *Mutually Agreeing on Plans* were proportionally the themes with most success factors with critical correlations to performance. However, certain success factors seem to be more critical in projects made with one or another knowledge source, such as *Mutually Agreeing on Technical Characteristics of Human Resources* which is part of a significant correlation just for science-based knowledge sources and *Joint Agreement on Appropriation Issues* is part of the ones for market-based knowledge sources.

## 2.5. Implication and future studies

This study contributes to innovation management literature in different ways. Firstly, it strengthens the integration of certain literature streams: project management literature, open innovation and innovation management. In the Innovation Management stream, scholars have traditionally tried to identify relationships between some variables and innovation performance. We followed this tradition by incorporating into it the open innovation challenge, which includes working with partner heterogeneity in the context of innovation. More specifically, we open the "black box" of project management to discuss its success factors and its relation to certain performance measures. However, we add project performance measures to evaluate the success of an R&D project due to the trend for the modern R&D function to be more responsive to organizational needs, which also involves delivering projects on time and within budget (Henttonen et al., 2016). By doing this, it also contributes to the discussion on evaluating project management success factors by relating them to R&D success in collaborative projects, as these results suggest that success varies according to the type of performance measurement. This might be a second contribution.

Finally, we advance the literature by identifying specific project management success factors that affect performance in R&D collaborative projects. We, therefore, recognized the dissimilarities that previous literature demonstrated (Bruneel et al., 2010; Estrada et al., 2016) and agree with the evidence that the knowledge source involved in an open innovation project should be a contingent factor in project management (Du et al., 2014), but, more specifically, we help to explore a broad range of project management practices in collaborative R&D setting with dissimilar partners by providing evidence of success factors that are dominant in a certain type of project characteristic, in terms of the knowledge source involved.

A practical implication of this study is to help managers involved in collaborative R&D to understand which are the success factors that are more suitable according to external partners involved in the project.

While certain researches are concerned with the effect of carrying out R&D projects with external partners, there is also a need to have a more fine-grained discussion on how these projects are being managed. It is not enough to know that dissimilarities between partners should be a concern when managing R&D projects with external partners. It is important to identify what approach should be used to overcome dissimilarity challenges and truly take advantage of collaboration for innovation.

Therefore, a great number of research opportunities appear in this context. Specifically, in relation to these findings, we suggest evaluating the use of project management activity in the following ways: examine more detailed data about the execution of project management; explore diverse performance measures and diverse cultural, industrial and other contexts and also evaluate projects with different levels of innovation comparing breakthrough innovation and incremental projects. In general, the opportunity involves bringing traditional management approaches to the context of Open Innovation.

Some limitations of this study are mainly related to the methodology. The study used an exploratory quantitative approach, which does not allow us to generalize the findings. This also brings the opportunity to move forward in terms of the insights that this study provides. We highlight the research opportunity related to having more focused research on the PMSFs that presented critical correlations in these results.

**References**

Barnes, T., Pashby, I. a N., Gibbons, A. (2002). "Industry Interaction : A Multi-case Evaluation of Collaborative R & D Projects". *Eur. Manag. J.* 20, 272–285.

Barnes, T., Pashby, I., Gibbons, A. (2006). "Managing collaborative R&D projects development of a practical management tool." *Int. J. Proj. Manag.* 24, 395–404. https://doi.org/10.1016/j.ijproman.2006.03.003

Bjerregaard, T. (2010). "Industry and academia in convergence: Micro-institutional dimensions of R&D collaboration." *Technovation* 30, 100–108. https://doi.org/10.1016/j.technovation.2009.11.002

Bruneel, J., D'Este, P., Salter, A. (2010). "Investigating the factors that diminish the barriers to university–industry collaboration." *Res. Policy* 39, 858–868. https://doi.org/10.1016/j.respol.2010.03.006

Calamel, L., Defélix, C., Picq, T., Retour, D. (2012). "Inter-organisational projects in French innovation clusters: The construction of collaboration." *Int. J. Proj. Manag.* 30, 48–59. https://doi.org/10.1016/j.ijproman.2011.03.001

Chesbrough, H. (2003). *Open Innovation The New Imperative for Creating and Profiting from Technology.* Harvard Business School Press, Boston, MA.

Clark, K.B., Wheelwright, S.C. (1993). *Managing New Product and Process Development: Text and Cases.* The Free Press, New York, NY.

Davis, J.P., Eisenhardt, K.M. (2011). "Rotating Leadership and Collaborative Innovation: Recombination Processes in Symbiotic Relationships." *Adm. Sci. Q.* 56, 159–201. https://doi.org/10.1177/0001839211428131

Du, J., Leten, B., Vanhaverbeke, W. (2014). "Managing open innovation projects with science-based and market-based partners." *Res. Policy* 43, 828–840. https://doi.org/10.1016/j.respol.2013.12.008

Estrada, I., Faems, D., Martin Cruz, N., Perez Santana, P. (2016). "The role of interpartner dissimilarities in Industry-University alliances: Insights from a comparative case study." *Res. Policy* 45, 2008–2022. https://doi.org/10.1016/j.respol.2016.07.005

Faems, D., Van Looy, B., Debackere, K. (2005). "Interorganizational collaboration and innovation: Toward a portfolio approach." *J. Prod. Innov. Manag.* 22, 238–250. https://doi.org/10.1111/j.0737-6782.2005.00120.x

Hagedoorn, J. (2002). "Inter-firm R & D partnerships : an overview of major trends and patterns since 1960." *Res. Policy* 31, 477–492.

Henttonen, K., Ojanen, V., Puumalainen, K. (2016). "Searching for appropriate performance measures for innovation and development projects." *R D Manag.* 46, 914–927. https://doi.org/10.1111/radm.12178

Kim, Y., Lee, K. (2003). "Technological collaboration in the Korean electronic parts industry: patterns and key success factors." *R D Manag.* 33, 59–77. https://doi.org/10.1111/1467-9310.00282

Lippe, S., vom Brocke, J. (2016). "Situational Project Management for Collaborative Research Projects." *Proj. Manag. J.* 47, 76–96. https://doi.org/10.1002/pmj.21561

Littler, D., Leverick, F., Bruce, M. (1995). "Factors Affecting the Process of Collaborative Product Development: A Study of UK Manufacturers of

Information and Communications Technology Products." *J. Prod. Innov. Manag.* 12, 16–32.

Mailhot, C., Gagnon, S., Langley, A., Binette, L.-F. (2016). "Distributing leadership across people and objects in a collaborative research project." *Leadership* 12, 53–85. https://doi.org/10.1177/1742715014543578

Mora-Valentin, E.M., Montoro-Sanchez, A., Guerras-Martin, L.A. (2004). "Determining factors in the success of R&D cooperative agreements between firms and research organizations." *Res. Policy* 33, 17–40. https://doi.org/10.1016/S0048-7333(03)00087-8

Morandi, V. (2013). "The management of industry-university joint research projects: how do partners coordinate and control R&D activities?" *J. Technol. Transf.* 38, 69–92. https://doi.org/10.1007/s10961-011-9228-5

Parkhe, A. (1991). "Interfirm diversity, Organizational learning, and Longevity in global strategic alliances." *J. Int. Bus. Stud.* 22, 579–601.

Ruuska, I., Teigland, R. (2009). "Ensuring project success through collective competence and creative conflict in public-private partnerships - A case study of Bygga Villa, a Swedish triple helix e-government initiative." *Int. J. Proj. Manag.* 27, 323–334. https://doi.org/10.1016/j.ijproman.2008.02.007

Smith, P. (2016). "Boundary emergence in inter-organizational innovation: The influence of strategizing, identification and sensemaking." *Eur. J. Innov. Manag.* 19, 47–71. https://doi.org/10.1108/EJIM-04-2015-0024

van Eck, N., Waltman, L., Dekker, R., van den Berg, J. (2010). "Writing information literacy assessment plans: A guide to best practice." *J. Am. Soc. Inf. Sci. Technol.* 61, 2405–2416. https://doi.org/10.1002/asi

vom Brocke, J., Lippe, S., (2015). "Managing collaborative research projects: A synthesis of project management literature and directives for future research." *Int. J. Proj. Manag.* 33, 1022–1039. https://doi.org/10.1016/j.ijproman.2015.02.001

Chapter 3

# Location Preferences and Innovation Dynamics of Knowledge-Intensive Business Services: The Case of Ankara Metropolitan City

Mehmet Tahsin Şahin

*Ankara University, Turkey*

**Abstract:** At the end of the 1960s and the beginning of the 1970s, a new division of labor emerged throughout the world, particularly in Western Europe. The decline of the manufacturing industry as a prominent economic sector and the emergence of information-intensive activities as a driving force of the economy are among the main reasons for this change. Within Knowledge Intensive Services, the transformation of Knowledge Intensive Business Services (KIBS) from other services to information-driven productivity and value-added services is very important in order to maintain high income and high financial capacity in the region. By using the survey method, the location preferences, network relations for innovation capacity and knowledge production of KIBS firms in Çankaya district of Ankara province is analyzed. By doing so, it is aimed to redefine the spatial pattern and innovation capacity emerging in the metropolitan area. The results show that spatial pattern and innovative capacity changes due to the types of KIBS firms; Professional KIBS (P-KIBS) and Technical-KIBS (T-KIBS).

**Keywords:** Knowledge Intensive Business Services, Professional-KIBS, Technical-KIBS, Innovation, Location Preferences, Urban Economy, Ankara.

## 3.1. Introduction

The structural transformation in the economy has created a new division of labor, also called the Second Global Transformation (Wood, 2002). The increasing complexity of the industrial sector has created many different and improved service demands. The service sector, which has the highest share of employment and value added in developed countries, has also been affected by this change and divided into many sub-sectors within itself. The role and importance of the service sector in this transformation is worth exploring. However, it is more important to define the sub-sectors of the service sector in this complex structure and to determine the area of the Knowledge Intensive Producer Services (KIBS) sectors.

In general, knowledge-intensive producer services within the producer services are categorized as technology intensive, business intensive and financial intensive services Within this categorization Knowledge Intensive Producer Services (KIBS) appear as the leading one in urban economics (Doloreux and Shearmur, 2012, Koch and Stahlecker, 2006, Kozar, 2012, Romero De Avila Serrano, 2014, Shearmur and Doloreux, 2014, Strambach, 2008, Amara et al., 2009, Corrocher et al., 2009). The increasing use of knowledge-intensive input in production processes is an indication of the fact that the KIBS sector is an important dynamic of economic growth. KIBS is an important sector not only for regional and national development but also for effective support to companies in the determination of innovation and formation of new activities and adaptation of local companies to new conditions of market and production (Moyart, 2005).

Another problem that this study deals with is that economic development studies generally focus on the manufacturing industry. While economic development is expressed through the increase in employment and the number of manufacturing industry firms, it has not been concerned whether this actually creates a production that provides knowledge and innovative activity. Most of the development policies have been implemented in this way and they have been practiced with rational models. Policy-makers and planners have considered the services sector as non-productive sector thus they have indicated that investments in services have little impact on increasing capital accumulation and have seen the manufacturing industry as the basis of capital accumulation and development (Chan, 1994, Kirkby, 1985). As a result of this approach, which is compatible with the basic theory of economics, the KIBS sector, which is an important component of the city and regional economy, has not received the necessary attention.

In recent years, rapidly growing information and communication technologies (ICT) sector and its related services sectors have revealed new information requirements and different sub-sectors. In addition, the ever-changing social, political and business structure has increased the demand for expert knowledge. As a result, the concepts of "inevitable transformation and fluid space" with the ICT revolution have gained importance (Castells, 2009). Although the ICT revolution has also led to debate as the "end of geography" (O'Brien, 1992) and "death of distance" (Cairncross, 1997) by some researchers, the economic activities involving KIBS evolved or clustered in specific spaces. The most important deficiencies of development policies are the uncertainty of the capacity of the KIBS activities in the country, region or city, the redefinition of clustering and cluster patterns, the determination of cluster species and the generation of innovation.

Being one of the most important drivers of innovation, the KIBS activities have changed the structure of the economy in cities after the 2000s and the fact of its being the most important player in the knowledge economies made it necessary to investigate the sector. In this context, this chapter provides an important contribution to the field of science by providing a systematic analysis from the national scale to the company scale both in terms of the sector and the space. In addition, it analyses the innovation capacities and forms of the KIBS firms in the socio-spatial framework and analyses the dynamics behind the innovation process in KIBS.

This study investigates the development, distribution, location preferences and innovation dynamics of the KIBS sector, which was previously underestimated by geographers and economists.

**Table 3.1:** Main targets and spatial scales of the stud.

| | *Targets* | *Spatial Scale* |
|---|---|---|
| 1 | To analyze the change in the employment in KIBS activities in the 2009-2015 period and the number of businesses with turnover indicators of NUTS Level-2 | Regional |
| 2 | To analyze the location preferences of the KIBS in the metropolitan city scale (Ankara) and to determine the KIBS clusters whether they locate in the city center or in different regions. | Urban |
| 3 | To analyze the characteristics, network connections, innovation dynamics and location preferences of KIBS firms in the district (Çankaya) scale. | Firm |

In this context, first of all, the KIBS activities were redefined and classified according to the changing economic structure. Secondly, the urban location preferences of the KIBS activities was discussed within the scope of location theories and the location preferences were compared with the innovation capacities of KIBS activities. Finally, the city of Ankara, Turkey's most important service provider and one of the hubs of KIBS with its clustering and innovation dynamics (the transfer of manufacturing/know-how and access to commercialization/co-resources and R & D structure) was chosen as the case study. In this stage, it was aimed to define the role of firms in the KIBS sector in Ankara regarding location preferences, competitiveness, back and forth connections and innovation sources.

Within the framework of these objectives, targets of the study are summarized below together with their spatial scales.

### 3.2. Background

In spite of the importance of producer services and KIBS activities, research involving sector-specific service industries decreased with only a few exceptions in the 2000s (Currid and Connolly, 2008, Kay et al., 2007, Shearmur and Doloreux, 2008). The location of the KIBS activities and their contribution to the regional economy have been studied at a macro-geographical level (Coffey and Shearmur, 1997, Goe, 1991, Huallacháin and Reid, 1991). However, their location in the urban system and their susceptibility to agglomeration economies (Eberts and Randall, 1998, Wernerheim and Sharpe, 2003) and clustering trends (Coe, 1998, Keeble and Nachum, 2002) were analyzed using a variety of methodological tools. Recently in Turkey, innovation studies and their relation with space (Eraydın and Köroğlu, 2007, Şahin and Altuğ, 2017, Tuncel, 2012, Yavuz, 2010, Varol; et al., 2011) have been receiving increasing attention.

The studies which analyze the service sector with statistical methods make an inference with the comparative methods among the countries. Wang's work in 2009 is derived from the Economic Background Theory. In his study, Wang examines the development of the service sector in the Chinese economy at both national and regional levels. In the first part of his study, he compared China with other countries and then discussed the contribution of the service sector to regional development in the 31 regions of China (Wang, 2009). Immediately after this study, a study by Yang and Yeh in 2013 analyzed the spatial distribution and development of the sub-branches of the service sector in China. The results of the analysis emphasized that the producer services are more concentrated in the urban system and the production services should be in big urban centers in a productive economy. Another finding is the accumulation of producer services in the Eastern regions where the industry is at the forefront (Yeh and Yang, 2013). This result differs from Western literature with the conclusion that the producer services in China follow the manufacturing industry. In the Western literature, it is accepted that the services of the producers do not follow the manufacturing activities and that they are distributed outside the urban and urban periphery (Beyers and Lindahl, 1996, Gong, 2001). In China, the opposite is localized in the center of large metropolises. This situation is explained by the living conditions and education level between urban and rural regions (Yeh and Yang, 2013).

Levent's doctoral thesis, which was prepared in 2007, analyzes the spatial organization of service activities in Ankara from the perspective of relational evolutionary economic geography and he discusses how to use the results in planning as a result of this analysis. In the study, the author shows both concentration and dispersion characteristics of the services sector with clustering analysis and adaptation analyzes on the neighborhood scale based on the number of firms. It is stated in the study that the services sector location preferences are shaped according to the market mechanism and that the planning and arrangements in Ankara force the city into a single centered structure (Levent, 2007).

In a study conducted by Doloreux and Shearmur in 2012, analyzes whether the innovations occurring in KIBS activities differ due to the metropolitan area. In the study, according to the survey conducted in Quebec in 2007, 1124 KIBS company sample was evaluated. When choosing the company, criteria such as distance to a metropolitan area, size of firm and code of economic activity were taken into consideration. The study was investigated with 51 variables and 16 factors, it was observed that geographic distance was one of the factors affecting innovation, and other local spatial patterns influenced the nature, cooperation and customer relations of the information sources of the institutions (Doloreux and Shearmur, 2012).

## 3.3. Research design

The study was carried out in four stages according to the determined targets. In the first phase, the distribution of the KIBS sector within the NUTS Level-2 regions is presented on a national scale. In the second stage, the spatial distribution of the KIBS sectors according to the districts of the city of Ankara was interpreted descriptively. In the third stage, the location patterns of the KIBS sector where located in the city of Ankara were analyzed distribution and concentration by means of the ArcGIS software program. In the last stage of the study, by using survey technique, 410 questionnaires were applied to KIBS firms to analyze their innovation dynamics, network connections (formal and informal network) and knowledge generation capacities (tacit information). Frequency and percentage analyses were made by independent chi-square and relationship level analyses (Table 3.2).

**Table 3.2:** Data and Method Stages.

| *Stages* | *Scale* | *Data Source* | *Data* | *Indicator* | *Years* | *Target* | *Method* |
|---|---|---|---|---|---|---|---|
| *1. Stage* | National | Turkish Statistical Institute | Employment Workplace Endorsement | Sectors According to KIBS Activities (Nace.Rev. 2) | 2009 - 2015 | To reveal the specialization of the KIBS sector in 26 NUTS 2 levels in Turkey | Location Coefficient |
| *2. Stage* | Urban | Social Security Institution | Employment Workplace | Sectors According to KIBS Activities (Nace.Rev. 2) | 2004 - 2016 | To reveal the location pattern of KIBS activities at Ankara district level | Descriptive Analysis Frequency-Percent |
| *3. Stage* | Neighborhood | Ankara Chamber of Commerce | Firm | Sectors According to KIBS Activities (Nace.Rev. 2) | 2017 | Demonstrate the clustering of KIBS activities within the borders of the metropolitan city of Ankara | Nearest Neighborhood Analysis Kernel Density Analysis (ArcGIS) |
| *4. Stage* | Firm | Firm | Survey | Sectors According to KIBS Activities (Nace.Rev. 2) | 2017 | To reveal the location preferences, innovation dynamics and network-information sources of KIBS activities within the borders of the metropolitan city of Ankara | Chi-square TestRelationship Level Test |

## 4. Conclusion

This section presents the results of the analyses that have been defined in the data and method section. Defining the location of the services sector as a priority in the world, Turkey highlights its place in the economy. KIBS activities put themselves forward in the next stage of specialization trends within the NUTS-2 Turkish regions. Hence, firstly, in order to put some light on these specialization trends, the areas of specialization in the KIBS sector are presented. In a second step, the distribution of the two subclasses of the KIBS activities, namely the P-KIBS and T-KIBS sectors, in the Ankara districts are compared for the years 2004 and 2016. A concentration analysis of the KIBS activities in the region of the Ankara metropolitan area is performed to highlight the most intensive regions. Finally, the outcomes deriving from the questionnaire, P-KIBS and T-KIBS activities, the location selection preferences and the innovation dynamics are analyzed comparatively.

### 3.4.1. Specialization Patterns of KIBS activities by Turkey NUTS-2 Regions

When we first out of three indicators (Employment, Workplace, Endorsement) P-KIBS sector consolidation of 2009, shows that of the 69 coded law and accounting activities showing the highest specialization in the sector in Turkey. Secondly, there are 74 code professional, scientific and technical activities. The industry with the least specialization is 59 coded motion picture, video and television programs, sound recording and music publishing activities. TR10 Istanbul is the region with the highest specialization in P-KIBS sectors. Istanbul region is followed by TR51 Ankara.

The specialization trends of P-KIBS sectors for 2015 do not show a different structure than in 2009. Although the number of regions specialized in three indicators increased compared to 2009, the sectors with the highest level of specialization are not different. In addition, the TR10 Istanbul region has been specialized in all three indicators of the P-KIBS sectors in 2015, while the TR51 Ankara region is noteworthy compared to 2009.

T-KIBS sectors in 2009, the number of NUTS-2 areas of specialization distribution in Turkey, 61 coded Telecommunications sector activities are showing the greatest expansion area. In contrast, 63 coded information service activities did not show specialization in any NUTS-2 region in 2009 due to data confidentiality. Other T-KIBS activities, computer programming and consulting activities, architecture and engineering activities, R & D services specialize in Ankara-Eskişehir-Istanbul line. In this case, it can be said that the formation of the corridor of T-KIBS activity between Ankara and Istanbul.

In 2015, unlike 2009, 63 coded information service activities were observed to be specialized in Ankara and Istanbul regions. In addition, 61 coded telecommunications activities, which were dominant in 2009, are accompanied by 71 coded architecture and engineering activities and 72 coded R & D activities in 2015. Another important point is that while the TR10 Istanbul region was the region with the highest level of specialization in T-

KIBS sectors in 2009, the TR51 Ankara region became the most specialized region in 2015. In this case, it is seen that the Ankara region is a leading city in technology-intensive KIBS activities in 2015.

### 3.4.2. Distribution and Concentration Analysis of KIBS Companies in Ankara Metropolitan Municipality

According to the K-Density Analysis of P-BYIH firms, the first-degree clustering is observed on CBD towards the south. Although P-KIBS firms show first and second-degree clusters within the 3 km radius CBD area T-KIBS firms show first-degree clustering in a very small area in CBD, but highly out of CBD borders (Figure 3.1).

**Figure 3.1:** KIBS Activities Kernel Density Analysis Map.

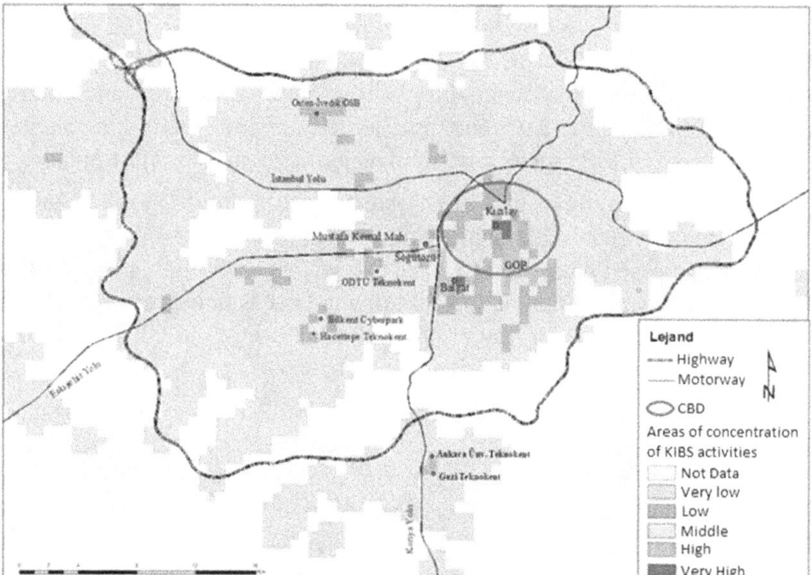


### 4.3. Location and Innovation Dynamics of KIBS Activities

The survey was applied to the KIBS companies within the Çankaya district. Of the 410 companies, 146 were P-KIBS, 264 were T-KIBS. The two classes have a total of five sub-sectors. In order to give more meaningful results, sample distribution was made proportionally according to the sub-sector number of firms.

The employees of KIBS are divided into 5 classes according to their qualifications. The highest share of these 5 classes is owned by the Engineers (42.2%) and the shareholders (shareholder) with a minimum share of 4.2%. While T-KIBS firms reflect the general structure, this situation is different in P-KIBS firms. T-KIBS firms are 45.9% Engineer, 20.2% Administrative Personnel, 15.4% Technician, 13.6% Owned and 4.9% Shareholders. P-KIBS companies are 37.3% Administrative Personnel, 34.2% are Engineers, 15.5% are Owners, 10.2% are Technicians and 2.8% are shareholders (Table 3.3).

69.1% of the persons working in KIBS companies have a bachelor's degree, 12.6% associate degree, 10.5% secondary education and 7.7% graduate degree. While P-KIBS and T-KIBS firms reflect this general structure, the only remarkable difference is that the share of graduate students in P-KIBS is 5,5% while this rate is 8,1 for T-KIBS firms (Table 3.3).

The number of firms established after 2000, in general, has increased. P-KIBS firms between the ages of 1-5 have a share of 34.2%, while this rate is 31.8% for T-KIBS firms. The age group with the second-highest accumulation is 11-25. In this group, P-KIBS firms have a share of 26% and T-KIBS firms have a share of 32.2% (Table 3.3).

In terms of the employment structure of the companies, the firms employing 2-9 people have a high share with 67.3%. In general, SMEs in the second piling group of KIBS firms with a 21.7% share of 10-49 people operating enterprises. The group showing the highest increase in P-KIBS is 2-9 people with a share of 68.5% and the second group is working with 0-1 people with 15.8%. The first group of T-KIBS firms were 2-9 people with 66.7%; the second group consisted of 10-49 people with a share of 25.8% (Table 3.3).

10 items under the 10 headings affecting the location preferences of KIBS companies were formed and these items were evaluated on five-point Likert scale. In this context, KIBS firms think that Easy Accessibility is more important than other items. Accordingly, the Easy Accessible item has an average of 4.23 over 5. The second important factor is to be close to the Central Business Area with an average of 3.86 and the third important item is the Power Infrastructure Facilities (parking space - the technology and comfort of the building) with an average of 3.65. On the other hand, there are 2 items with an average below 3. These are Labor and Production Costs with an average of 2.85; the other one is being close to similar sectors with an average of 2.97. The other five items have an average value of 3 to 4.

**Table 3.3:** Demographic Characteristics of KIBS Firms

| *Firm Demographic Features* | *P-KIBS* | *T-KIBS* | *KIBS* | *Firm Demographic Features* | *P-KIBS* | *T-KIBS* | *KIBS* |
|---|---|---|---|---|---|---|---|
| **Quality of Employees** | % | % | % | **Age of the Firm** | % | % | % |
| Owner | 15,5 | 13,6 | 14,2 | 1-5 Age | **34,2** | 31,8 | **32,7** |
| Engineer | 34,2 | **45,9** | **42,2** | 6-10 Age | 24,7 | 26,5 | 25,9 |
| Technical staff | 10,2 | 15,4 | 13,7 | 11-25 Age | 26 | **32,2** | 30 |
| Administrative staff | **37,3** | 20,2 | 25,7 | 26+ Age | 15,1 | 9,5 | 11,5 |
| Partner (Shareholder) | 2,8 | 4,9 | 4,2 | **Total** | **100** | **100** | **100** |
| **Total** | **100** | **100** | **100** | | | | |
| **Education status** | % | % | % | **Employment** | % | % | % |
| High school | 10,5 | 9,6 | 10,5 | 0-1 Employee | 15,8 | 5,3 | 9 |
| Associate of Science | 14,2 | 12,6 | 12,6 | 2-9 Employees | **68,5** | **66,7** | **67,3** |
| Bachelor's Degree | **69,8** | **69,8** | **69,1** | 10-49 Employees | 14,4 | 25,8 | 21,7 |
| Master and Ph.D. Degree | 5,5 | 8,1 | 7,7 | 50-249 Employees | 1,4 | 2,3 | 2 |
| **Total** | **100** | **100** | **100** | **Total** | **100** | **100** | **100** |

The distribution of innovation type is given in Table 4. When the results of this analysis are examined, 24,63% of the KIBS companies have product innovation, 19,76% process innovation, 16,34% organization innovation and 11,71% strategy / marketing innovation. In P-KIBS companies, product innovation is 15,75%, process innovation is 11,64%, organization innovation is 13,01% and strategy / marketing innovation is 7,53%; In T-KIBS companies, it is observed that there is 29,55% in product innovation, 24,24% in process innovation, 18,18% in organization innovation and 14,02% in strategy/marketing innovation. (Table 3.4).

The next analysis is the rate of R & D expenditures in 2016 on the realization of the innovation of KIBS companies. In total KIBS, 24,88% of the firms, did not allocate shares over annual turnover to R & D. Among P-KIBS activities 30,82% of the firms P-KIBSdo not allocate a share for R & D, 21,92% share between 1% and 5%, 17,12% share between 6% and 10%, and among T-KIBS activities 21,59% of the firms do not allocate R & D shares, 21,21% between 1% and 5%; 18,18% share between 6% and 10%.

**Table 3.4:** Distribution of Innovation Type of P-KIBS and T-KIBS Companies

| *Class* | *Indicator* | *N* | *Average* (0 = no innovation, 1 = innovation) | *Standard deviation* |
|---|---|---|---|---|
| *P-KIBS* | Application of product innovations | 146 | 0,16 | 0,37 |
| | Application of process innovations | 146 | 0,12 | 0,32 |
| | Application of organizational innovations | 146 | 0,13 | 0,34 |
| | Application of marketing innovations | 146 | 0,08 | 0,26 |
| *T-KIBS* | Application of product innovations | 264 | 0,30 | 0,46 |
| | Application of process innovations | 264 | 0,24 | 0,43 |
| | Application of organizational innovations | 264 | 0,18 | 0,39 |
| | Application of marketing innovations | 264 | 0,14 | 0,35 |
| *KIBS* | Application of product innovations | 410 | 0,25 | 0,43 |
| | Application of process innovations | 410 | 0,20 | 0,40 |
| | Application of organizational innovations | 410 | 0,16 | 0,37 |
| | Application of marketing innovations | 410 | 0,12 | 0,32 |

*Source*: calculated by the authors.

### 3.5. Implications and future research

The doctoral dissertations of Levent (2007) and Gökçe (2008), which analyze the spatial pattern of the service activities of the producer and the sub-sector, are an important reference for us to see the change in the location preferences of the KIBS in the city of Ankara (Levent, 2007, Gökçe, 2008). In this context, the new clustering fields in the form of safe, prestigious, technological infrastructure and skilled labor pool, which started with METU Technopolis in 2005, have changed the city macro form. However, this applies only to T-KIBS activities. T-KIBS activities have chosen place independent of location. In these preferences, factors such as a socio-cultural structure of the region, income level, and transportation are not taken into consideration. However, the economies of scale, the economy of the same sector, close to the qualified workforce and technological infrastructure are effective. Whereas the factors such as the socio-cultural structure of the region, income level, and transportation are important factors for P-KIBS activities; economies of scale, coexistence with firms of the same sector, close to qualified workforce and dynamics such as technological infrastructure are not important.

T-KIBS activities reveal a concentration area independent from CBD; P-KIBS firms show an aggregation within or near the CBD. There is no excessive dependence on CBD in the structure of general KIBS activities. The KIBS sectors are the first to place the settlements with high-income levels, the areas opened to the new settlement, security and prestigious areas close to the major public institutions.

Considering that KIBS activities are the most important dynamics of innovation and knowledge production, it is inevitable for them to cooperate with universities. Many studies in the Western literature point to this. However, in the city of Ankara, the minimum number of KIBS companies cooperate. This is the biggest proof that the government policy, which started with university-industry cooperation, is still not fully established. It is also clear that firm owners still have great doubts about trusting universities. The KIBS activities give more importance to the internal dynamics in the process of producing the information. In-firm dynamics can be understood as helping to produce new information up to a certain extent, and the capacity of KIBS activities to realize innovation is below 40%.

KIBS activities are defined as sectors that create high added value, perform innovation and play an important role in the production of new information. But in Ankara, this structure is different than it looks. P-KIBS activities have a mission to provide a customer-oriented and routine service. Although this situation is different from P-KIBS activities in T-KIBS activities, the ratio, in general, is not more than 50%. In Turkey, KIBS activities that reflect the mission of the structure is not fully understood, and we can understand by looking at the Ankara metropolitan city.

According to these results, national and regional plans (urban transformation-urban development plans) affect the location decisions of the sector, while local planning decisions (road routes and public investments) of local administrators affect the location preferences of the sector. In addition, the investments made by public institutions and what they do to the district are some of the reasons for this sectoral concentration.

The dynamics such as population density and income level determine the clustering areas of P-KIBS firms; Factors such as information security, prestige and close to qualified labor force determine the clustering areas of T-KIBS firms. While P-KIBS firms show clustering within the CBD, T-KIBS firms are concentrated outside the CBD area.

When we look at the general location of the companies, it is seen how important accessibility is in the selection of location. KIBS firms emphasize the Accessibility factor and they actually imply the concept of visibility. In particular, P-KIBS firms prefer a location that their customers can easily reach and can see while walking on the street. On the other hand, BYIH companies want to be close to the Central Business District. We can support this result from the findings of the distribution and concentration analysis of KIBS firms. As a result of the general structure, the KIBS companies, which are clustered within the CBD, are localized in Sogutozu and Eskisehir route. The general location preference of KIBS firms is CBD, but some firms choose the location outside the CBD, but these areas are in the extension of the CBD.

One of the important dynamics underlying the capacity of firms to realize innovation is the fact that firms have an independent R & D department and investments in R & D. In this context, there are some differences when we compare the Professional and Technological KIBS sectors. Only 8,9% of the P-KIBS firms have an R & D department. When we evaluate the innovation capacities of the P-KIBS sector in this context, only 26% of them realize innovation. The large share of this innovation constitutes the type of organizational innovation. Organizational innovation, which is the type of innovation carried out by P-KIBS companies, is known as the use of a new organizational structure in the business practices, planning, education structures, internal and external relations of the company or region (Yavuz, 2010, Tuncel, 2012).

Considering that T-KIBS activities consist of sectors with the analytical knowledge base, it is normal to have a more technical and mechanical structure compared to P-KIBS sectors. This difference affects the distribution of engineers working in two sectors. The rate of engineers employed in P-KIBS firms is lower than in T-KIBS firms.

The differences between the two sectors were determined according to the field study applied to reveal the cooperation structure of the P-KIBS and T-KIBS sectors. Only 30% of P-KIBS firms cooperate with another institution; this rate is quite high in T-KIBS firms. The main issue that needs to be discussed here is what institutions P-KIBS and T-KIBS have been cooperating with. P-KIBS companies have cooperated intensively with R & D centers. This result can be evaluated from two different perspectives. First of all, P-KIBS sector does not need R & D activities due to its general structure and technical personnel is few. Therefore, P-KIBS activities should outsource for analytical or technical service. Secondly, P-KIBS is not innovative due to its formation. Service offerings consist of a common structure that requires routine knowledge. Therefore, it does not want the cooperation network, its structure or different types of sectors due to its competitive advantage. As a result, the cooperation of the P-KIBS sectors with R & D centers means that they are receiving analytical and technical support for their customers in the service delivery rather than being innovative.

One of the important dynamics that prepares or triggers innovation is localized or implicit information. The methods and processing capacities of KIBS firms to obtain this implicit information influence or shape their innovation forms. In order to discuss the relationship between implicit knowledge and innovation, the data collected from the field study of the internal and external social activity frequencies of the firms were analyzed. While there is no significant relationship between innovation and internal social network in the P-KIBS sector, it has been found that there is a moderate level relationship between innovation and intra-company social network in T-KIBS sector. These results are parallel to the same sector or non-company social network and innovation relationship. In other words, the frequency of social network activities in the P-KIBS sector supports the type of information it uses and does not show an innovation relationship. In the T-KIBS sector, the frequency of social network activity supports the type of information it uses, and it has a significant relationship with innovation, unlike the P-KIBS sector.

Customer relations of P-KIBS and T-KIBS sectors are important within the framework of competitive advantages, planning, strategy, and marketing innovation. The type of strategy/marketing innovation among the companies that make innovation among KIBS sectors has the lowest share among both P-KIBS and T-KIBS companies. The fact that the two sectors cannot produce innovations in the field of marketing techniques is one of the most important reasons for establishing relations with their customers through traditional methods. The institutional structures of the KIBS companies in Ankara are also seen in customer relations. The 2 sub-sectors of KIBS activities establish customer relations through familiar means or relations based on long years. According to the results of the field application, the lowest means is fair / meeting means and advertising.

**Urban Policy and Planning Proposal**

1. In the planning works, due to the abstract output, the service sector is not given the necessary importance. This study is a guiding and facilitating guide in the policy-making processes of policymakers. Because different regions have different innovation and knowledge capacities, each region has its own socio-cultural structure, economic and political dynamics. Since some regions have an innovative structure different from the others, the policies to be implemented in each region must also differ. In this context, it is necessary to take into account the activities of the KIBS in the plans to be prepared for the

metropolitan city of Ankara. These plans should be aimed at increasing the development and competitiveness, mobilizing all actors, and promoting the culture and innovation of innovation.

2. Policies such as the establishment of R & D clusters may be required in economies based on ICT and information activities.
3. Protocols should be strengthened and strengthened with the support of public policies in order to strengthen cooperation between universities and KIBS firms.
4. In order to provide information network among the companies, it is necessary to support and/or promote the works for the development of relations between KIBS firms.
5. Steps should be taken in order to institutionalize KIBS firms which are at SME level and should be managed more professionally.
6. In the next zoning plan for Ankara, it is necessary to take into consideration the election preferences of the KIBS sectors and to plan the infrastructure and carrying capacity of the new settlements to be opened.

## Notes

This paper is written on the basis of the project titled "Location Preferences and Innovation Dynamics of Knowledge Intensive Business Services: The Case of Ankara Metropolitan City" which was supported by Ankara University Scientific Research Projects (SRP) Coordinator (Project number: 18L0649001) and the doctoral thesis of M. Tahsin Şahin completed in Ankara University Social Sciences Institute under the supervision of Associate Professor Mutlu Yılmaz.

## References

Amara, N., Landry, R. & Doloreux, D. (2009). "Patterns of innovation in knowledge-intensive business services." *The Service Industries Journal*, 29, 407-430.

Beyers, W. B. & Lindahl, D. P. (1996). "Explaining The Demand For Producer Services: Is Cost -Driven Externalization The Major Factor?" *Papers in Regional Science*, 75, 351-374.

Cairncross, F. (1997). *The Death of Distance: How the Communications Revolution Is Changing Our Lives*, London, Orion Business Books.

Castells, M. (2009). *The Rise of the Network Society: The Information Age: Economy, Society, and Culture*, Oxford, Wiley-Blackwell.

Chan, K. W. (1994). *Cities with Invisible Walls: Reinterpreting Urbanization in Post-1949 China*, Hong Kong and New York, NY: Oxford University Press.

Coe, N. M. (1998). "Exploring Uneven Development in Producer Service Sectors: Detailed Evidence from the Computer Service Industry in Britain." *Environment and Planning A*, 30, 2041-2068.

Coffey, W. & Shearmur, R. (1997). "The Growth and Location of High-Order Services in the Canadian Urban System, 1971-1991." *Professional Geographer*, 49, 404-418.

Corrocher, N., Cusmano, L. & Morrison, A. (2009). "Modes of innovation in knowledge intensive business services evidence from Lombardy." *Journal of Evolutionary Economics*, 19, 173-196.

Currid, E. & Connolly, J. (2008). "Patterns of Knowledge: The Geography of Advanced Services and the Case of Art and Culture." *Annals of the Association of American Geographers*, 98, 414-434.

Doloreux, D. & Shearmur, R. (2012). "Collaboration, information and the geography of innovation in knowledge intensive business services." *Journal of Economic Geography*, 12, 79-105.

Eberts, D. & Randall, J. E. (1998). "Producer Services, Labor Market Segmentation and Peripheral Regions: The Case of Saskatchewan." *Growth and Change*, 29, 401-422.

Eraydın, A. & Köroğlu, B. A. (2007). "Increasing Role of Services in Competitive Power and Innovativeness of Firms and Industrial Clusters." *European Planning Studies*, 15, 905-925.

Goe, W. R. (1991). "The Growth of Producer Services Industries: Sorting Through the Externalization Debate." *Growth and Change*, 22, 118-141.

Gong, H. (2001). "A Hierarchical Change Model Of Business And Professional Services In The United States." *Urban Geography*, 22, 340-359.

Gökçe, B. (2008). *Spatial Dynamics of Producer Services in Ankara.* Doktora, ODTÜ.

Huallacháin, B. Ó. & Reid, N. (1991). "The Location and Growth of Business and Professional Services in American Metropolitan Areas, 1976–1986." *Annals of the Association of American Geographers*, 81, 254-270.

Kay, D. L., Pratt, J. E. & Warner, M. E. (2007). "Role of Services in Regional Economy Growth." *Growth and Change*, 38, 419-442.

Keeble, D. & Nachum, L. (2002). "Why do business service firms cluster? Small consultancies, clustering and decentralization in London and southern England." *Transactions of the Institute of British Geographers*, 27, 67-90.

Kirkby, R. J. R. (1985). *Urbanization in China: Town and Country in a Developing Economy, 1949–2000 A.D*, New York, NY:Columbia University Press.

Koch, A. & Stahlecker, T. (2006). "Regional innovation systems and the foundation of knowledge intensive business services. A comparative study in Bremen, Munich, and Stuttgart, Germany. "*European Planning Studies*, 14, 123-145.

Kozar, J. M. (2012). *Knowledge intensive business services and metropolitan economic growth: An examination of the computer service industry.* Ph.D. Dissertations & Theses, The University of North Carolina at Charlotte.

Levent, T. (2007). *Spatial Organization Of Service Activities In Ankara.* Ph.D. Thesis Ph.D. Thesis, Middle East Technical University.

Moyart, L. (2005). "The role of producer services in regional development: what opportunities for medium-sized cities in Belgium?" *The Service Industries Journal*, 25, 213-228.

O'Brien, R. (1992). *Global Financial Integration : The End of Geography*, United States, Council on Foreign Relations Press

Romero De Avila Serrano, V. (2014). *Knowledge-Intensive Business Services in Los Angeles: Patterns, Interpretation, Consequences*. Master Master Thesis, University of California.

Shearmur, R. & Doloreux, D. (2008). "Urban Hierarchy or Local Buzz? High-Order Producer Service and (or) Knowledge-Intensive Business Service Location in Canada, 1991-2001." *The Professional Geographer*, 60, 333-355.

Shearmur, R. & Doloreux, D. (2014). "Knowledge-Intensive Business Services (KIBS) Use and User Innovation: High-Order Services, Geographic Hierarchies and Internet Use in Quebec's Manufacturing Sector." *Regional Studies*, 49, 1654-1671.

Strambach, S. (2008). "Knowledge-Intensive Business Services (KIBS) as drivers of multilevel knowledge dynamics." *International Journal of Services Technology and Management* 10, 152-174.

Şahin, M. T. & Altuğ, F. (2017). "Türkiye'de Yenilik Faaliyetlerinde Yenilikçi Uzmanlaşma Eğilimleri: İstanbul, Ankara ve İzmir Bölgeleri İmalat Sanayi Patent Göstergeleri." *Coğrafi Bilimler Dergisi*, 15, 157-166.

Tuncel, C. O. (2012). *İnovasyon Sistemleri ve Ekonomik Gelişme: Bursa Bölgesi İmalat Sanayinde İnovasyon Süreçleri Üzerine Bir Alan Araştırması*, Bursa, Nilüfer Akkılıç Kütüphanesi Yayınları.

Varol;, Ç., Sat, N. A., Üçer, Z. A. G. & Yılmaz, G. (2011). *Yenilikçilik ve Mekan: Ankara'daki Teknoloji Geliştirme Bölgeleri*, Ankara, Tmmob Makine Mühendisleri Odası.

Wang, E. (2009). "The Service Sector in the Chinese Economy: A Geographic Appraisal." *Eurasian Geography and Economics*, 50, 275-300.

Wernerheim, C. M. & Sharpe, C. (2003). "High Order Producer Services in Metropolitan Canada: How Footloose Are They?" *Regional Studies*, 37, 469-490.

Wood, P. (2002)."Introduction: Knowledge-intensive services, consultancy and innovation." *In:* WOOD, P. (ed.) *Consultancy and Innovation: The Business Service Revolution in Europe*. London: Routledge.

Yavuz, Ç. (2010). "İşletmelerde İnovasyon-Performans İlişkisinin İncelenmesine Dönük Bir Çalışma." *Girişimcilik ve Kalkınma Dergisi*, 5, 143-174.

Yeh, A. G. O. & Yang, F. (2013). "Spatial Development of Producer Services in the Chinese Urban System." *Environment and Planning A*, 45, 159.

Chapter 4

# Impact of Internal Crowdsourcing Contests on the Development of an Innovation Culture in Large Organizations

Juan R. Campos

*ESIC Business & Marketing School, Spain*

**Abstract:** There are few studies which provide empirical evidence of the use of collaborative technologies within organizations as an element which favors the participation of all employees in the innovation process, and, consequently, helps develop a culture which fosters innovation and becomes an adaptive system which favors the survival of the organization. The purpose of this research is to explore the impact of internal crowdsourcing contests on the development of an innovation culture in large organizations. We adopted a qualitative research using a multiple case study of four large organizations with headquarters in Spain. In addition to in-depth interviews, we built an instrument based on the Rao and Weintraub (2013) innovation culture framework to test which elements are influenced by an internal crowdsourcing contest. The findings indicate that internal crowdsourcing contests foster the commitment of most employees within the organization and encourage them to act as true innovation agents.

**Keywords:** Competitive advantage; innovation culture; internal ideation contests; internal crowdsourcing; innovation management; co-creation; intrapreneurship; large organizations.

## 4.1. Introduction

The acceleration in globalization and the resulting increase in competition, as well as an increase in market complexity, uncertainty and turbulence, characterized, among other aspects, by shorter product life cycles, changing customer demands and intense and radical technological advances, have created an environment in which it is difficult, if not impossible, to maintain a competitive advantage over a long period of time. Consequentially, some companies, particularly large organizations, are changing the way processes are organized and are focusing resources to achieve transitory competitive advantages (McGrath, 2013).

The capacity of the internet to promote the worldwide flow of information and knowledge creates the conditions for a more enriching and open ecosystem, but also a much more complex one. Technological disruption and social transformation have gone hand-in-hand in recent decades and caused radical changes to the viability of business strategies. This continuous change, happening with unprecedented speed, forces organizations to better anticipate, and be more prepared to adopt, new ways of creating, innovating, manufacturing, commercializing and even financing.

These changes are making companies more permeable to the outside world and its ideas. This new approach can be seen in the concept of Open Innovation (OI), a term coined by Henry Chesbrough (2003), who describes it as the paradigm of innovation which assumes that firms can and should use both internal and external ideas, as well as consider both internal and external paths to market, as organizations look to advance (Domingo, 2013).

Over the last 15 years open innovation processes have been broadly studied from many perspectives, such as: leveraging external knowledge and experience through crowdsourcing platforms for generating ideas and solving problems (Howe, 2006; Brabham, 2013); managing external and own intellectual property (Chesbrough, 2003, 2006; Resnick, 2011; Chesbrough and Ghafele, 2014); or emphasizing the importance of the business model as the key aspect for capturing value from innovation (Chesbrough, 2003, 2006; Boudreau and Lakhani, 2009; Teece, 2010). There are, however, few studies which provide empirical evidence of the use of collaborative technologies and their associated processes within organizations as an element which favors the participation of all employees in the innovation process. Some of these examples describe how the *wikis* can be used throughout the different stages of the innovation process from idea generation to commercializing the product or service developed (Standing and Kiniti, 2011), or how Swarovski created the *i-flash* community for generating and selecting employee ideas (Füller *et al.*, 2010), or how the implementation of an internal ideas management platform was the element which allowed a service company to change its organizational culture (Scupola and Nicolajsen, 2014).

Likewise, competitive advantage is usually obtained by making good use of technology, but it has a short life cycle, since products and services are almost immediately copied by competitors (Fawcett *et al.*, 2008). For this reason, organizations are looking at their employees as a source of competitive advantage which will allow them to differentiate themselves for longer periods of time (Fawcett *et al.*, 2008; Bolino *et al.*, 2010). This sustainability is gained by knowing how to exploit the tangible productive resources available, achieved through the knowledge, skills and attitudes of people. From this perspective, the participation of all members of the organization would not only increase the idiosyncratic nature of the competencies developed for the generation of sustainable and difficult-to-imitate competitive advantage but would also produce adaptive advantages, given that new ideas would serve to solve problems or satisfy evident or dormant needs detected outside and inside organizations. If this imperative is not fulfilled, ideas would not be selected. Consequently, an innovation culture not only fosters innovation, but also becomes an adaptive system which favors the growth and survival of organizations. Ultimately, it means the innovation culture forms part of the DNA of the whole organization, and not only in silos (Morcillo, 2007).

Hence, the research pursues a "micro-perspective", which has been repeatedly demanded in the literature (Zuchowski *et al.*, 2016). It then matches this perspective with an organizational level analysis of capabilities and culture.

This study responds to the overarching research question: *how does the implementation of an internal crowdsourcing contest influence the development of an innovation culture in large organizations?* This main question is related to four operational objectives:

1. Understand the characteristics, and key factors of an internal crowdsourcing initiative, as well as the rationale behind it.
2. Develop or select a model which groups together the main components of internal crowdsourcing contests.
3. Develop or select an innovation culture model and estimate its reliability and validity.
4. Test which components of an innovation culture are strengthened in organizations where an internal crowdsourcing contest has been implemented.

## 4.2. Background

### Innovation Culture

For the purpose of this research, a culture of innovation is defined in a multi-dimensional context. We have chosen the Rao and Weintraub (2013) innovation culture framework to explore which elements of an organizational culture improve in an organization which provides resources for managing ideas to stimulate employee co-creation around intrapreneurship. This choice was driven by our own literature review as well as the conclusions obtained by Danks (2015) and Danks *et al.* (2017) during their assessment process as to which was the most appropriate instrument to measure an innovation culture in an organization, along with two significant facts: on the one hand, it is the instrument selected by the Spanish Association for Quality (Asociación Española para la Calidad or AEC) to carry out the yearly study on the Innovation Culture Index (ICI) in Spain since 2014 (AEC, 2014) and, on the other hand, it is the one used by one of the four case studies analysed in this research, specifically Repsol Group .

This conceptual framework considers that an innovative culture rests on a foundation of six blocks: resources, processes, values, behaviors, climate and success (Figure 4.1). Each of the six building blocks is composed of three factors (18 in all), and each of those factors incorporates three underlying elements (54 in all). As we move from those abstract building blocks towards more concrete elements, the innovative culture becomes more measurable and manageable – for example, the abstract building block of values involves the entrepreneurial factor, which can be further divided into hungry, ambiguity and action-oriented.

The building blocks are dynamically linked. Thus, the values of the organization have an impact on people's behaviors, on the climate of the workplace and on how success is defined and measured.

**Figure 4.1:** Components of the innovation culture conceptual framework.

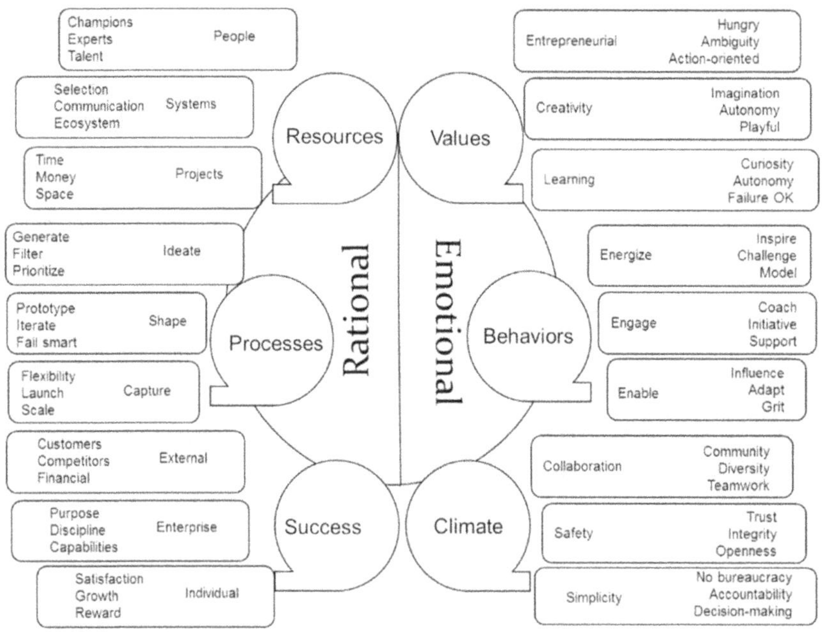


Source: Own elaboration adapted from Rao and Weintraub (2013).

When it comes to fostering innovation, organizations have generally focused considerable attention on resources, processes, and success-measures, and have often paid less attention to people-oriented dimensions, such as values, behaviors and working environment. As many managers have discovered, people values, behaviours and the working environment are less tangible and difficult to manage.

**Crowdsourcing**

Over the course of the last decade, the literature on innovation management has devoted much attention to new open models of innovation that facilitate knowledge exchange among the different actors in the innovation process (Villarroel and Reis, 2010). Crowdsourcing (Howe, 2006) is one of the new types of Open Innovation (Chesbrough, 2003) of which organizations are increasingly seeing the potential.

Brabham (2013: p. xix) defines crowdsourcing as "an online, distributed problem-solving and production model that leverages the collective intelligence of online communities to serve specific organizational goals".

Crowdsourcing is a relatively new practice that has developed considerably during the last decade. Nevertheless, as a concept, it is still considered to be "under construction" (Schenk and Guittard, 2011), and as such, remains underexplored. Many taxonomies of crowdsourcing can be found in the literature, such as explicit and implicit crowdsourcing (Doan *et al.*, 2011), external and internal crowdsourcing, and so on, but for the purpose of this research we are focused on internal crowdsourcing (Simula and Ahola, 2014) or intra-corporate crowdsourcing (Villarroel and Reis, 2010) with employees, in the form of an internal ideation contest.

According to the literature review by Zuchowski *et al.* (2016), internal crowdsourcing has several unique characteristics that make it distinct from other forms of crowdsourcing, as for example, [1] "the crowd" is made up of identifiable employees, [2] competitive and confidential issues can be addressed, and [3] there is the need in internal crowdsourcing for change and culture management skills. Zuchowski *et al.* (2016: p. 168) define internal crowdsourcing as an "IT-enabled group activity based on an open call for participation in an enterprise". Villarroel and Reis (2010: p. 2) provide a more complete definition: "intra-corporate crowdsourcing refers to a distributed organizational model used by the firm to extend problem-solving to a large and diverse pool of self-selected contributors beyond the formal internal boundaries of a multi-business firm: across business divisions, geographical locations, and hierarchical positions".

Furthermore, we selected the internal crowdsourcing model (Figure 4.2) of Zuchowski *et al.* (2016) as a way of synthesizing the analyzed internal crowdsourcing contests, allowing the schematic representation of the six main components which characterize these initiatives.

**Figure 4.2:** Conceptual framework for internal crowdsourcing.

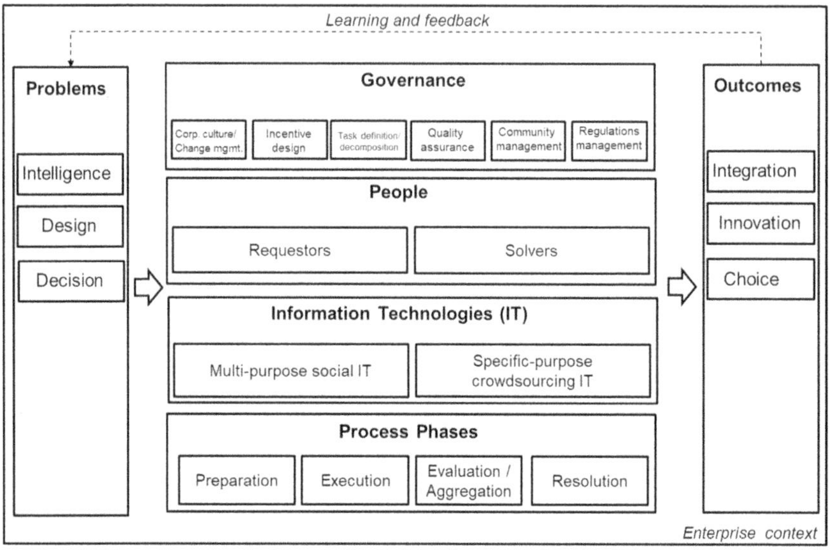


Source: Zuchowski *et al.* (2016: p. 170).

## 4.3. Research design

The basic methodology applied in this research has been *contemporary multiple case studies* (Eisenhardt, 1989; Yin, 1989, 1998) with an essentially *inductive* – and partially *deductive* – scientific approach (Yin, 1998). Yin (1989: p. 13) defines case study research as "an empirical inquiry that investigates a contemporary phenomenon within its real-life context, especially when the boundaries between phenomenon and context are not clearly evident". These are common circumstances in the object of study of this research (Table 4.1). Its application in this research is based on an exploratory, descriptive and explanatory study.

Prior to data gathering and the analysis process, a structured literature review was conducted to identify the key issues, to steer the research process and, more importantly, to establish how the empirical findings enrich understanding of current internal crowdsourcing practices and their impact on an innovation culture.

As mentioned above, we selected both the internal crowdsourcing model of Zuchowski *et al.* (2016) and the innovation culture framework developed by Rao and Weintraub (2013). To empirically estimate the reliability and validity of said innovation culture model, the company DicereGlobal provided us with an extract from their database which they created to help the AEC to measure the ICI in Spain, which bases its results on the Innovation Quotient Instrument developed by Rao and Weintraub (2013).

With the 12,496 observations of that database[1], once it had been confirmed that the sample and the validation of measurement scales were representative, a multivariate analysis was carried out consisting of a first phase in an Exploratory Factorial Analysis (EFA) and concluding with a Third-Order Confirmatory Factorial Analysis (3O-CFA).

From the perspective of the phenomenon under study, the units of analysis considered were large organizations with presence in Spain that have implemented an internal ideation contest. The following four large organizations were studied: Madrid City Hall, Banco Sabadell, Endesa and Repsol group. The selection of the cases was based on a theoretical sample, rather than statistical and random, to enable an analytical (not statistical) generalization of the results (Yin, 1989) and, therefore, it does not follow the rules of a random sample with statistical generalization capability.

For this purpose, following the methodological design proposed by Villarreal (2007, 2017) and Villarreal and Landeta (2010), based on the findings of the literature review (Eisenhardt, 1989; Maxwell, 1996; Yin, 1998), several sources of evidence were used, obtained in two complementary phases of research. The first one, essentially qualitative, was carried out to describe the rationale and characteristics behind each stage of an internal idea management initiative in the four cases analyzed. Using methodological triangulation to validate the data, we will gather the evidence from: (i) internal and external documentation review; (ii) multiple in-depth interviews with key informers; and (iii) use of physical, technological and cultural artefacts for recording interviews and for producing photographs.

For the second – quantitative – phase, we built an instrument based on the innovation culture model of Rao and Weintraub (2013), to empirically test what elements, factors and dimensions of said model evolved as a direct influence of each initiative. Using a Likert-type response scale with degrees of influence ranging from 1 = without influence to 5 = very positive, the questionnaire allowed the analysis of the initiative's influence on each of the 54 items corresponding to the six dimensions of the innovation culture framework selected.

---

[1] Respondents belong to large organizations (≥ 250 employees) based in Spain.

**Table 4.1:** Case studies data

| | |
|---|---|
| Purpose of research | Understand motivations, characteristics and key factors of an internal idea management initiative.<br>Analyze which aspects of an internal crowdsourcing contest have a positive impact on the development of a culture of innovation in four large organization and its inherent components. |
| Methodology of research | Multiple holistic case studies. Descriptive, exploratory and partially explanatory study. |
| Unit of analysis | Four organizations which have implemented an internal crowdsourcing contest. |
| Geographical coverage | Spain |
| Type of sample | Logical and theoretical sample (capacity of transferability of the phenomenon studied), non-random (sampling and statistical generalisation). |
| Sample | Madrid City Hall, Banco Sabadell, Endesa and Repsol Group. |
| Evidence-gathering methods | Documentary review (documentation and archives).<br>Multiple semi-structured interviews with open and closed questions.<br>Use of physical, technological and cultural artefacts. |
| Information sources | *Internal*: reports and studies.<br>*External*: publications, reports, own websites and other websites. |
| Key informers | Relevant employees, project managers and directors dealing with the internal crowdsourcing contests. |
| Methods of analyzing the evidence | Essentially qualitative:<br>• Search for key factors<br>• Search for critical difficulties<br>• Identification and description of the steps to implement such an initiative.<br>• Analysis of critical decisions. |
| Scientific approach | Analytical induction through replication logic (analytical generalization).<br>Deductive processes insofar as they arise from the literature review. |
| Evaluation of the methodological rigor and quality | Validity (constructive, internal and external), reliability, consistency (contextual and theoretical – interpretative). |
| Date conducted | January 2015 – August 2017 |

Source: Own elaboration based on Villarreal and Landeta (2010).

## 4.4. Conclusion

An employee ideation contest is focused on the fuzzy front end of the innovation process, so that once the organizations' challenges are identified, original ideas are sought to solve them. Within an innovative and open ecosystem, there are a series of characteristics which make employees ideal candidates for this type of initiative, since they know how the business works (Simula and Ahola, 2014), what issues arise, how they are managed, and, if they want to be competitive in their roles, it is likely that they have already carried out part of the market research needed to be familiar with the issues relating to the challenge.

However, they do not have access to significant research resources, so if organizations aim for employees to become true innovation agents, they must clearly communicate the type of challenges to be included in these initiatives and what will be required from employees.

The justification for implementing an internal idea management initiative is directly linked to what the company expects to gain from it. Said expectations are very similar in the four case studies analyzed and can be summarized as follows (Campos and Calderón-Martínez, 2016):

- Encourage the participation and involvement of all employees during the initial phases of the innovation process, to obtain more and better business ideas through collective intelligence (Simula and Ahola, 2014).
- Allow hidden talent to emerge from within the organization and identify intrapreneurs.
- Favor internal communication (Linke and Zerfass, 2011) and encourage employee ideas to be recognized, as well as increasing the collaboration between different business units (Simula and Vuori, 2012).
- Promote the development of an innovation culture within an organization (Scupola and Nicolajsen, 2014).

The key factors of this kind of initiative are related to learning obtained in previous editions. It is worth differentiating between those which are associated with matters of leadership and people, and those which are more involved in designing the support processes.

With regards to the leadership aspects required for the development of these initiatives, the following are noted:

- The support of *top management* is critical (Hassard and Sharifi, 1989, cited in Brown, 1998).

- The role of a *challenge sponsor/owner* is key and should be at an operational hierarchical level where ideas are implemented.
- The *definition of the challenge* needs to be worked on at length with the sponsor.
- It is very important to create and train *initiative management teams*, since they are responsible for monitoring the whole process and making sure that it is functioning correctly (*governance* component).
- The commitment of *middle managers* must be encouraged to ensure they support the participation of employees in their respective departments.
- *Expectations* must be well managed. The whole organization must be clear on the purpose of these type of initiatives. They cannot be considered as the company's whole innovation plan.
- With a view to generating credibility around the initiative, *results* must be achieved in the short term, and be made visible.

Regarding factors related to the design of supporting processes (*process* component), it is worth mentioning the following:

- The use of a *specific online platform* for encouraging the participation of all employees is recommended.
- One of the cornerstones of the process is a strong *communication plan* (Linke and Zerfass, 2011) which embraces the whole process, invigorates and encourages participation.
- It is beneficial to communicate who will form part of the *jury* responsible for assessing ideas and selecting the winners.
- *Transparency* of the whole process is another of the key factors. Special emphasis should be placed on explaining the challenge itself and clarifying the criteria for idea evaluation and selection.
- Another important aspect is *simplicity*. User experience should be very friendly. The process for presenting ideas, voting, and possibly adding comments, must be simple.
- The best *reward*, along with recognition, is the implementation of the ideas selected.

### 4.5. Implications and future research

This research contributes to theory in five major ways. First, it confirms important statements on the objectives and reasons for implementing an internal crowdsourcing contest but shows an interesting and novel contribution with regards to the objective of companies to build a better innovation culture.

Second, it emphasizes the importance of leadership for OI – an often mentioned but rarely researched topic in the field. With regards to this point, the following aspects stand out: (i) the first requirement to note is the **support of top management**, as well as the critical role played by the figure of **sponsor or challenge owner**, able to provide the financial and human resources required to make the selected ideas a reality, and who should be very much involved in addressing the challenge; (ii) it should be recommended that the whole organization clearly understands that this type of initiative cannot be considered the company's whole innovation plan, since it focuses only on the initial stages of the innovation process; (iii) a very important aspect is gaining the commitment of **middle managers and supervisors** so that they, in turn, support those in their teams who decide to participate in the initiative; finally, with a view to generating credibility around the initiative, (iv) **results must be achieved** in the short term, and **made visible**, since the best reward is the implementation of the selected ideas.

Third, it selects a conceptual framework which allows the main components of an internal crowdsourcing contest, with their respective decisions, to be represented schematically (Zuchowski *et al.*, 2016). The six main components are: the problems, the governance, the people, the IT, the processes to be developed for its implementation, and the expected outcomes.

Fourth, it provides empirical evidence of the reliability and validity of the InnoQuotient instrument selected as a tool for appraising an innovation culture within an organization. Finally, from a methodological point of view, this research provides a robust argument that justifies the use of this case study methodology, as well as substantial elements for building appropriate and rigorous designs for scientifically-based and focused case study research.

Furthermore, this research offers some implications and practical recommendations for practitioners, especially for business managers, and OI intermediaries and platform providers. The main conclusion is that a systematic and focused gathering of ideas leads to a normalized process (Pedersen *et al.*, 2013), which comprises eight stages: Planning, Promotion, Launch, Participation, Evaluation, Selection, Reward model, and Post-campaign analysis. With regards to this stage model, the results have shown some important key factors. For example, the use of a specific online platform that encourages the participation of all employees is important (Ebner *et al.*, 2009; Bullinger *et al.*, 2010; Brabham, 2013), but not the critical factor for these initiatives. The most important factor is an **effective process design** and the ability to adapt it based on the learning acquired from previous editions.

One of the cornerstones of the process is a strong **communication plan** (Linke and Zerfass, 2011), which is essential for bringing it to life and for encouraging participation, together with a team of innovation **facilitators** or **ambassadors** to provide support and motivation.

On the other hand, the internal crowdsourcing framework used (Zuchowski *et al.*, 2016) is proposed as a guide to action at the disposal of the internal crowdsourcing contest management team to help them decide which are the analytical and decisional units with enough weight to lead the design and roll-out of this type of initiative, without losing the necessary rational coherence among the different components.

Based on the results obtained through the quantitative phase, it is expected that business managers who are considering developing or improving an innovation culture in their organization might rely on an internal crowdsourcing contest, as it provides a common vehicle for the emergence of hidden employee talent, for intrapreneurs to be identified and their creativity leveraged in solving real organizational challenges, creates a favorable climate for communication between departments, thus fostering the commitment of most of the employees, and encouraging them to act as true innovation agents.

Lastly, we want to emphasize the importance of assuming that there is no single solution, as has become patently clear in the four cases analyzed. In this regard, we advise managers who are considering using an internal crowdsourcing initiative for developing an innovation culture in their organization, to take these recommendations as a guide for good practice but not as a magic formula nor a rigid pattern to follow. What is key is to train and support effective teams of professionals who know how to analyze, interpret and adapt the initiative in line with the learning acquired during implementation.

With regards to future research, internal crowdsourcing contests as a cultural statement are an interesting value proposition, however a challenging one, as internal crowdsourcing contests can build an innovation culture, but also demand an existing open culture for innovation to be successful in the first place. Following this trade-off is a promising area for future innovation research.

Conversely, the stage model mentioned above has rather little academic novelty with regards to theory development, however, it has a large value for management practice and also provides a very good framework for a more fine-grained study of internal crowdsourcing contests. For future innovation practice, a contingency perspective could be assumed here, for example, assessing in more detail how situational factors or characteristics of the host organization influence the design and execution of the stages.

Finally, we want to mention that although the multiple case study methodology used has been ideal for analyzing the phenomenon, we are aware it has several limitations related to the sample selection, geographical scope, the amount of time that longitudinal research takes, but especially related to statistical generalization. Nevertheless, given the objectives of this research, the benefits that the case study has brought to the research far outweigh its limitations.

## Acknowledgements

We greatly appreciate the contributions of all those professionals from Madrid City Hall, Banco Sabadell, Endesa and Repsol Group, who have participated so actively in this research. All errors and omissions remain ours.

## References

Asociación Española para la Calidad (AEC) (2014). Metodología del Primer Estudio Cultura de la Innovación. *AEC*, [online] Available at: www.aec.es/web/guest/cultura-innovacion/primer-estudio-cultura-innovacion/metodologia [Accessed 9 Dec. 2016].

Bolino, M., Valcea, S. and Harvey, J. (2010). "Employee, manage thyself: The potentially negative implications of expecting employees to behave proactively." *Journal of Occupational and Organizational Psychology*, 83(2), pp. 325-345.

Boudreau, K. and Lakhani, K. (2009). "How to Manage Outside Innovation." *MIT Sloan Management Review*, 50(4), pp. 69-75.

Brabham, D. (2013). *Crowdsourcing*. Cambridge: MIT Press.

Brown, A. (1998). *Organizational Culture*. 2nd ed. Financial Times - Prentice Hall.

Bullinger, A., Neyer, A., Rass, M. and Moeslin, K. (2010). "Community-Based Innovation Contests: Where Competition Meets Cooperation." *Creativity and Innovation Management*, 19(3), pp. 290-303.

Campos, J. and Calderón-Martínez, G. (2016). "Internal Idea Management Contest as a Catalyst for a Culture of Innovation in the Public Sector. The Case of Madrid City Hall (Spain)." *Proceedings of the 14th International Open and User Innovation Conference, August 1-3*. Boston: Harvard Business School. https://oui2016.exordo.com/files/papers/145/final_draft/Campos-Calderon_2016_OUI-Conference-Final.pdf (Accessed 15 Mar. 2018).

Chesbrough, H. (2003). *Open Innovation: The New Imperative for Creating and Profiting from Technology*. Boston: Harvard Business School Press.

Chesbrough, H. (2006). "Open Innovation: A New Paradigm for Understanding Industrial Innovation." In: H. Chesbrough, W. Vanhaverbeke and J. West, eds., *Open Innovation: Researching a New Paradigm*, New York: Oxford University Press, pp. 1-12.

Chesbrough, H. and Ghafele, R. (2014). "Open Innovation and Intellectual Property: A Two-Sided Market Perspective." In: H. Chesbrough, W. Vanhaverbeke and J. West, eds., *New Frontiers in Open Innovation,* Oxford: Oxford University Press, pp. 191-207.

Danks, S. (2015). *Measuring Culture of Innovation: A Validation Study of the Innovation Quotient Instrument.* Doctoral thesis: University of North Texas, Denton, Texas.

Danks, S., Rao, J. and Allen, J. (2017). "Measuring Culture of Innovation: A Validation Study of the Innovation Quotient Instrument (Part One)." *Performance Improvement Quarterly,* 29(4), pp. 427-454.

Doan, A., Ramakrishnan, R. and Halevy, A. (2011). "Crowdsourcing Systems on the World-Wide Web." *Communications of the ACM,* 54(4), pp. 86-96.

Domingo, C. (2013). *El viaje de la innovación: La guía definitiva para innovar con éxito.* Barcelona: Gestión 2000, Ediciones Grupo Planeta.

Ebner, W., Leimeister, J. and Krcmar, H. (2009). "Community engineering for innovations: the ideas competition as a method to nurture a virtual Community for innovations." *R&D Management,* 39(4), pp. 342-356.

Eisenhardt, K. (1989). "Building Theories from Case Study Research." *The Academy of Management Review,* 14, pp. 532-550.

Fawcett, S., Brau, J., Rhoads, G., Whitlark, D. and Fawcett, A. (2008). "Spirituality and Organizational Culture: Cultivating the ABCs of an Inspiring Workplace." *International Journal of Public Administration,* 31(4), pp. 420-438.

Füller, J., Lenz, A. and Pirker, C. (2010). "Innovation management 2.0: how to organize innovation in the era of social media." *Performance,* 3(2), pp. 28-35.

Hassard, J. and Sharifi, S. (1989). "Corporate culture and strategic change." *Journal of General Management,* 15(2), pp. 4-19.

Howe, J. (2006). "The Rise of Crowdsourcing." *Wired,* [online] Volume 14 (6). Available at: http://www.wired.com/2006/06/crowds/ [Accessed 9 Dec. 2016].

Linke, A. and Zerfass, A. (2011). "Internal communication and innovation culture: developing a change framework." *Journal of Communication Management,* 15(4), pp. 332-348.

McGrath, R. (2013). *The End of Competitive Advantage: How to Keep Your Strategy Moving as Fast as Your Business.* Boston: Harvard Business Review Press.

Maxwell, J. (1996). *Qualitative Research Design: An Interactive Approach.* Sage Publications: Thousand Oaks.

Morcillo, P. (2007). *Cultura e Innovación Empresarial. La Conexión Perfecta.* Madrid: Thomson Editores Spain.

Pedersen, J., Kocsis, D., Tripathi, A., Tarrell, A., Weerakoon, A., Tahmasbi, N., Xiong, J., Deng, W., Oh, O. and deVreede, G-J. (2013). "Conceptual Foundations of Crowdsourcing: A Review of IS Research." *Proceedings of the 46th Annual Hawaii International Conference on System Sciences,* Maui, HI, USA, pp. 579-588.

Rao, J. and Weintraub, J. (2013). "How Innovative Is Your Company's Culture?" *MIT Sloan Management Review,* 54, pp. 29-37.

Resnick, D. (2011). Managing Legal and IP Issues. In: P. Sloan, ed., *A Guide to Open Innovation and Crowdsourcing*. London: Kogan Page Ltd., pp. 148-159.

Schenk, E. and Guittard, C. (2011). "Towards a characterization of crowdsourcing practices." *Journal of Innovation Economics & Management*, 1(7), pp. 93-107.

Scupola, A. and Nicolajsen, H. (2014). "The Impact of Enterprise Crowdsourcing on Company Innovation Culture: The Case of an Engineering Consultancy." In: T. Commisso, J. Nørbjerg and J. Pries-Heje eds., *Nordic Contributions in IS Research*. Switzerland: Springer International Publishing, pp. 105-120.

Simula, H. and Vuori, M. (2012). "Benefits and Barriers of Crowdsourcing in B2B Firms: Generating Ideas with Internal and External Crowds." *International Journal of Innovation Management*, 16(6), pp. 1-19.

Simula, H. and Ahola, T. (2014). "A network perspective on idea and innovation crowdsourcing in industrial firms." *Industrial Marketing Management*, 43(3), pp. 400-408.

Standing, C. and Kiniti, S. (2011). "How can organizations use wikis for innovation?" *Technovation*, 31(7), pp. 287-295.

Teece, D. (2010). "Business Models, Business Strategy and Innovation." *Long Range Planning*, 43, pp. 172-194.

Villarreal, O. (2007). *La Estrategia de Internacionalización de la Empresa. Un Estudio de Casos de Multinacionales Vascas* (Tesis Doctoral). Universidad del País Vasco-Euskal Herriko Unibertsitatea, Bilbao.

Villarreal, O. (2017). "Is it desirable, necessary and posible to perform research using case studies?" *Cuadernos de gestión*, 17(1), pp. 147-171.

Villarreal, O. and Landeta, J. (2010). "El estudio de casos como metodología de investigación científica en economía de la empresa y dirección estratégica." *Investigaciones Europeas de Dirección y Economía de la Empresa*, 16 (3), 31-52.

Villarroel, J. and Reis, F. (2010). "Intra-Corporate Crowdsourcing (ICC): Leveraging Upon Rank and Site Marginality for Innovation." *CrowdConf 2010*. CA: San Francisco.

Yin, R. (1989). *Case Study Research. Design and Methods*. Applied Social Research Methods Series. 1st ed. London: SAGE Publications, Inc.

Yin, R. (1998). "The Abridged Version of Case Study Research." In *Handbook of Applied Social Research Methods*, edited by Leonard Bickman and Debra Rog. Sage Publications: Thousand Oaks.

Zuchowski, O., Posegga, O., Schalagwein, D. and Fischbach, K. (2016). "Internal crowdsourcing: conceptual framework, structured review, and research agenda." *Journal of Information Technology*, 31(2), pp. 166-184.

Chapter 5

# Innovation through Cross-Fertilization: Serious Games and Gamification in the EU-Funded Research Projects

Manel González-Piñero

*Universitat de Barcelona, Spain*

**Abstract:** Ecosystems of innovation have gained substantial momentum in academic research. As a response to recent calls in open innovation literature for novel research, this doctoral thesis extends the study of the process and ecosystems of innovation in projects that include serious games and gamification by considering the cross-fertilization of knowledge and technologies. Organizations' orchestration of activities within their activity systems and transformation of their business models through innovation to realize opportunities with the objective to increase value creation are part of the topic of this dissertation. It has endeavoured to improve the understanding of how cross-fertilized alliances are formed, what their outcomes are, what causes them to generate value (or not) and what capabilities organizations need in order to successfully manage and reap value from the innovation process. For this purpose, two approaches that support innovation have been complementarily taken into account: the knowledge-technological perspective and the management perspective.

**Keywords:** Open innovation; Innovation management; Technology management; Knowledge management; Cross-fertilization of knowledge and technologies; Serious games; Gamification; End user; Multidisciplinarity; Cultural diversity

## 5.1. Introduction

Open innovation has impacted and enhanced organizations' collaboration strategies and public policy programs as EU-H2020. This new paradigm emerged from businesses' needs to adapt to changing circumstances after a global recession. In this new wave of innovation, companies refocused on organic growth and on their customers and consumer markets to enrich their business units and new corporate venturing initiatives. So, open innovation gained importance in organizations' innovation and new strategies as the cross-fertilization of knowledge and technologies became a path to develop new technological applications and market opportunities. Moreover, given the need for innovation systems that require the collaboration between organizations on local and international levels, governments are designing new programs and strategies to capture the benefits of investing in R&D programs. The EU-H2020 Framework Programme provides a balanced response to the main challenges faced by Europe: firstly, the need to maintain a strong expertise in key technology value chains; secondly, the necessity to move quicker from research excellence to market.

The video game industry is in constant evolution, concerned to know better the end user and incorporate him/her in the development process, integrating the latest technological advances in creation and distribution, cross-fertilizing with other fields to provide the user with better gaming experiences, thereby obtaining significant economic returns. This innovative characteristic of the field generates new relationships that push companies to determine the best approach for managing direct-to-consumer relationships, troubleshooting game issues, reducing gamer churn and preventing loss of gamer engagement. The digital endpoints, the lower barriers to entry for low-cost alternatives, and the need to innovate and join the group of disruptors are more critical than ever. This innovative character makes gaming one of the most competitive and attractive investment sectors, with an audience that grows from year to year in non-existing percentages in any other sector. Two of the video game applications that generate great opportunities in terms of cross-sector applications and impact on the market are serious games and gamification.

The serious games market is promising in terms of research and development; however, it also represents a scattered industry with a variety of application areas and characteristics. As of today, there is no serious games market breakthrough. Reasons for these grand challenges include socio-economic aspects (development costs, quality, cost-benefit ratio), legal aspects (data protection and privacy), and a number of research and technical development related issues. Nevertheless, serious games provide a good opportunity for developer studios to cross-finance their own technology development or to bridge time between big(ger) entertainment productions eventually popping up due to unforeseen events. Gamification, as opposed to serious gaming, focuses on the integration of certain elements and mechanics from the field of gaming and game design into an existing (non-gaming) environment (Klevers *et al.*, 2016). The business community is starting to realize the power it has to improve customer engagement, build loyalty, and incentivize employees and partners to perform at high levels. And the concept has the potential to solve a variety of problems outside the business world as well, in areas such as: health, education, public policy, tourism, sustainability, personal development –and the list continues to grow.

This chapter seeks to get insights about the innovation and technology challenges existing in the cross-fertilization of technologies when serious games or gamification are included, from basic research through technological commercialization, exploring the specificities of capabilities required to get a successful technology transfer process. In fact, the complete technological and innovative lifecycle of new products must solve the gap between academia, industry and market known as the "Valley of Death" (Debackere, 2000; Flynn and Wei, 2005; Linton and Walsh, 2008; European Commission, 2012; Mahroum and Al-Saleh, 2013) and the so-called "European paradox" (Pavitt, 1998; Debackere, 2000; Flynn and Wei, 2005; Linton and Walsh, 2008; Mahroum and Al-Saleh, 2013) which suggests a contradiction between higher levels of scientific performance on the one hand and the minimal contributions to industrial competitiveness and new venture entrepreneurship in Europe on the other (Paez-Aviles, 2017).

Overcoming this gap to reach commercial success and the social return of research could be a difficult process if innovation challenges are not addressed. In fact, the future of the industry will rely on its ability to innovate in high-tech activities that can offer a differential added value, rather than improving existing technologies and products (Juanola-Feliu *et al.*, 2012; Motyl and Filippi, 2014). Cross-fertilization of knowledge and technology is an innovation strategy. Most of the approaches of cross-fertilization have been focused on inter-disciplinarity (Egenfeldt-Nielsen, 2008; Frans, 2009; Hacklin *et al.*, 2009; Porter and Youtie, 2009; Rafols and Meyer, 2010; Pilon and Tremblay, 2013; Sedighi, 2013; Schummer, 2004) and partial technological convergence (Dang *et al.*, 2010; No and Park, 2010). Previous works have also analysed the cross-fertilization process by focusing on the inter-disciplinarity of research collaboration (Rafols and Meyer, 2010; Van Rijnsoever and Hessels, 2011; König *et al.*, 2013; Sedighi, 2013) but little attention has been paid to address innovation and technology transfer challenges for the successful commercialization of outcomes including serious games or gamification applications. This work contributes to a better understanding of the processes and ecosystems of innovation and thus, to reduce the Valley of Death gap between research and market.

## 5.2. Background

The rapidly changing competitive landscape challenges organizations to become more innovative. Instead of falling prey to ever-changing market forces, some firms show great agility and strategic renewal as they relentlessly change and transform their business models in terms of innovation. Driven by a continuous quest for opportunities that put their activities and resources to better and more profitable use and allow them to create and capture more value, companies (but not only) frequently and consistently introduce new value propositions and new ways of value appropriation. Organizations' orchestration of activities within their activity systems and transformation of their business models through innovation to realize opportunities with the objective to increase value creation is part of the topic of this dissertation. Especially, how cross-fertilization of knowledge and technology creates adequate multidisciplinary knowledge and technology (Van der Bergh, 2008; Adler and Heckscher, 2006; Van Rijnsoever *et al.*, 2015) to ensure the success of an emerging technology, and how important is the research and innovation that takes place in the practitioners' communities (Starkey and Madan, 2001; Søraa *et al.*, 2017); and a second view, how the management perspective presents the analysis of the innovation management strategies that boost the cross-fertilization of technologies (Almeida and Phene, 2004; Maine *et al.*, 2014).

Funding instruments can be used as a tool for policy makers to influence organizations and their level of technological diversity (Adler and Heckscher, 2005; Edquist and Hommen, 1999) and thus to secure the long-term viability of technology. Also, the use of specific technologies is encouraged to be recombined with others creating new applications or developing new uses to existing technologies. From an innovation perspective, concepts as serious gaming or gamification are an example. The creation and persistence of knowledge and technological multidisciplinarity depend on learning from their neighbourhood and network externalities. There is little empirical evidence about the characteristics of innovation projects that influence multidisciplinarity. Van Rijnsoever *et al.* (2015) demonstrated that diversity created by an innovation project is related to the network position and organization composition of a project. Adding to insights from innovation systems (Edquist, 1997), Van Rijnsoever *et al.* (2015) argue that it is also important to consider the structure of the network to make a technology successful in the long term.

The international multidisciplinarity of collaborative research projects should be beneficial to technological diversity creation, but this implication has not been tested empirically. From this knowledge and technology perspective, these current approaches are extended by the study of the influence of the characteristics of EU-funded serious games and gamification related projects on the creation of multidisciplinarity. Additional novel variables that have a plausible influence on diversity creation are included in the study.

Furthermore, to understand technological multidisciplinarity, a deep analysis of the content of the documents is needed. An approach is to look at the network of citations of the documents (Rafols and Meyer, 2010). A different one is using pre-existing categories like patent classes to measure diversity (Jonard and Yfldizoglu, 1998; Rafols and Meyer, 2010). Yet, these approaches are mainly applicable to patent, Web of Science categories or publication data, and not to H2020 projects. Hence, to study multidisciplinarity, topic modelling was applied (Leydesdorff *et al.*, 2014) as a novel approach to categorize the most relevant topics and thematic areas that are described in 87 projects including 519 organizations. This method allows calculating multidisciplinarity in an efficient manner (Paez-Aviles, 2017).

The change in knowledge and technological diversity caused by a project was related to the independent variables mentioned above and results have shown that the largest contribution to diversity comes from the multidisciplinary nature of a project and the knowledge base of the organizations in a project. Moreover, the obtained results largely confirm the results by Van Rijnsoever *et al.* (2005) and Paez-Aviles (2017). These results aim to open the reflection as to how policy makers can use public subsidies to influence the level of diversity in a technological field.

The importance of having mechanisms for systematic management of innovation has been widely recognized and investigated (Burns and Stalker, 1961; Parker, 1982; Kanter, 1983; Leonard-Barton, 1992; Christensen, 1997). Chiesa et al. (1996) developed an innovation audit model that tests a set of organizational innovation management good practices, in order to determine the firm's innovation capabilities. This model is based on the exploration of "key" innovation processes (new concept generation, new product development, process redefinition, technology acquisition) plus other "support" activities (leadership and culture, resource allocation, organizational systems). Other models of functional analysis were proposed by Yam *et al.* (2004) and Heinz *et al.* (2006).

Technological diversity leads to opportunity creation (Pisano, 2006; Subramanian and Soh, 2010) and there is enormous potential for innovation from the confluence of technologies (Sharp *et al.*, 2011). Maine *et al.* (2014) go a step forward and explore how the convergence of technologies can lead to the creation of radical innovation and subsequently, the emergence of new industries. According to Maine *et al.* (2014), there are three central innovation management strategies in this convergence: i) to import ideas from broad networks, ii) to create environments for deep collaboration and iii) technology-market-matching. The first strategy refers to the search and synthesis of ideas that could be taken up from networks with different technology streams. The second strategy involves the dynamic collaborative flow of knowledge between R&D groups. Finally, these two strategies need to be complemented by considering market needs, which is the third strategy (Paez-Aviles, 2017).

## 5.3. Research design

### 5.3.1 Sample selection

The study focused on those projects in which serious games and gamification are one of the technologies included. Specifically, all the projects including serious games and/or gamification and funded by the European Union through any Horizon 2020 work programme have been selected as the subject of study.

Horizon 2020 is the EU Research and Innovation programme with nearly €80 billion of funding available over 7 years (2014 to 2020). The study sample was the granted projects covering the period between 2014 and 2016 (April), selecting only the 87 projects, including serious games and/or gamification technologies. The EU contribution received by these 87 projects was 201,714,160 €.

### 5.3.2 Methodology

#### 5.3.2.1 Database

In early 2016, the information retrieved from the selected projects was used to create a new database including the 87 projects with their 519 organizations and 597 observations, detailing any characteristic. Clearing, filtering and detection of errors took months of work to obtain the final database. Later, it was analysed in-depth through descriptive statistics, network graphs and text mining approaches in order to have a complete overview of the elements of study. Next, to analyse the creation of multidisciplinarity, the Topic Modelling approach was used. This method allows the calculation of multidisciplinarity creation in a more efficient manner than in conventional qualitative approaches. Finally, the analysis was complemented with the use of external databases, indexes and rankings.

#### 5.3.2.2 Survey

In order to get insights about the Innovation Management Strategies, in middle 2017, a project coordinators survey was conducted for the second section of the study. They were contacted mainly by e-mail (in some case a phone contact was required) and this information was retrieved from the projects web sites, institutions web sites and in some cases contacting directly with the administration of their institutions.

The hypotheses formulated for this section were mainly tested through an in-depth statistical analysis. This survey was only addressed to the coordinators of the 62 collaborative projects, including serious games and/or gamification technologies and funded by H2020. A total of 46 complete responses were received resulting in a 74.1% response rate. This response rate is extremely superior to those of e-mail surveys involving senior executives – typically with very lower response rates (Kriauciunas *et al.*, 2011).

### 5.3.2.3 Personal Interviews

Moreover, two types of personal interviews were conducted: (1) with experts of the video game ecosystem to help define the object of study and design of the thesis; and (2) with independent experts to understand and have elements for the subsequent analysis and discussion of the findings.

The methodology applied in the three sections is summarized in **Figure 5.1**.

**Figure 5.1:** Summary of the methodology used in the empirical study.

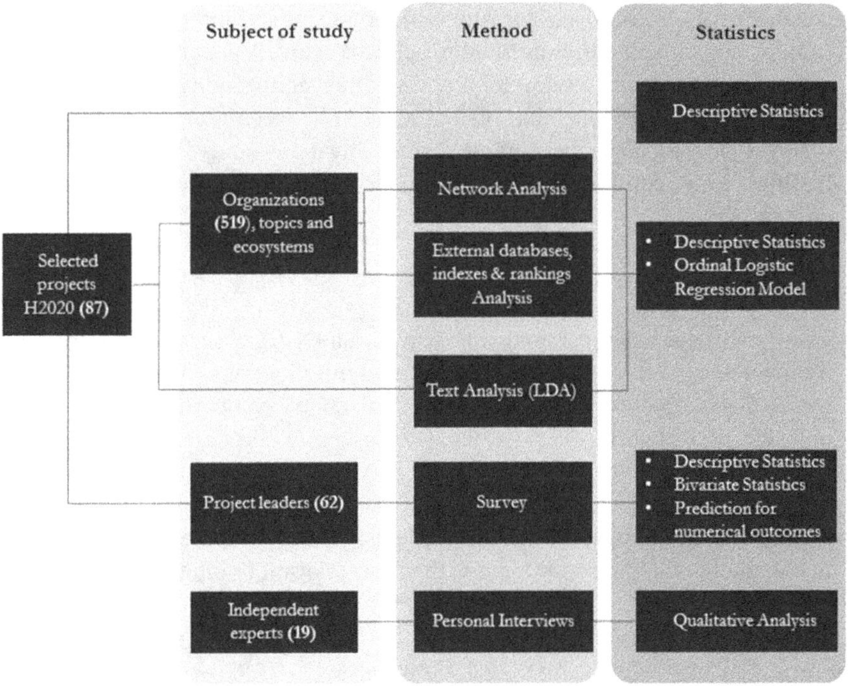

### 5.3.3 Analysis

#### 5.3.3.1 Database

In the first place, an in-depth descriptive statistical analysis was performed for the entire sample of projects (87 projects with their 519 organizations and 597 observations) in order to get insights into the characteristics of the elements of analysis. Second, the subsequent focus on the organizations required the use of Lattice plot correlation, network graphs and text mining approaches to complement the previous descriptive statistical analysis. Finally, some variables required to be complemented by the analysis of external databases, indexes and rankings.

#### 5.3.3.2 Survey

Firstly, a descriptive analysis was performed for the entire sample of collaborative projects' coordinators in order to get information on the projects consortia. Later, I decided to select certain exogenous variables that influence directly in the development of other endogenous variables. So, I chose some key variables that firstly I crossed between them and then with the rest of variables, developing diverse bivariate statistical tests. These findings were complemented by statistics for predictions of numerical outcomes.

#### 5.3.3.3 Personal Interviews

This qualitative analysis used the data obtained from several face-to-face interviews, all of them following a structured questionnaire. This information was written up into a report and a final chart, comparing the answers between the different interviewees who represent the Catalan video game ecosystem according to the Triple Helix Model. Complementarily, shorter interviews took place with additional independent experts to discuss or getting knowledge of some specific findings. Finally, all these data were used to complement and discuss some of the most relevant findings of this present study.

## 5.4. Conclusion

This doctoral thesis has analysed the process and ecosystems of innovation in projects that include serious games and/or gamification by considering the cross-fertilization of knowledge and technologies. It has endeavoured to improve the understanding of how cross-fertilized alliances are formed, what their outcomes are, what causes them to generate value (or not) and what capabilities organizations need in order to successfully manage and reap value from the innovation process. For this purpose, two approaches that support innovation have been complementarily taken into account: the knowledge-technological perspective and the management perspective.

Organizations' orchestration of activities within their activity systems and transformation of their business models through innovation to realize opportunities with the objective to increase value creation is part of the topic of this dissertation. Especially, how cross-fertilization of knowledge and technology creates adequate multidisciplinary knowledge and technology (Van der Bergh, 2008; Adler and Heckscher, 2006; Van Rijnsoever *et al.*, 2015) to ensure the success of an emerging technology, and how important is the research and innovation that takes place in the practitioners' communities (Starkey and Madan, 2001; Søraa *et al.*, 2017).

Key issues and current concerns of innovation and technology transfer have been addressed. By doing so, this work has sought to extend scientific, industrial and innovation knowledge attempting to answer the new challenges that publicly-funded research is facing. Additionally, the relevance of collaborative interaction and the environmental factors associated with the success of gaming-related emerging technology were highlighted in this chapter by consolidating the redefinition of the video game value chain and how it affects the business and monetization models.

Findings from this research could have implications for evolutionary economics regarding technological diversity creation in innovation systems. The data obtained supports once again the idea that innovation system literature is connected with the social network approaches. In this regard, it has been shown that external collaboration plays an important role in emerging technologies.

Moreover, this chapter exhibits a methodological original contribution, which is the implementation of the probabilistic text modelling method LDA for analysing the degree of a project's multidisciplinarity. Even though this method is well accepted by the research community, text analysis is less frequent and has been only used once for studying technological diversity (Paez-Aviles, 2017). Nevertheless, this is the first work that used topic modelling for analysing technological diversity in serious games and gamification-related European projects in a convergent scenario of technologies. Additionally, since project information has been used as the source of data, this study offers a differentiated methodology compared with publications and patents, which have been the common source of data used for analysing information. Therefore, this work has considered complementary techniques by utilizing from the increasing power of machine learning and computation.

The combination of newness and often asymmetric dispersion of knowledge suggests that relevant knowledge will most likely reside in networks of organizations, rather than in individual members of a technology innovation system (Powell *et al.*, 1996). This doctoral thesis has attempted to explore and define theoretically and empirically two characteristics found in the innovation ecosystems: the level of multidisciplinarity and the level of cross-fertilization, by distilling its enablers of knowledge-technology and management strategies to ensure the robustness of my conceptualizations. Furthermore, the study is focused on projects that combine diverse technologies but always including serious games and/or gamification in order to identify the benefits and advantages provided by these technologies.

Another contribution of this work is related to the significant role of serious games and gamification in the cross-fertilization of knowledge and technologies. The presence of those technologies in a project is seen as very important and important for the 73% of the respondents. In a redefinition of the previous EU-funding Programs[1], the current H2020 could help to address the European Paradox, fostering the market orientation of the projects; in fact, serious games and gamification are seen in the majority of cases as a tool for developing market-oriented solutions closer to commercialization and better oriented to customer needs. Furthermore, the important role of end users along the value chain is emphasized by this study. From an open innovation perspective, the end user becomes a co-creator and/or a co-developer.

### 5.5. Implications and future research

From the **knowledge and technology perspective**, the main contribution to the literature is that the degree of multidisciplinarity of a project and a large knowledge base enhances recombinant innovation, increasing the possibilities of emerging and transferring new technologies into the market. These results clearly support that the degree of multidisciplinarity of a project and the size of the joint knowledge base are positively associated with the creation of multidisciplinary knowledge and technology.

Secondly, findings suggest that larger project teams provide a larger chance of recombining different types of knowledge, expertise and ideas, and thus innovation (Powell *et al.*, 1996; Ruef, 2002). Thus, results show how Rijnsoever arguments are not supported and there is a positive association between the number of organizations and the creation of multidisciplinary knowledge and technology in projects including serious games and gamification.

---

[1] FP1 (1984-1987), FP2 (1987-1991), FP3 (199o-1994), FP4 (1994-1998), FP5 (1998-2002), FP6(2002-20006

Furthermore, every organization brings to the project unique knowledge and skills that can be recombined to form novel concepts and designs (Mo 2016), creating more technological multidisciplinarity and diversity (Rijnsoever *et al.*, 2015).

Thirdly, the study has tried to make a contribution to the open debate about the degree and the effect of clustering on innovation. Results suggested that the degree of clustering around a project is negatively associated with the creation of multidisciplinary knowledge and technology. In fact, excessive cognitive resemblance may limit innovation opportunities, since there would be little left to learn (Boschma, 2005; Nooteboom, 1999). Homogeneity of knowledge must be avoided venturing further afield but balancing the composition of clustered networks. Fourthly, the innovation intensity was measured by the Global Innovation Index, supporting a positive association with the creation of multidisciplinary knowledge and technology.

The results obtained from the knowledge and technology perspective can serve as guidelines to policy makers, especially at the EU-level, for fostering the success of emerging technologies on the basis of their cross-fertilization and the creation of multidisciplinary knowledge and technology. In order to encourage the creation of multidisciplinarity, emphasis should be placed on subsidizing the following projects: (1) involving or developing different disciplines, (2) including a large knowledge base for enhancing the ability of organizations to make novel combinations, (3) including different typologies of organizations giving unique knowledge and skills, (4) with a different number of partners but not too closely connected with each other, (5) with balanced consortia in terms of innovation intensity. The first three are already explicit or implicit criteria in H2020, although findings recommend reducing the size of some consortia for not overlapping knowledge and capacities. In fact, the fourth recommendation introduces that partners must provide diversity of knowledge that later could be used by the consortium to make novel combinations. Finally, the fifth contribution also emphasizes the importance of innovation intensity because the local network influences the chances of developing new knowledge and technology.

The **second perspective** analysed in this study, the **management** one, takes as a starting point Maine's (2014) exploration of how the convergence of technologies can lead to the creation of radical innovation and subsequently the emergence of new industries. According to her, there are three central innovation management strategies in this convergence that have been explored in this study: i) *to import ideas from broad networks*, ii) *to create environments for deep collaboration* and iii) *technology-market matching*. Also, other aspects related to network theories, absorptive capacity and dynamic capabilities' literature have been considered.

The first strategy refers to the search and synthesis of ideas that could be taken up from networks with different technology streams. This strategy was studied by the analysis of the knowledge and technological distance, the technological effort, the access to external information and the participation of end users along the value chain. Results show that the level of cross-fertilization is higher when there are larger knowledge and technological distances in the network, when organizations make stronger knowledge and technological efforts, when organizations open up the innovation process to external knowledge flows (because belonging to the network is critical to access to external information and so having a competitive advantage) and when end users participate in the process of development along the value chain.

The second strategy involves the dynamic collaborative flow of knowledge between R&D groups. The existence of these collaborative networks has been explored by the analysis of the partners' previous collaborative experiences, the knowledge intensity, the types of collaboration networks and the cultural diversity. Findings suggest that cross-fertilization is boosted when: organizations tend to collaborate from the beginning of the process, there is knowledge intensity and organizations tend to concentrate efforts in the employability of doctorate holders, there are formal collaborations between partners, and teams celebrate and reflect cultural diversity. Therefore, this team-based collaboration fosters cross-functional activities, creates innovative value, often leads to new ways of working (Ashkenas, 2012) and has a positive impact on creativity.

The third strategy complements the previous two by considering market needs. The technology-market matching is analysed through the level of orientation to market, the customer prioritization and the experience of higher TRLs. Findings suggest that market-oriented and customer prioritized projects boost higher levels of cross-fertilization. In fact, this continuous understanding of the needs of both the current and potential target customers and the use of that knowledge for creating superior value for companies is indissoluble from the market orientation strategy.

**Managing innovation** is essential to increase the creation of knowledge, to understand the competitive implications of partners' selection and to develop strategies or actions in order to influence the productivity, to develop collaborative strategies and to create and reinforce customer loyalty for a better understanding of the end-user needs. Therefore, in order to encourage this process of cross-fertilization and innovation management strategies, findings suggest considering projects where: (1) partners have different knowledge and technologies, (2) there is a capacity for establishing an open prioritization for importing knowledge that could accelerate the commercialization, (3) value generation is possible thanks to co-creation with current and potential users of our products or services, (4) organizations have had previous collaborations at early stages of the value chain and greater knowledge intensity, (5) cultural diversity is an opportunity for generating creativity and added-value technologies, (6) market orientation improves organizational, product performances and satisfies better end-user needs and demands.

Considering this contribution, new scientific policies and strategies could be inspired by some of the results presented in this study to redefine, support and reward those collaborative projects that include the cross-fertilization of knowledge and technologies -including serious games and gamification. I not only provide the variables to understand the innovation management strategies in a particular moment in time, but I also reflect on how they evolve over time and allow organizations to adapt to changing and evolving ecosystems. I also provide some insights to understand the factors that influence and the outputs derived from the cross-fertilization strategy. In fact, I consider the cross-fertilization of knowledge and technologies a strategy that, thanks to the research performed in this chapter, has shown what elements can be influenced to favour the process of innovation.

The conclusions summarized here, and the detailed conclusions of each chapter, could have practical implications for all the stakeholders involved in innovation and technology transfer. On the one hand, it could be particularly useful for researchers wishing to transfer their basic research, and on the other hand, industrial entrepreneurs challenged to scale and bring new knowledge and technologies into the marketplace. Innovation managers and project leaders could also benefit from the insights presented in this work in order to apply adequate innovation strategies in the development of cross-fertilized outputs. Also, game developers could work on the design and development of new methodologies and technologies that favour the engagement of users with new products; designing new tools that favour the cohesion of knowledge and technologies between partner organizations; and giving more efficient answers to the real needs of users. Furthermore, this work could guide policy makers in reshaping and improving priority lines related to serious games and gamification. In this context, it is suggested that policies could: i) foster an open, collaborative, integrative and balanced ecosystem; ii) influence the level of diversity in groups and projects; and iii) foster excellent science and technological quality, but also strategic innovation management capacities of all the stakeholders that participate in the innovation ecosystem of serious games and gamification. Following these guidelines, this work contributes to redefining innovation strategies and long-term success when commercializing new (serious) gaming and gamified solutions applied to any field.

## References

Adler, P. S. and Heckscher, C. (2006). 'Towards Collaborative Community." In: C. Heckscher and P. S. Adler, eds., *The firm as a collaborative community: Reconstructing trust in the knowledge economy*, ed. Oxford: Oxford University Press, pp. 11–106.

Almeida, P. and Song, J. (2004). "Subsidiaries and knowledge creation: The influence of the MNC and host country on innovation." *Strategic management journal*, 25(8-9), pp. 847-864.

Ashkenas, R. (2012). "Why teams don't collaborate." *Forbes*, [online]. Available at: http://www.forbes.com/sites/ronashkenas/2012/03/21/why-teams-dont-collaborate/ [Accessed 9 April 2018].

Boschma, R. A. (2005). "Proximity and innovation: A critical assessment." *Regional Studies*, 39, pp. 61-74.

Burns, T. and Stalker, G. (1961). *The Management of Innovation*. Tavistock Publications, London.

Chiesa, V., Coughlan, P. and Voss, C. A. (1996). "Development of a technical innovation audit." *Journal of Product Innovation Management*, 13(2), pp. 105-136.

Christensen, C. M. (1997). "The Innovator's Dilemma: When New Technologies Cause Great Firms to Fail." *Harvard Business School Press*, Boston.

Dang, Y., Zhang, Y. and Fan, L. (2010). "Trends in worldwide nanotechnology patent applications: 1991 to 2008." *Journal of Nanoparticle Research*, 12(3), pp. 687-706.

Debackere, K. (2000). "Managing academic R&D as a business at K.U. Leuven: context, structure and process." *R D Manag.*, 30(4), pp. 323–328.

Edquist, C. (1997). "Systems of innovation approaches - their emergence and characteristics." *Syst. Innov. Technol. Institutions Organ* 1989, pp. 1–35.

Edquist, C. and Hommen, L. (1999). "Systems of innovation: Theory and policy for the demand side." *Technol. Soc.*, 21(1), pp. 63–79.

Egenfeldt-Nielsen, S., Smith, H. J., Pajares Tosca, S. (2008). *Understanding video games: the essential introduction.* New York: Routledge Taylor and Francis.

European Commission (2012). *Regional Innovation Scoreboard 2012 Report.*

Flynn, T. and Wei, C. (2005). "The pathway to commercialization for nanomedicine." *Nanomedicine* 1(1), pp. 47–51.

Frans, M. (2009). "Getting into the Game: Doing Multidisciplinary Game Studies." In: Bernard Perron and Mark J.P.Wolf (eds.), *The Video Game Theory Reader 2.* New York: Routledge, pp. 313-329.

Hacklin, F., Marxt, C. and Fahrni, F. (2009). "Coevolutionary cycles of convergence: An extrapolation from the ICT industry." *Technol. Forecast. Soc. Change*, 76(6), pp. 723–736.

Heinz, U., Baga, T., Diether, G. and Kearney, E. (2006). "Leadership and cooperation as success factors in innovative R&D projects on electronic platforms." *Team Performance Managament: An International Journal*, 12(3/4), pp. 66-76

Jonard, N. and Yfldizoglu, M. (1998). "Technological diversity in an evolutionary industry model with localized learning and network externalities." *Struct. Chang. Econ. Dyn.*, 9, pp. 35–53.

Juanola-Feliu, E., Colomer-Farrarons, J., Miribel-Catala, P., Samitier, J. and Valls-Pasola, J. (2012). "Market challenges facing academic research in commercializing nanoenabled implantable devices for in-vivo biomedical analysis." *Technovation*, 32(3–4), pp. 193–204.

Kanter, R. M. (1983). *The change masters: Innovation for productivity in the American corporation.* New York: Simon and Schuster.

Klevers, M., Sailer, M., and Günthner, W. (2016). "Implementation Model for the Gamification of Business Processes: A Study from the Field of Material Handling." In: *Simulation and Gaming in the Network Society*, 9, pp. 173-184.

König, J., Müller, F. and Fromm, M. F. (2013). "Transporters and drug-drug interactions: important determinants of drug disposition and effects." *Pharmacol Rev.*, 65 (3), pp. 944-66.

Kriauciunas, A., Parmigiani, A. and Rivera-Santos, M. (2011). "Leaving our Comfort Zone: Integrating Established Practices with Unique Adaptations to Conduct survey – based Strategy Research in Nontraditional Context." *Strategic Management Journal*, 32(9), pp. 994-1010.

Leonard-Barton, D. (1992). "Core capabilities and core rigidities: A paradox in managing new product development." *Strategic Management Journal*, 13(S1), pp. 111–125.

Lettl, C. (2007). "User involvement competence for radical innovation." *J. Eng. Technol. Manag.*, 24 (1–2), pp. 53–75.

Leydesdorff, L., Kushnir, D. and Rafols, I. (2014). "Interactive overlay maps for US patent (USPTO) data based on International Patent Classification (IPC)." *Scientometrics*, 98(3), pp. 1583–1599.

Linton, J. D. and Walsh, S. T. (2008). "Acceleration and Extension of Opportunity Recognition for Nanotechnologies and Other Emerging Technologies." *Int. Small Bus. J.*, 26(1), pp. 83–99.

Mahroum, S. and Al-Saleh, Y. (2013). "Towards a functional framework for measuring national innovation efficacy." *Technovation*, 33(10–11), pp. 320–332.

Maine, E., Thomas, V. J. and Utterback, J. (2014). "Radical Innovation from the Confluence of Technologies: Innovation Management Strategies for the Emerging Nanobiotechnology Industry." *Journal of Engineering and Technology Management*, 32, pp. 1-25.

Mo, G. Y. (2016). "Examining cross-disciplinary communication's impact on multidisciplinary collaborations: implications for innovations." *Information Commun. Soc.*, 19(5), pp. 673–690.

Motyl, B. and Filippi, S. (2014). "Integration of Creativity Enhancement Tools in Medical Device Design Process." *Procedia Engineering*, 69, pp. 1316-1325.

No, H. J. and Park, Y. (2010). "Trajectory Patterns of Technology Fusion: Trend Analysis and Taxonomical Grouping in Nanobiotechnology." *Technology Forecasting Social Change,* 77(1), pp. 63-75.

Nooteboom, B. (1999). "Innovation and inter-firm linkages: new implications for policy." *Research Policy,* 28, pp. 793-805.

Paez-Aviles, C. (2017). *Innovation on Nanoscience: Processes and ecosystems of innovation with a multi-KET approach to foster technology transfer and commercialization of nanotechnologies in the field of healthcare.* PhD. Universitat de Barcelona.

Parker, R. (1982.) *The management of innovation.* Chichester, UK: Wiley.

Pavitt, K. (1998). "The inevitable limits of EU R&D funding." *Research Policy,* 27(6), pp. 559–568.

Pilon, S. and Tremblay, D. G. (2013). "The Geography of Clusters: The Case of the Video Games Clusters in Montreal and in Los Angeles." *Urban Studies Research,* Vol. 2013, 9 pp.

Pisano, G. (2006). *Science Business: The Promise, the Reality, and The Future of Biotech.* Cambridge, MA, USA: Harvard Business Press.

Porter, A. L. and Youtie, J. (2009). "How interdisciplinary is nanotechnology?." *J. Nanoparticle Res.,* 11(5), pp. 1023–1041.

Powell, W. W., Koput, K. W. and Smith-Doerr, L. (1996). "Interorganizational Collaboration and the Locus of Innovation: Networks of learning in biotechnology." *Administrative Science Quaterly,* 41(1), pp. 116–145.

Rafols, I. and Meyer, M. (2010). "Diversity and network coherence as indicators of interdisciplinarity: case studies in bionanoscience." *Scientometrics,* 82(2), pp. 263–287.

Ruef, M. (2002). "Strong ties, weak ties and islands: structural and cultural predictors of organizational innovation." *Ind. Corp. Chang.,* 11(3), pp. 427–449.

Schummer, J. (2004). "Multidisciplinarity, interdisciplinarity, and patterns of research collaboration in nanoscience and nanotechnology." *Scientometrics,* 59(3), pp. 425–465.

Sedighi, M. (2013). "Interdisciplinary relations in some high-priority fields of science and technology: An analytical study." *Libr. Rev.,* 62(6), pp. 407–419.

Sharp, P. *et al.* 2011. "The Third Revolution: The Convergence of the Life Sciences, Physical Sciences, and Engineering." [Whitepaper on convergence, Massachusetts Institute of Technology (MIT), Washington, DC].

Søraa, R. A., Ingeborgrud, L., Suboticki, I. and Solbu, G. (2017). "Communities of peer practitioners, Experiences from an Academic Writing Group." *Nordic Journal of Science and Technology Studies,* 5(1).

Starkey, K.. and Madan, P. (2001). "Bridging the Relevance Gap: Aligning Stakeholders in the Future of Management Research" *British Journal of Managament* 12(S3-S6).

Subramanian, A. and Soh, P. H. (2010). "An empirical examination of the science-technology relationship in the biotechnology industry." *Journal of Engineering and Technology Management,* 27(3-4), pp. 160-171.

Van den Bergh, J. C. J. M. (2008). “Optimal diversity: Increasing returns versus recombinant innovation.” *Journal of Economic Behaviour and Organization*, 68(3–4), pp. 565–580.

Van Rijnsoever, F. J. and Hessels, L. K (2011). “Factors associated with disciplinary and interdisciplinary research collaboration.” *Reearch. Policy*, 40(3), pp. 463–472.

Van Rijnsoever, F. J., Van den Berg, J. C. J., Koch, J. and Hekkert, M. P. (2015). “Smart innovation policy: How network position and project composition affect the diversity of an emerging technology.” *Res. Policy*, 44(5), pp. 1094–1107.

Yam, R. C. M., Guan, J. C., Pun, K. F. and Tang, E. P. Y. (2004). “An audit of technological innovation capabilities in Chinese firms: Some empirical findings in Beijing, China.” *Research Policy*, 33(8), pp. 1123-114

Chapter 6

# Towards a Dynamic Knowledge-Based Theory of the Firm: An Activity System Perspective

Yasmina Khadir

*Nyenrode Business Universiteit, Netherlands*

**Abstract:** The continued interest in the field of the knowledge-based view of the firm has been linked to the constant attempts in understanding the mechanisms and dynamics supporting organisational knowing and knowledge emergence and / or creation. While the concepts and principles associated with organisational knowing are underpinned by a broad range of theoretical and practical knowledge-based approaches and prescriptive models in the literature, current research paradigms do not provide an adequate methodological perspective to explore the processes involved in organisational knowing and knowledge emergence and / or creation. To address this problem, this chapter proposes a novel methodological approach that uses activity theory. Relying on a combination of epistemological knowledge approaches and an activity system perspective, the mechanisms and dynamics involved in organisational knowing and knowledge emergence and /or creation are explored.

**Keywords:** Organisational knowing; organisational knowledge; knowledge-based view of the firm; activity theory; activity system; theory of knowledge; theory of the firm, Marx dialectical materialism, knowledge-intensive organisations; critical realism.

## 6.1. Introduction

As knowledge-economies gathered momentum, the nature of the engine of economic growth changed profoundly to become the new dominant societal and economic paradigm. Knowledge has emerged as a central feature of post-industrial societies (Bell, 1973), an essential element of the production function, and the only meaningful resource today in our societies (Drucker, 1993, Quinn, 1992), the driver of productivity and economic growth and a major pillar of knowledge-based economies (OECD, 1996). Consistent with the advent of knowledge economies and the unprecedented shift away from the industrial paradigm, the idea of a firm as a body of knowledge or a knowledge system has gained credence in organisation studies (Spender, 1996, Grant, 1996, Tsoukas, 1996, Nonaka et al., 2006) and consolidated the field of the knowledge-based view of the firm (KBV). This evolution in organisational theory originated in the works of scholars such as Simon (1947), Selznick (1957) or Penrose (1959) who had initially questioned the prevailing theory of the growth of the firm. Drawing on Knight (1921), the authors endeavoured to integrate a more realistic epistemological orientation towards a theory of the firm. One of the major building blocks in the field is the distinction Penrose (1959) made between the firm's tangible resources that are finite by nature and the services those resources provided. The latter are infinite and *'mediated by endlessly extensible body of knowledge management capabilities'* (Spender, 1996: 46). At the centre of this new development in organisation theory are the concepts of organisational knowledge and its possible creation.

The knowledge-based view of the firm concept has attracted a lot of interest and a substantial body of research has developed. However, these contributions are fragmented, partial and often bearing the imprint of positivism, reducing knowledge to an object to be studied scientifically (Spender, 1996). Following Brown and Duguid (2001: 198), *'these contrary descriptions of knowledge reflect different, partial, and sometimes 'balkanised' perspectives from which knowledge and organisations are viewed'.* Indeed, according to these authors, common images of knowledge in organisations and models of knowledge creation co-exist in literature and constitute the base of most current speculations. This leads to the emergence of a compartmentalised and static approach on the subject.

The existing models and perspectives suggested in the literature that are concerned with unveiling the intricacies of knowledge management and its creation, tend to be presented as solutions that can be simply implemented in any organisation. These suggestions fail to present convincing supporting dynamics and mechanisms such as the Nonakian *'knowledge-creating company'* concepts and principles (Tsoukas, 2005). Similar to the literature, we concur that Nonaka and Takeuchi (1995) have made a substantial contribution that allowed the field of the KBV to evolve beyond the resource-based view paradigm. The two authors have coined the term *'organisation knowledge'* and provided managers with a language to envisage a knowledge-based understanding of their organisations (Spender, 2013). However, their theory has been criticised for being too centred on the individual and failed to provide insights on how to conceptualise the boundaries of a firm (Spender, 1996). Hence, to date, no satisfactory dynamic and holistic knowledge-based theory a firm exists. This is what this research attempts to address.

The kernel of organisational knowledge / knowing emergence and / or its creation should be concerned about understanding the underpinning mechanisms (or the set of processes), and dynamics (or the force that stimulates change or progress within a process). In an attempt to progress the field of the

KBV, this chapter suggests implementing a Cultural-Historical Activity Theory (CHAT) or activity theory (AT) in its shorter version (Vygotsky, 1978, Engeström, 1987, 2001) perspective. Consequently, the following overarching research question is proposed:

> *How can we understand the mechanisms and dynamics of organisational knowledge emergence and creation using activity theory in asset management firms?*

The epistemological and methodological perspectives encapsulated in AT enables a practical study of how organisational knowledge / knowing emerge and / or is created that transcends the focus on types of knowledge and static stances. AT is a powerful theory-method that is particularly suited for the study of work in complex environments (Yamagata-Lynch, 2010). In this research, AT is used for a theory-building perspective and as a descriptive device to address the research question. AT fundamental principle consists in the study of mechanisms and dynamics underpinning cognitive development. It also envisages the existence of possible tensions and contradictions stimulating or hindering knowledge / knowing emergence and / or creation. The activity theoretical mechanisms consist of subject-object mediated relationships of which the dynamics have different origins, such as the history of the organisation and goal-oriented activities. Moreover, AT lends itself naturally to representing the emergence of personal knowledge within collective settings and on an individual level.

The following paragraphs introduce respectively (2) an overview of the literature, (3) the methodological choices guiding the research, (4) and the major findings before closing on (5) the implications for practice and further research.

## 6.2. Background

The knowledge-based view of the firm is rooted in Simon's (1947) concept of bounded rationality and his endeavour to connect the economic and organisational lines of argument. Both Grant (1996) and Spender (1996) consider the KBV as an outgrowth of the resource-based view of the firm but also that this paradigm rests necessarily on two pillars: a theory of knowledge and a theory of the firm. While Grant (1996) takes an economist perspective, puts the emphasis on the theory of the firm and contends that the management of knowledge pertains to organisational theory, it is Spender (1996) that gives consistency to the double nature of the KBV. As such, Spender (1996: 45) found a way to *'make knowledge the basis of dynamic theory of the firm'* and has framed *'make knowledge the basis of a dynamic theory of the firm'* (Spender, 1996: 45); and he framed the theory of organisation in terms of theory of knowledge.

In relation to the first pillar, organisational theories concentrate on the analysis of the internal structure of the firm and the relationships and mechanisms bounding its different constituent units and departments (Grant, 1996). It is in this area that the literature focuses, particularly in relation to knowledge creation/innovation, and organisational learning (Spender, 1996, Grant, 1996). Addressing the question of the existence of the firm when knowledge is the major asset, Grant (1996) attempts to counterbalance the emphasis of the earlier literature on knowledge creation and organisational knowledge by stressing knowledge application and the role plays in it the individual. So, departing from mainstream literature, Grant (1996: 112) is more concerned with the firm as a *'knowledge-integrating institution'*, and the *'application of existing knowledge to the production of goods and services'*. In his view, knowledge creation is primarily a person's attribute. In contrast, considering the firm as a *'body of knowledge'* (Spender, 1989: 185), Spender (1996: 46) argues that *'since the origin of all tangible resources lies outside the firm, it follows that competitive advantage is more likely to arise from the intangible firm-specific knowledge which enables it to add value to the incoming factors of production in a relatively unique manner. Thus it is the firm's knowledge, and its ability to generate knowledge, that lies at the core of a more epistemologically sound theory of the firm'*. As such, the author reconciles the firm with the individual in a relationship bounded within a body of knowledge that integrates, keeps and generates knowledge. He has settled the KBV in its own paradigm where firms are not anymore *'primarily concerned with predicting the behaviour of firms in external markets'* (Grant, 1996: 109), and addressed its counterpart, the theory of organisations as a theory of knowledge.

Concerning this second pillar of the KBV, the theory of knowledge, a general consensus acknowledges that it is rooted in the distinction between tacit and explicit knowledge (Nonaka and Takeuchi, 1995, Spender, 1996, Grant, 1996, Venkitachalam and Busch, 2012, Nonaka and von Krogh, 2009). Moreover personal knowledge cannot be conceived without collective knowledge. Grant (1996: 115) refers to the previous as *'common knowledge'* while Cook and Brown (1999: 386) defines it as *'the body of knowledge'* that is *'held in common by the group'*. Thus, personal and collective knowledge ought to be considered as inseparable.

In order *'to move towards a dynamic knowledge-based theory of the firm'* (Spender, 1996: 54) additional elements are introduced. Coexisting next to the *'sticky'* view of knowledge (Brown and Duguid, 2001: 198) or knowledge as a possession (Cook and Brown, 1999), some scholars underscored the *'active'* or practice-oriented dimension of knowledge, referring to it as *'knowing'* (Spender, 1996, Cook and Brown, 1999, Brown and Duguid, 2001) as knowledge translates into actions (Orlikowski, 2002). Causal mechanisms articulating the different types of knowledge in the firm (Spender, 1996, Cook and Brown, 1999, Grant, 1996, Nonaka and Takeuchi, 1995) and understanding organisational conflicts and tensions as sources of knowledge creation (Nonaka and Takeuchi, 1995, Cook and Brown, 1999, Spender, 1996) are also of importance.

In conclusion, the foundational elements that could constitute the basis of a *dynamic knowledge-based theory of the firm* have been identified in the literature. They are encapsulated within (i) a theory of the firm and a theory of organisations (Grant, 1996, Tsoukas, 1996), (ii) a theory of the organisations and a theory of knowledge (Tsoukas and Vladimirou, 2001, Nonaka and Takeuchi, 1995, Cook and Brown, 1999), and (iii) a theory of the firm and organisations and a theory of knowledge (Spender, 1996). (i) In the first case, the emphasis is on the nature of the firm and its boundaries, and the mechanisms supporting knowledge flows. While the question of *'what is knowledge'* is considered, it is not explored satisfactorily. (ii) In the second case, the emphasis is on mechanisms and epistemologies of knowledge that are represented in Tsoukas and Vladimirou's (2001) *'from-to'* structure, Nonaka and Takeuchi's (1995) SECI model, and Cook and Brown's (1999) *'generative dance'* between knowing as a practice and knowledge as a possession. Within these approaches, it is the theory of the firm and more particularly the question of its boundaries that is overlooked.

Thus, while fundamental in the construct of a dynamic knowledge-based theory of the firm, these previous approaches are incomplete. However, Spender (1996) provides some useful insights: while he combines both a theory of the firm and a theory of knowledge, the author introduces an original theory of organisations articulated around its *'knowing entities'* and bounding issues. Hence, Spender's (1996) insight appears to be the most comprehensive and insightful in terms of foundational principles as the author decisively manages to craft a new paradigm supporting a *dynamic* KBV. Therefore, it is within this path that this chapter engages while developing further Vygotsky's contributions. Thus, one of the originalities of this dissertation is to draw from, and combine management and organisation studies with principles and concepts from development psychology. This study also addresses the issue of developing and operational dynamic knowledge-based theory of the firm.

## 6.3. Research design

### Research philosophy

This study uses activity theory as the methodological perspective to study the mechanisms and dynamics of organisational knowing/knowledge emergence and/or creation. Consistent with Marx dialectical materialism, Russian revolutionary psychologists Vygotsky (1978, 1987), Luria (1961) and Leontiev (1978, 1981) initiated the movement that is now referred to as Cultural-Historical Activity Theory. CHAT approaches human activity as a dialectic relationship between subject and object mediated by tools and the community setting the rules and roles within which the different participants act (Hasan, 2002). According to Kuutti (1996), activity theory is a philosophy and cross-disciplinary framework that lends itself to the study of the different forms of human practices and provides a set of concepts, structures and terms that are perfectly suited to any research undertaken within communities of practice.

The elicited research philosophy is Bhaskar's (1978) critical realist paradigm. Indeed, critical realism and activity theory share many aspects. Both are situated in a tradition embracing Marxian themes, transcending positivism and interpretivism concerning a dialectically evolving material and social reality. In addition, both are concerned with the generating processes underpinning phenomena.

## Research strategy

### Two-case comparative design

This study is positioned as a two-case comparative design. The comparative-case strategy or small N analysis (Lijphart, 1971) is also referred to as a case-oriented comparative method (Ragin, 1987). Considered as a basic method in its own right, alongside experimental, statistical and case study methods, the chosen design is *'a method of discovering empirical relationships among variables'* (Lijphart, 1971: 683). Similarly to AT, the case-oriented method is particularly concerned with understanding an individual situation in its historical specificity and its full context. Each case is envisaged as a whole, encompassing the total configuration or constellation of factors and conditions. Provided that *'theoretical complexity is needed to account for organisational complexity'* (Tsoukas, 2016: 1), the AT intricate framework has been elicited to investigate complex organisational settings. The previous aligns with the need to untangle the *'multiple conjunctural causation'* (Ragin, 1987: 20) characterising social phenomena (Tsoukas, 2016). Figure 6.1 delineates the conceptual framework enabling the study of the mechanisms and dynamics at the origin of knowing and knowledge emergence and/or creation.

### Case design

Two asset management companies were selected and the group of workers (i.e. Portfolio Managers, Chief Executive Officers...) who were identified as key to performance generation constituted the sample. Consistent with activity system analysis, semi-structured interviews *(n=37)* transcribed *verbatim* constituted the instrument for data collection (Yamagata -Lynch, 2010).

This study attempts to continue the works of the researchers that pioneered the KBV (Nonaka and Takeuchi, 1995, Spender, 1996, Grant, 1996, Cook and Brown, 1999). Accordingly, a point was made to identify a field of investigation comparable to that found in earlier works. Similarly, this chapter revisits an *'old'* industry (von Nordenflycht, 2010) and seeks to front stage the views and perspectives of these scholars. Therefore, Asset Management (AM) organisations in Ireland are identified as the suitable field for empirical study in this chapter. The Irish economic and social context was particularly suited for this study as the country went through the biggest financially driven economic shock in its history in the aftermath of the 2008 financial crisis.

## Data analysis and activity system modelling

Data was reduced using the constant comparative method (Glaser and Strauss, 1967); open, axial and selective codings were subsequently conducted.

**Figure 6.1:** An activity system for the understanding of OK emergence and creation (adapted from Engeström, 1987)

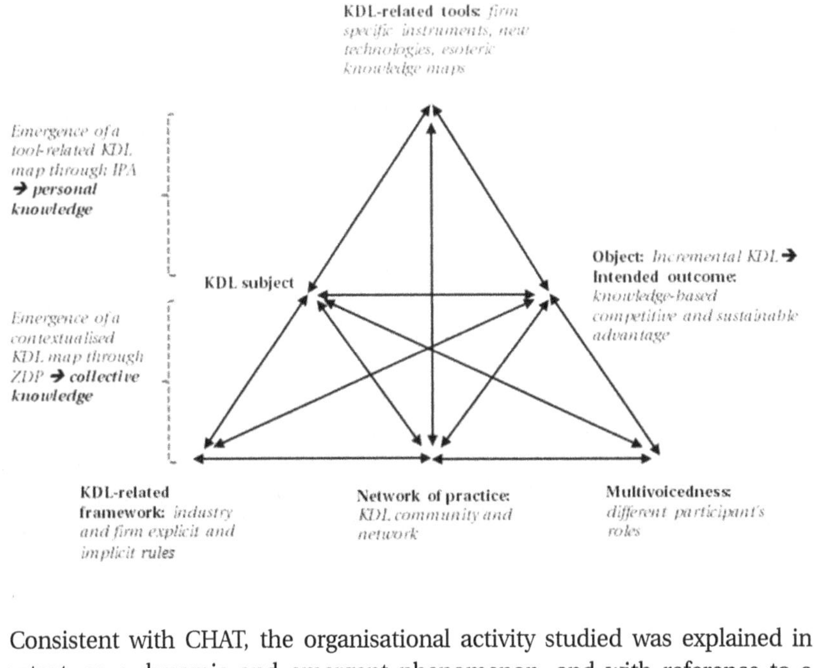


Consistent with CHAT, the organisational activity studied was explained in context, as a dynamic and emergent phenomenon, and with reference to a broader analysis of historical development and social relations. Activity systems models were drafted by identifying the themes fitting into the different nodes of the activity system triangle designed for this study. The models were finalised after a thick description of data written in a narrative format (Yamagata -Lynch, 2010).

## 6.4. Conclusion

### Rationale

The dissertation provides a new perspective in the field of KBV and suggests a dynamic and holistic knowledge-based theory of the firm. The study identifies a way in which individual knowledge advances as a result of the development of collective knowledge from a learning perspective. The research also successfully found a way to understand how knowing is integrated, emerges and/or is created. It considers the development of knowing in organisations in action as it is shaped by circumstances that are internal and external to the firm. This conceptual framework allows a consideration of organisational knowing that is *holistic* and *dynamic*. This tentative and exploratory methodological perspective proves applicable, as demonstrated in the comparative case study. While subjects translate their constructed cognitive abilities through goal-oriented actions, findings highlight enhancing and binding mechanisms. Finally, the two facets on which a dynamic and holistic knowledge-based theory of the firm ought to be resting, a theory of knowledge and a theory of the firm, are explored. The findings relating to both theories are introduced in the following sections.

### Theory of knowledge:

### Precedence of organisational knowing on organisational knowledge

The activity system triangle emphasises how the knowing from the two firms studied is integrated collectively and individually while being modelled by tools and artefacts, a framework and multivoicedness. Indeed, this study's primary focus is on *'knowing'* as it emerges and is shaped by mediators and crystallises in goal-oriented actions. This contrasts with an approach concerned with knowledge types and how they move from one state of development to another as instantiated in the works of Nonaka and Takeuchi (1995). Second, this study emphasises that knowing is partially derived from the broader industrial and societal context considering the firm in its organisational and societal environments.

## Knowing emergence and creation over the Nonakian knowledge creating model

This study shows that firstly, creation occurs on particular points of inflection in companies business as instantiated in the empirical study. Secondly, it takes the form of new learning and knowing (i.e. subjects learning new types of strategies or having to teach them to sub-contractors). No creation as such occurred during the time of the empirical study, even within the more innovative of the two firms investigated. Instead, subjects indicated that incremental steps in learning while doing took up most of their time. This finding is partially encapsulated in the object for both organisations studied. Thus, participants were concerned with improving their learning, knowing and doing contrasting with the Nonakian focus on an abstract and opaque knowledge creation process.

## Theory of the firm

Despite attempts to conceptualising a knowledge-based firm and understanding and predicting its structure and behaviours (Grant, 1996), no satisfactory solutions have been agreed upon. In this regard, this chapter has contributed to the (1) question of the unit of analysis, (2) the binding and coordinating mechanisms and (3) dynamics supporting these mechanisms.

(1) One major contribution of this study is the identification of a unit of analysis that is manageable within a dynamic knowledge-based approach of the firm. This is defined in terms of a series of goal-oriented actions that represent an object-oriented activity based on collective experiences, and described by multiple participant sources. The subjects that constitute the unit of analysis are identified based on a shared goal their actions addressed with no regard for the hierarchical levels or the specialisation subjects work into.

(2) The mediated relationship is a mechanism that centres on understanding how cognitive capabilities develop while the subject completes her or his action. Moreover, these mechanisms show how personal and collective knowledge are naturally intertwined and how one feed off the other.

(3) The existing literature has not singled out mechanisms from dynamics. However, they cannot be confused and dynamics supporting or able to support the mechanisms emerge from different origins such as systemic contradictions and tensions or object-oriented activity and goal-oriented actions.

## 6.5. Implications and future research

### Implications for practitioners

The findings suggest a new approach for envisaging an organisation if the latter wishes to innovate. This study provides a very comprehensive view on how to approach such an endeavour. Innovation is understood from the point of view of learning and particularly emphasizes the *kaizen* aspect whereby creation or creativity resides in everyday little routines. Knowledge creation as such in the Nonakian sense can be compared to breakthroughs and can occur only punctually. Thus, managing the learning process in the organisation and nurturing organisational knowing emergence over the more rhetorical knowledge creation foregrounds a truly innovative organisation, or a firm where creativity is part of its DNA. And this can ease off the pressure put on workers to come up with innovative ideas on a regular basis as this was observed in one of the two companies studied.

### An innovative conception of organisation structure

This study provides a way to operationalize a truly dynamic and holistic knowledge-based organisation. In terms of structure, firms should adopt the activity system approach and consider an interconnected network of these activity systems. This provides an opportunity to design a modular and efficient organisation that can evolve around changing objects or problem spaces. Hence, the concept of boundaryless organisation can take form. Indeed, the activity system Engeström (1987, 2001) introduced is intrinsically connected to the external environment. This study underscores the mechanisms that may constitute the base of a genuinely knowledge-intensive firm.

In addition, dynamics or impulses for change and innovation have been identified in the study. The first force driving innovation originates from the systemic tensions and contradictions that naturally emerge from day-to-day business. This study showed a way to capture these contradictions that eventually transforms into tensions. From there, an innovative dynamic and iterative circle can be organised and managed. And, systemic tensions are not anymore approached negatively urging the firm to suppress them. Indeed, any endeavour in that direction would be vain if the structure needs change or intend to stay at the forefront of innovation.

Finally, the modular approach encapsulated in the network of activity systems that are connected through a shared object within the firm but also with its external environment (Engeström, 2001) (boundaryless organisations) is in line with the principles of flatter and dematerialised organisation. This constitutes a dramatic shift away from the traditional organisational hierarchical structure.

### Stimulating organisational knowing emergence

Drawing on this study, managers are provided with an understanding of the factors and dynamics that influence innovation. This contribution allows the development of a learning and constructive dynamic that may become part of the corporate culture. In addition, the activity system approach provides a way to identify the means that influence and shape organisation knowing. For instance, technological endowments have been identified as one of the elements influencing knowing in the study.

Another aspect is that an activity system approach allows the identification of the real goal-oriented object of the activity system workers are pursuing, and manage it accordingly. Indeed, the organisation may believe that employees are working towards achieving the strategic vision while the true motive is totally different. This would be the case, particularly when a contradiction arises.

Finally, adopting an activity system perspective allows a reflection at a conceptual level that would not be possible without a proper perspective. This also enables companies to fully embrace the potential promised by the knowledge economy and a society that irremediably evolves towards more and more intangibility.

### Implications for scholars

This dissertation addresses the foundations of knowledge management and repositions this field in a relevant epistemological and ontological domain. In contrast with static views on knowledge that is regarded as the main asset, an activity system perspective is concerned with the mechanisms and dynamics supporting knowing emergence and creation. This alternative paradigm opens new opportunities for understanding how innovation occurs.

### Directions for future work

This research proposes new bases supporting a dynamic and holistic knowledge-based theory of the firm within a conjunctive philosophy that departs from mainstream literature. It has revisited the theory of knowledge and consolidated the theory of the firm. Based on this study and its findings, suggestions for future work are introduced hereafter.

The next step to undertake is to consolidate this activity theory-method in organisations that present different challenges. This study has shown that for both the units of analysis identified in the two firms investigated, the object and intended outcomes were similar because the two firms were comparable in terms of size and development. This does not mean that this result can be generalised to all firms. For instance, a firm that is struggling for survival might be motivated by another outcome and object. A firm in the pharmaceutical industry or in creative arts might have different concerns and a different knowledge-intensity profile. This chapter emphasises a theoretical and methodological perspective that requires more testing and more consolidation. Always in relation with the conceptual and analytical framework, each node of the activity system triangle and the elements composing it can be developed.

A major second development to consider is the use of the methodological perspective introduced in this study as an actual tool for managing knowing in an organisation. This was successfully implemented in education and medical care environments within the framework of development work research, as instantiated in the works of Engeström (1987), Yamagata-Lynch (2003) and Barab et al. (2002).

Third, in relation to the theory of the firm, further research is needed to conceptualise a firm in terms of network of activity systems. Different units of analysis would have to be determined in an organisation following the principle of a series of goal-oriented actions that are binding groups of workers together.

Finally, this study provides an opportunity to reflect on organisational knowledge-intensity as a distinctive field of its own. Further research could envisage organisational knowledge-intensity as a lens for interpretation rather than a definite list of characteristics that would qualify a firm as knowledge-intensive. Organisational knowledge-intensity constitutes perhaps a language that is more open and flexible to talk about knowledge and knowing in organisations compared to phrases such as tacit and explicit knowledge.

## References

Alvesson, M. (2004). *Knowledge work and knowledge-intensive firms,* Oxford, Oxford University Press.

Barab, S., Barnett, M., Yamagata-Lynch, L., K., S., & Keating, T. (2002). "Using Acivity Theory to understand the systemic tensions characterizing a technology-rich introductory astronom course." *Mind, Culture and Activity,* 9, 76-02

Bell, D. (1973). *The coming of post-industrial society: a venture in social forecasting,* New York, Basic Books.

Bhaskar, R. (1978). *A Realist Theory of Science,* Hassocks, Sussex, Harvester Press.

Brown, J. S. & Duguid, P. (2001). Knowledge and Organization: A Social-Practice Perspective. *Organization Science,* 12, 198-213.

Cook, S. D. N. & Brown, J. S. (1999). "Bridging Epistemologies: The Generative Dance between Organizational Knowledge and Organizational Knowing." *Organization Science,* 10, 381-400.

Drucker, P. F. (1993). *Post Capitalist society,* Oxford, Butterworth-Heinemann.

Engeström, Y. (1987). *Learning by expanding: An activity-theoretical approach to developmental research,* Helsinki, Orienta-Konsultit.

Engeström, Y. (2001). "Expansive Learning at Work: toward an activity theoretical reconceptualization." *Journal of education and work,* 14.

Glaser, B., G. & Strauss, A., L. (1967). *The discovery of grounded theory analysis: Strategies for qualitative research,* Hawthorne, NY, Aldine de Gruyter.

Grant, R. (1996). "Towards a knowledge-based theory of the firm." *Strategic Management journal,* 17, 109-122.

Hasan, H. (2002). "Relating knowledge management to business strategy by means of and activity theory framework." Third European Conference on Organisational Knowlegdge, Learning, and Capabilities, Athens.

Knight, F. (1921). *Risk, Uncertainty and Profit,* University of Chicago Press.

Kuutti, K. (ed.) (1996). *Activity theory as a potential framework for human-computer interaction research,* Cambridge, MA: The MIT Press.

Leontiev, A., N. (1981). *Problems of the Development of the Mind,* Moscow, Progress.

Leontiev, A. N. (1978). *Activity, consciousness and personality,* Englewood Cliffs, Prentice Hall.

Lijphart, A. (1971). "Comparative Politics and Comparative Method." *American Political Science Review,* 65, 682-93.

Luria, A. R. (1961). *The role of speech in the regulation of normal and abnormal behavior.*

Nonaka, I. & Takeuchi, H. (1995). *The knowledge-creating company: How Japanese Companies Create the Dynamics of Innovation,* Oxford, Oxford University Press.

Nonaka, I. & Von Krogh, G. (2009). "Tacit knowledge and knowledge conversion: Controversy and advancement in organizational knowledge creation theory." *Organization Science,* 20, 635-652.

Nonaka, I., Von Krogh, G. & Voelpel, S. (2006). "Organizational Knowledge Creation Theory: Evolutionary Paths and Future Advances." *Organization Studies,* 27, 1179-1208.

OECD (1996). "The knowledge-based economy. Organisation for Economic Co-operation and Development."

Orlikowski, W. J. (2002). "Knowing in Practice: Enacting a Collective Capability in Distributed Organizing." Institute for Operations Research and the Management Sciences.

Penrose, E. T. (1959). *The theory of the Growth of the Firm,* New York, NY., John Wiley & Sons.

Quinn, J. B. (1992). *Intelligent Enterprise: a knowledge and service based paradigm for industry,* New York, Free Press.

Ragin, C. C. (1987). *The Comparative method: moving beyong qualitative and quantitative strategies* Berkeley, CA, University of California Press.

Selznick, P. (1957). *Leadership in Administration: A Sociological Interpretation,* New York, Harper & Row.

Simon, H. A. (1947). *Administrative Behavior,* New York, Macmillan.

Spender, J.-C. (1989). *Industry Recipes: The Nature and Sources of Managerial Judgement,* Oxford, U.K., Basil Blackwell.

Spender, J.-C. (1996). "Making knowledge the basis of a dynamic theory of the firm." *Strategic Management Journal,* 17, 45-62

Spender, J.-C. (2013). Nonaka and KM's Past, Present and Future. In G. Von Krogh, H. Takeuchi, K. Kase, & C. G. Cantón (Eds.), *Towards Organizational Knowledge: The Pioneering Work of Ikujiro Nonaka.* London: Palgrave Macmillan.

Tsoukas, H. (1996). "The Firm as a Distributed Knoweldge System: A Constructionist Approach." *Strategic Management Journal,* 17, 11-25.

Tsoukas, H. (2005). *Complex Knowledge: Studies in Organisational Epistemology,* Oxford, Oxford University Press.

Tsoukas, H. (2016). "Don't Simplify, Complexify: From Disjunctive to Conjunctive Theorizing in Organization and Management Studies." *Journal of Management Studies,* 1-22.

Tsoukas, H. & Vladimirou, E. (2001). "What is Organizational Knowledge?" *Journal of Management Studies,* 38, 973-993.

Venkitachalam, K. & Busch, P. (2012). "Tacit knowledge: review and possible research directions." *Journal of Knowledge Management,* 16, 356-371.

Von Nordenflycht, A. (2010). "What Is A Professional Service Firm? Towards A Theory And Taxonomy Of Knowledge Intensive Firms." *Academy of Management Review,* 35, 154.

Vygotsky, L. S. (1978). *Mind and Society: The development of higher psychological processes,* Cambridge, Harvard University Press.

Vygotsky, L. S. (1987). "Thinking and speech." *In:* Rieber, R. W. & Carton, A. S. (eds) *The collected works of L. S. Vygotsky,* Volume 1: *Problems of general psychology.* New York: Plenum

Yamagata-Lynch, L.C. (2003). "Using Activity Theory as ana analytical lens for technology professional development in schools." *Mind, Culture and Activity,* 10, 100-119

Yamagata-Lynch, L., C. (2010). *Activity Systems Analysis Methods: Understanding Complex Learning Environments,* New York, Dordrecht, Heidelberg, London, Springer Science Business Media.

Chapter 7

# The Contribution of the Human Factor to Systems of Innovation and the Formulation of Regional Innovation Policies

George Martinidis

*Urban and Regional Innovation Research (URENIO), Greece*

**Abstract:** Innovation is usually studied in the form of systems, with the regional level being arguably the most important. Despite constantly improving technological infrastructure, the human-related aspects of innovation are still the most important part of the innovation process. The human factor in innovation essentially consists of three components: 1) Human Capital, which refers to education, knowledge and skills; 2) Social Capital, which refers to the strength of social links and social coherence; 3) Psychological Capital, which refers to peoples' values, attitudes and behaviors. The research findings confirmed this model and showed which specific indicators of the three types of capital had a significant impact on innovation output. A new, extended regional innovation scoreboard emphasizing the human factor, is proposed. Also, based on the findings and current EU policy, a number of measures are proposed for the formulation of "more human" innovation policies in order to increase innovation in European regions and coherence between them.

**Keywords:** innovation; regional development; innovation policy; human capital; human resources; social capital; psychological capital; innovation benchmarking; smart specialization

## 7.1. Introduction

Because of its impact, innovation is the central issue determining prosperity (Porter, 2008) and the main driver of progress and development throughout history (Godin, 2008a). All this, needless to say, means that innovation is a subject that is well worth studying and understanding. Since the production of innovations will directly or indirectly lead to growth and prosperity, innovation can be viewed as a catalyst for these benefits. Therefore, any kind of insight that can be put into practice to increase the rate at which innovation occurs is well worth researching and analyzing.

The first systematic attempt to measure innovation started in the 1950s with the pioneering work of Rupert Maclaurin. Since, at that time, innovation was measured at the level of firms, his proposed measures included indicators such as research budget, research workers, new products developed, new firms, and growth curves for products and firms (Godin, 2008b). By the 1980s, it was realized that innovation does not only take place in firms, and, even when it does, it is affected by external sources of knowledge and technology (Komninos, 2008). This led to a shift from firms to geographically defined systems of innovation (Freeman, 1987), which is reflected in the evolution of innovation metrics. In the 1980s and -mostly- 1990s measures incorporated system-related indicators, based on surveys and the integration of publicly available data (Do Carmo Costa, 2015). This emphasis on systems is even more noticeable in the fourth, post-2000, generation of metrics, which is based on a knowledge-based networked economy and pays close attention to knowledge, intangibles, networks, clusters, and systems dynamics (Milbergs & Vonortas, 2004).

As the forewords to the Global Innovation Index point out, while innovation is an inherently human endeavor which succeeds when people with experience, skills and capabilities come together, the existence of highly qualified individuals does not, by itself, guarantee scientific or technological breakthroughs. It is, however, an essential starting point, without which any kind of innovation would be virtually impossible (Cornell University, INSEAD & WIPO, 2014), and it is also what counts most in fostering innovation (Severijns, 2017).

Out of the various innovation metrics, it can be argued that the human factor is the aspect of innovation that is most difficult to measure. GDP expenditures on R&D, the percentage of employment on knowledge-intensive services, or patent applications, despite their own methodological difficulties, are easier to measure than, say, human knowledge, skills, attitudes and behavior. This might be why, in practice, when it comes to assessing innovation by benchmarking or influencing it via policies and other initiatives, the importance of the human factor is underestimated, underrepresented or even misrepresented. For example, the tendency of some parts of the research to attempt to capture the human factor via the number of patent applications (Godin, 2008b; McCann & Ortega-Argiles, 2013; Varsakelis, 2016) is rather problematic, not just because patents are a blunt benchmarking measure (Nicholas, 2014), but also because in the market climate of the 21st century, they depend on many external factors and do not only reflect human capabilities (Basulto, 2015).

This problem is also reflected in innovation measurement, as the leading innovation benchmarking indices such as the European Innovation Index and its regional level variant, the Regional Innovation Index (Hollanders, Es-Sadki & Kanerva, 2015) or the Global Innovation Index (Cornell University, INSEAD & WIPO, 2014) only take the human factor into account only via education and -sometimes- skills, which are only a small part of the complex and comprehensive ways in which deep-seated human features shape innovation, and may not be representative on its own, as the results of the dissertation indicate.

This problem is compounded by the lack of available data at the regional level, which is arguably the most important scale of innovation systems (Todtling & Trippl, 2011). Despite the crucial role that regions hold for innovation as well as for EU policy, most of the indicators used by the EIS are not available at the regional level (Hollanders, Es-Sadki & Kanerva, 2015). This severe lack of data means that the RIS captures the impact of human resources solely by the percentage of people between the ages of 30 and 34 with tertiary education... This is only one indicator and a very dubious one at that, since the quantity of higher education degrees does not really reflect the quality of education (Asteriou & Agiomirgianakis, 2001). Similarly, policy recommendations (e.g. World Bank, 2010) as well as actual policies for fostering innovation, including the EU's highly lauded Smart Specialization (Foray et al., 2011) only take the human factor into account by improving the knowledge, education and skills of the workforce, which is a crucial part of the process, but again, far short of the whole.

## 7.2. Background

While, as the section above indicates, the tools for properly measuring the human contribution to innovation and subsequently taking it into account when formulating innovation policies seem to be missing, the theoretical constructs required to do so are present.

The approach through which the major indices mentioned above take the human factor into account is essentially the concept of human capital. ***Human Capital*** was invented to refer to the value of human capacities (Schultz, 1971). It can be defined as a collection of knowledge, talents, skills, abilities and training possessed by individuals (Carbaugh, 2013). The notion of human capital recognizes that not all labor is equal, as the education, experience and abilities -the skill set- of an employee can vary and has an economic value for employers and for the economy as a whole (Schwab, 2017). Like any other kind of capital, human capital could be invested in. In this case, the investment can take place through education and training, and the resulting benefits are expected to lead to an improvement in the level and quality of production (Becker, 1962; Schultz, 1971). The creation of sustainable, inclusive growth requires a broad investment in human capital across society. Investment in small subsections of highly skilled labor cannot achieve this, and it is an unrealistic and outdated approach (Schwab, 2017).

***Social Capital*** was developed to complement human capital by reflecting the added dimensions of trust, relationships, and contact networks between people (Luthans et al., 2004). Social capital provides a value-added contribution to other types of capital, or functions as a multiplier of their own effect (Akcomak & Ter Weel, 2009). According to the social network theories of innovation, social capital functions as a moderator in the relationship between expenditure on innovation and innovation output (Barrutia & Echebarria, 2010). Like human capital, investment in social capital can be vital to the success of employers, organizations, as well as entire economies (Luthans et al., 2004). Social capital is particularly relevant for innovation as it is part of the mediating mechanism that transforms innovation to economic growth (Akcomak & Ter Weel, 2009). Social capital influences innovative activity, with different dimensions of social capital having different effects on innovation (Kaasa, 2009). This provides a powerful reason to foster strong social relationships within the modern networked economy (Doh & Acs, 2010).

***Psychological Capital*** complements human and social capital by demonstrating, that, in the same way, that human beings do not work in isolation from their external surroundings, they also do not work in isolation from their internal characteristics, capacities and identities. This concept is drawn from the approach known as positive psychology (Luthans et al. 2007). According to Luthans et al. (2004), psychological capital is measurable, open to development, and can be invested in and managed in the same way as for human capital. On an individual level, psychological capital is assessed via factors such as intelligence, motivation and personality (Patterson, 2002; Sternberg & Lubart, 1999). On a grander scale, as in the case of large enterprises, regions and nations, culture can be used as a substitute for personality (Hofstede, 2011), a fact which has been backed by research showing that culture can reflect personality on a mass level (Hofstede & McCrae, 2004).

It seems that several aspects of human capital are often underrepresented and social and psychological capital are downright ignored in current innovation benchmarking scales (e.g. Hollanders, Es-Sadki & Kanerva, 2016). The three types of capital which comprise the human factor and the suggested approaches for their measurement are summarised in figure 7.1.

In effect, the dissertation used various sources in the literature to propose a comprehensive model which accurately captures the human contribution to innovation via these three types of capital. The central idea was to test this model to see whether these constructs have a significant impact on innovation performance in Europe. To do this, two hypotheses were formulated. The main research hypothesis was that human, social and psychological capital, as measured through the indicators that were chosen, have a significant impact on regional innovation performance in the EU, explaining a major part of the variation in innovation performance between different regions. A second hypothesis was that social and psychological capital, which are not represented in major innovation scoreboards, are as important to innovation as human capital, so social and psychological capital will prove to be no less significant than human capital in its impact on innovation performance.

**Figure 7.1:** The three types of capital comprising the human factor in innovation (concept taken from Luthans et al., 2004) (credit to A. Psaltoglou for the graph).

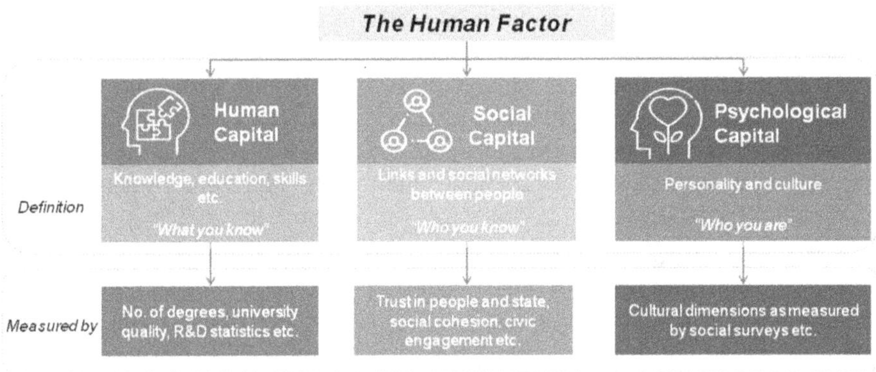


## 7.3. Research design

The research used data from all European regions. The complete dataset consisted of 208 NUTS 1, NUTS 2 or country-level regions, depending on country size and data availability. The Regional Innovation Scoreboard (Hollanders, Es-Sadki & Kanerva, 2016) also uses those particular scales. The research was restricted to EU countries due to the common statistical approach of NUTS regions, the availability of the same data in sources such as Eurostat, and the fact that the findings can be used to recommend policies inside the EU's existing framework; mainly, the EU cohesion policy, which supports the economic convergence of member states through measures implemented at the regional level (Bachtler & Turok, 2013; Carayannis et al., 2018).

Human Capital was measured according to the approaches recommended by the literature and followed by major indices. The Regional Innovation Scoreboard approach of assessing the percentage of university graduates in the population was supplemented with other indicators such as the percentage of researchers and participation rates in education and vocational training, and -in order to take the quality of education into account as well- with the rankings of the world's universities. Social Capital was measured by following both the approach recommended by the field of sociology and the one recommended by the field of economics. A number of indicators recommended by the literature, and also determined by the availability of data at the regional level, were taken for each approach. Psychological Capital was calculated by taking a number of statements from the European Social Survey, which includes data at regional level, and using them as proxies for Hofstede's five cultural dimensions, as they were described by him (Hofstede, 2001).

Innovation Output Measures were calculated by following the same approach as the Regional Innovation Scoreboard, taking the five indicators that it uses in the Innovation Outputs dimension to assess the innovative output of a region's firms. Since all these indicators have an equal importance for innovation output and are all measured in the same way, as percentages, their mean was used to calculate an "overall regional innovation output score" which was the dependent variable in the research.

The issue of missing data, usually encountered due to incomplete datasets in Eurostat and other sources, was handled by the recommended statistical procedure of multiple imputations, which can enormously improve the quality of estimation (Ader & Ader, 2008). Regression analyses were run in order to establish the relationship between the three aspects of the human factor and innovation output, and identify the indicators which could significantly predict innovation output. The assumptions and conditions for the use of linear regression appear to be present. The data are quantitative, and seem to be approximately linear. Most importantly, the use of regression for this type of demographic data on the scale of regions and countries seems to be well established in the literature, both from official sources such as the European Commission (Hollanders, 2003), as well as from a multitude of scientific papers (e.g. Asteriou & Agiomirgianakis, 2001; Bilbao-Osorio & Rodriguez-Pose, 2004; Dall'Erba & Le Gallo, 2008; De Dominicis, Florax & De Groot, 2013; Doh & Acs, 2010; Hofstede & McCrae, 2004; Komninos & Tsamis, 2008; Lee & Rodriguez-Pose, 2013; Peiro-Palomino, 2017; Pinto, 2009; Sleuwaegen & Boiardi, 2014).

The 37 indicators selected as the best available measures of human, social and psychological capital were the independent variables, while the innovation output composite indicator created by calculating the mean of RIS output indicators was the dependent variable. The regression analysis can demonstrate how the typical value of the regional innovation output changes when any indicator of the human factor is varied while the other indicators are held fixed (Gelman & Hill, 2006).

Note, however, that with 37 independent variables, if a single regression were used, the model could have been considered overfitted, i.e. being excessively complex due to too many predictor variables relative to the number of observations, resulting in a poor predictive performance (Babyak, 2004). In order to prevent overfitting, four separate regressions were run for each facet of the human factor, including separate regressions for the economics approach and the sociology approach to social capital. This resulted in four different regression models.

## 7.4. Results & Conclusion

Overall, 20 out of the 37 independent variables selected to capture the human factor in innovation were found to significantly predict variations in the innovation output total score. The significant predictors, and their impact on innovation output, are summarized in table 7.1. The findings indicated that human, social and psychological capital all have a significant impact on regional innovation performance in the EU. Moreover, social and psychological capital were at least as important for innovation as human capital (which is the one most benchmarking scales take into account), if not more so, meaning that overlooking them can be a major shortcoming.

More specifically, with regard to human capital, more R&D personnel and researchers, higher rates of training and a closer connection between academic institutions and industry predict a higher innovation output. Interestingly, the only finding which was contrary to assumptions was that a higher rate of tertiary education graduates predicts a lower innovation output. This might very well be due to the fact that European economies are oversaturated with qualified people, which tends to have a negative impact on growth (Asteriou & Agiomirgianakis, 2001).

With regard to social capital, several variables of both the economics-based approach, using "distal", demographic indicators not directly related to the key concept, and the sociology-based approach, using "proximal" indicators more closely related to the key concept -albeit in the form of self-reports- were significant predictors of innovation output. Finally, with regard to psychological capital, measured via Hofstede's (2001) cultural dimensions, it was found that high Individualism (but also, high friends-related Collectivism), high Masculinity, low Uncertainty Avoidance, and a Long-Term Orientation, successfully predict a high innovation output.

**Table 7.1**: Results of the four regressions.

| *Indicator (and name from Tables 1-3)* | *β (se)* |
|---|---|
| Human Capital | |
| -Population % Tertiary Education (HC1) | -0.005** (0.001) |
| -R&D personnel & researchers % (HC2) | 0.072** (0.009) |
| -Participation in education & training (HC3) | 0.003* (0.001) |
| -THE Industry Income Scores (HC4) | 0.001* (0.000) |
| $R^2$ | 0.530 |
| $F(9,208)$ | 24.838 |
| Social Capital (sociology approach) | |
| -Trust in country's legal system (SC2) | 0.035** (0.009) |
| -TV Watching news - politics (SC3) | -0.053* (0.021) |
| -Interest in Politics (SC5) | -0.099** (0.034) |
| -Voluntary work for charity (SC7) | -0.072** (0.017) |
| $R^2$ | 0.472 |
| $F(7,208)$ | 25.516 |
| Social Capital (economics approach) | |
| -Population % Secondary Education (SC8) | 0.002** (0.001) |
| -Unemployment Rate (SC9) | -0.011** (0.001) |
| -Life Expectancy (SC10) | 0.033** (0.003) |
| $R^2$ | 0.590 |
| $F(4,208)$ | 72.900 |
| Psychological Capital | |
| -Make own decisions, be free (PC2) | -0.150** (0.038) |
| -Be loyal to friends (PC2) | -0.088* (0.040) |
| -Show abilities, be admired (PC3) | -0.091** (0.031) |
| -Help people, care for well-being (PC3) | 0.133** (0.046) |
| -Be successful, achievements (PC3) | -0.052* (0.023) |
| -Live in secure & safe surroundings (PC4) | 0.076** (0.029) |
| -Think new ideas and be creative (PC4) | -0.134** (0.039) |
| -Adventures & Exciting life (PC4) | 0.128** (0.027) |
| -Traditions and customs (PC5) | 0.132** (0.034) |
| $R^2$ | 0.610 |
| $F(17,208)$ | 17.495 |

*Note:* * Significant at 5%, ** Significant at 1%

These findings indicate that the dissertation terms as the "human factor" plays a crucial role in determining regional innovation output, and this is often overlooked. As the literature already notes, even the most widely-used existing approaches to innovation benchmarking should not be applied in an isolated manner, without complementing it with other types of indicators and information regarding the system being assessed (Foray & Hollanders, 2015). Indicators capturing the human factor clearly belong to this category of essential additional information.

### 7.5. Implications and future research

The findings lead to two major practical implications. First of all, the knowledge gained points towards a need for expanding current approaches to the benchmarking of innovation. In practice, this can entail the creation of a new index or the modification of an existing one, in order to produce a measurement instrument which does not overlook the significance of human factor-related variables. This should be considered essential, since the best and most widely-used instrument for measuring regional innovation currently available, the RIS, has received significant criticism (Edquist & Zabala-Iturriagagoitia, 2015).

Actually creating such an index is no easy task, however, as the process would face a number of obstacles, such as the unavailability of data and various methodological issues. The RIS, for example, follows a particularly strict methodological approach, only using data from official and reliable sources such as Eurostat, OECD and the UN (Hollanders & Es-Sadki, 2014) and only measuring indicators directly. Straying from this approach would mean that the extended index would be weaker in terms of validity, yet, Hugo Hollanders himself stated that the RIS should not be applied in an isolated manner or without relying on other types of indicators and information on the system considered" (Foray & Hollanders, 2015 p.214), including other statistical evidence as well as qualitative insights. This is what is needed to provide the underrepresented human component of innovation with the prominence it deserves (Martinidis, 2017). This can be true for innovation policies as well as for innovation benchmarking tools.

Secondly, the findings can lead to the redesign of policies and strategies fostering innovation. Jean Severijns (2017, p.6) states clearly in his review of the history and future of regional innovation policy in Europe that "at the end of the day the human factor counts most". It is therefore essential to take it into account for the formulation of innovation policies. This can be done in the context of the EU's highly successful Smart Specialization Strategy which, in a nutshell, builds on the strengths of each region and focuses support and investments on a number of key priorities.

European innovation policy has evolved and progressed considerably since its origins in 1994. Over this time, the nature of innovation policies has changed from linear and supply-driven research to mission-oriented research and from infrastructure-supporting regional policies to user-driven innovation and smart growth. Smart specialization strategies (S3) is a key component of the EC Cohesion Policy for the period 2014-2020 in the field of innovation and constitutes an ex-ante conditionality for the EU Member States for receiving financial support from the European Structural and Investment Funds. With smart specialization, the focus has shifted to public-private partnerships in R&D and innovation, a critical mass of innovation support actions, pilot actions and scale-up, monitoring and assessment.

As a new regional development policy, smart specialization is aligned to characteristics of each region and promotes a transformation of the regional economy through an entrepreneurial discovery process (EDP) for diversification and opportunities in the international market. The basic principle of the new approach is the place-based policy design, defined by specificities of regional features and innovation systems (Carayannis, Grigoroudis & Goletsis, 2016). EDP, entrepreneurial knowledge and the private sector have a leading role and lead the specialization priorities across sectors with cognitive proximity.

The main conclusion from the dissertation is the need to fine-tune innovation policy by strengthening the role of the human factor, namely human, social and psychological capital, in order to produce an "updated," "more human" or human-centric version of smart specialization. In terms of human capital, apart from the obvious solutions of investing the workforce by improving R&D, education and skill training (Agiomirgianakis, Asteriou & Monastiriotis, 2002), which are already part of existing policies (Thomas, 2017), the main implication would be a shift towards an outcome-based education (OBE), connected more closely to its real-world application (Spady, 1994). In order for the knowledge generated by universities to be translated into innovation output –and, later, innovation output to regional growth- (Cavallini et al., 2016), the main target should be to connect them to enterprises, government and society by a more cohesive and comprehensive user and stakeholder engagement process achieved via quadruple helix networks (Carayannis & Campbell, 2009; Carayannis, Goletsis & Grigoroudis, 2018; Komninos, 2018; Thomas, 2017).

Fostering social capital is widely discussed in the innovation literature. In general, social capital requires healthy communities and strong civic engagement (Ekman & Amna, 2012; Putnam, 1995) but it is difficult to build social capital "from scratch", where little social capital exists (Dillahunt, 2014). Weak ties can be encouraged by increasing shared spaces with heterogeneous communities and then strengthened by building trust and identity within these communities (Dillahunt, 2014). New developments, such as ICT, can also assist in this, via platforms and apps that enhance social capital (Komninos, 2018) along the lines of the sharing economy, participatory democracy (Saughet, 2015) or e-governance solutions (Angelopoulos, Kitsios & Papadopoulos, 2010). Social innovation can also be an important policy instrument, as it extends and strengthens civil society (Gerometta, Haussermann & Longo, 2005) and provides potential solutions to pressing social, economic and environmental challenges that cities and regions have come to face in recent times (Angelidou & Psaltoglou, 2017). Social innovation initiatives, by definition, need to have a bottom-up direction, being generated by the needs of the local environment instead of being the result of top-down processes (Howaldt & Schwarz, 2010), which makes them ideal for smart specialization strategies, whose strongest point is the fact that they are adapted to the local environment and its needs. There are multiple reasons to give more visibility to social innovation in smart specialization strategies as a distinct and crucial component.

Psychological capital can prove to be a more complex issue. Since, on the mass level, psychological capital is reflected by culture, a reasonable question is to what extent culture can be changed or "strengthened". While European innovation policies included the stated aim of building an ingrained innovation culture in European regions since the mid-1990s (Thomas, 2017), the European Commission has never provided sufficient policy guidelines on what innovation culture is and how it can be cultivated. While the literature offers several solutions for fostering an innovation culture in organizations (e.g. Jimenez-Jimenez, Sanz Valle & Hernandez-Espallardo, 2008), there seems to be no existing set of policy recommendations or even suggestions for doing the same in regions or countries.

This should come as no surprise. Whether cultural differences, as reflected in the differences between the characteristics of their members, can be attributed to the impact of historical-cultural geography or to more practical differences in urbanization, income and education (Brons, 2006), their change will inevitably be a slow and challenging process. These dimensions outline the features of a liberal society with a free market and an opportunity for social mobility and achievement. Fostering such a society cannot be done directly, but it is possible to promote policies that have an indirect beneficial effect on psychological capital, even if they have different primary aims. This might include applying the principles of equal rights and opportunities and equal access to the involvement of people and staff, providing opportunities for migrants, promoting an open society. This is already being done in the case of smart specialization strategies, like the EU, in the context of its pillar of social rights, attempts to ensure equal opportunities in all its initiatives, including policies, research funding and other domains (The European Commission, 2018).

Yet another implication of this line of research, is that a closer examination of the levels of human, social and psychological capital across regions can perhaps highlight any significant differences between regions that have high and low levels of these types of capital, resulting in customized, "bespoke" approaches for increasing innovation according to the specific human factor profiles and specific needs of these regions. In general, since the human factor is the most crucial component of the innovation process in several ways, its cultivation and optimization can have a major positive effect on innovation, and, by extension, economic growth and prosperity. A lot of research is required on the topic, but its potential applications can be extremely important.

## References

Adèr, H. J., & Adèr, M. (2008). *Advising on research methods: A consultant's companion.* Huizen, the Netherlands: Johannes van Kessel Publishing.

Akcomak, I. S., & Ter Weel, B. (2009). "Social capital, innovation and growth: Evidence from Europe." *European Economic Review, 53*(5), 544-567.

Agiomirgianakis, G., Asteriou, D., & Monastiriotis, V. (2002). "Growth effects of human capital and stages of economic development: a panel data investigation of different country experiences." *The ICFAI Journal of Applied Economics, 1*(1), 31-47.

Angelidou, M., & Psaltoglou, A. (2017). "An empirical investigation of social innovation initiatives for sustainable urban development." *Sustainable Cities and Society, 33,* 113-125.

Asteriou, D., & Agiomirgianakis, G. M. (2001). "Human capital and economic growth: time series evidence from Greece." *Journal of Policy Modeling, 23*(5), 481-489.

Babyak, M. A. (2004). "What you see may not be what you get: a brief, nontechnical introduction to overfitting in regression-type models." *Psychosomatic medicine, 66*(3), 411-421.

Bachtler, J., & Turok, I. (2013). *The coherence of EU regional policy: Contrasting perspectives on the Structural Funds.* London: Routledge.

Barrutia, J. M., & Echebarria, C. (2010). "Social capital, research and development, and innovation: An empirical analysis of Spanish and Italian regions." *European Urban and Regional Studies, 17(4),* 371-385.

Basulto, D. (2015, July 14). "Patents are a terrible way to measure innovation." *The Washington Post.* Retrieved from: https://www.washingtonpost.com/news/innovations/wp/2015/07/14/patents-are-a-terrible-way-to-measure-innovation/?utm_term=.db502c8c2a82

Becker, G. S. (1962). "Investment in human capital: A theoretical analysis." *The journal of political economy,* 9-49.

Bilbao-Osorio, B., & Rodriguez-Pose, A. (2004). "From R&D to innovation and economic growth in the EU." *Growth and Change, 35*(4), 434-455.

Brons, L. L. (2006). "Indirect measurement of regional culture in the Netherlands." *Tijdschrift voor economische en sociale geografie, 97*(5), 547-566.

Carayannis, E. G., & Campbell, D. F. (2009). "'Mode 3' and 'Quadruple Helix': toward a 21st century fractal innovation ecosystem." *International journal of technology management, 46*(3-4), 201-234.

Carayannis, E. G., Grigoroudis, E., Campbell, D. F., Meissner, D., & Stamati, D. (2018). "The ecosystem as helix: an exploratory theory-building study of regional co-opetitive entrepreneurial ecosystems as Quadruple/Quintuple Helix Innovation Models." *R&D Management, 48*(1), 148-162.

Carayannis, E.G., E. Grigoroudis, & Y. Goletsis (2016). *A Multi-level and Multi-stage Efficiency Evaluation of Innovation Systems: A Multi-objective DEA Approach,* Expert Systems with Applications, 62, 63-80.

Carbaugh, R. J. (2013). *Contemporary economics: an applications approach.* Armonk, NY: M.E. Sharpe.

Cavallini, S., Soldi, R., Friedl, J. & Volpe, M. (2016). *Using the quadruple helix approach to accelerate the transfer of research and innovation results to regional growth.* Brussels: European Union Committee of the Regions.

Cornell University, Insead & Wipo (2014). *The Global Innovation Index 2014: The Human Factor In innovation.* Fontainebleau, Ithaca, and Geneva.

Dall"Erba, S., & Le Gallo, J. (2008). "Regional convergence and the impact of European structural funds over 1989–1999: A spatial econometric analysis." *Papers in Regional Science, 87*(2), 219-244.

De Dominicis, L., Florax, R. J., & De Groot, H. L. (2013). "Regional clusters of innovative activity in Europe: are social capital and geographical proximity key determinants?." *Applied Economics, 45*(17), 2325-2335.

Dillahunt, T. R. (2014, April). "Fostering social capital in economically distressed communities." In *Proceedings of the SIGCHI Conference on Human Factors in Computing Systems* (pp. 531-540). ACM.

Do Carmo Costa, P. (2015). *Measuring innovation. A framework for getting it done.* Lisbon, Portugal: Exago.

Doh, S., & Acs, Z. J. (2010). "Innovation and social capital: a cross-country investigation." *Industry and Innovation, 17*(3), 241-262.

Edquist, C., & Zabala-Iturriagagoitia, J. M. (2015). *The Innovation Union Scoreboard is Flawed: The case of Sweden–not being the innovation leader of the EU.* Lund University, CIRCLE-Center for Innovation, Research and Competences in the Learning Economy.

Ekman, J., & Amnå, E. (2012). "Political participation and civic engagement: Towards a new typology." *Human affairs, 22*(3), 283-300.

Foray, D., Goddard, J., Goenaga, X., Landabaso Belderrain, M., McCann, P., Morgan, K., Nauwelaers, C., Ortega-Argiles, R., Mulatero, F. (2011) *RIS3 Guide.* Seville: European Commission/Joint Research Centre.

Foray, D., & Hollanders, H. (2015). "An assessment of the Innovation Union Scoreboard as a tool to analyse national innovation capacities: The case of Switzerland." *Research Evaluation,* rvu036.

Freeman, C. (1987). *Technology Policy and Economic Performance: Lessons from Japan.* London: Pinter Publishers.

Gelman, A., & Hill, J. (2006). *Data analysis using regression and multilevel/hierarchical models.* Cambridge: Cambridge University Press.

Gerometta, J., Haussermann, H., & Longo, G. (2005). "Social innovation and civil society in urban governance: Strategies for an inclusive city." *Urban Studies, 42*(11), 2007-2021.

Godin, B. (2008a). "Innovation: the History of a Category." *Project on the Intellectual History of Innovation Working Paper*, (1).

Godin, B. (2008b). "In the shadow of Schumpeter: W. Rupert Maclaurin and the study of technological innovation." *Minerva, 46*(3), 343-360.

Hofstede, G. (2001). *Culture"s consequences – comparing values, behaviours, institutions and organizations across nations.* Thousand Oaks, CA: Sage Publications.

Hofstede, G. (2011). "Dimensionalizing Cultures: The Hofstede Model in Context." *Online Readings in Psychology and Culture, 2(1).* Retrieved, October 23 2016, from: http://dx.doi.org/10.9707/2307-0919.1014

Hofstede, G. & McCrae, R. R. (2004). "Culture and personality revisited: Linking traits and dimensions of culture." *Cross-Cultural Research, 38,* 52-88.

Hollanders, H. (2003). *2003 European Innovation Scoreboard: Technical Paper No 3 Regional Innovation Performances.* Maastricht, Netherlands: Maastricht Economic and Social Research Institute on Innovation and Technology (UNU-MERIT).

Hollanders, H. & Es-Sadki, N. (2014). *Regional Innovation Scoreboard (RIS) 2014.* Maastricht, Netherlands: Maastricht Economic and Social Research Institute on Innovation and Technology (UNU-MERIT).

Hollanders, H., Es-Sadki, N. & Kanerva, M. (2015). *Innovation Union Scoreboard 2015.* Maastricht, Netherlands: Maastricht Economic and Social Research Institute on Innovation and Technology (UNU-MERIT).

Hollanders, H., Es-Sadki, N. & Kanerva, M. (2016). *Regional Innovation Scoreboard (RIS) 2016.* Maastricht, Netherlands: Maastricht Economic and Social Research Institute on Innovation and Technology (UNU-MERIT).

Howaldt, J. & Schwarz, M. (2010). *Social innovation: concepts, research fields and international trends.* Aachen, Germany: RWTH Aachen University.

Jimenez-Jimenez, D., Sanz Valle, R., & Hernandez-Espallardo, M. (2008). "Fostering innovation: the role of market orientation and organizational learning." *European Journal of Innovation Management, 11*(3), 389-412.

Kaasa, A. (2009). "Effects of different dimensions of social capital on innovative activity: Evidence from Europe at the regional level." *Technovation, 29*(3), 218-233.

Komninos, N. (2008). *Intelligent cities and globalisation of innovation networks.* London: Routledge.

Komninos, N. (2018). "Internet Platforms, Innovation and Growth under the Smart Everything Paradigm." 20th Conference of the Greek Regional Scientists, pp. 119-125.

Komninos, N., & Tsamis, A. (2008). "The system of innovation in Greece: structural asymmetries and policy failure." *International Journal of Innovation and Regional Development, 1*(1), 1-23.

Komninos, N., Kakderi, C., Panori, A., Garcia, E., Fellnhofer, E., Reid, A., Cvijanović, V., Roman, M., Deakin, M., Mora, L., and Reid, A. (2018).

*Intelligence and co-creation in Smart Specialisation Strategies: Towards the next stage of RIS3.* Online S3 White Paper.

Lee, N., & Rodríguez-Pose, A. (2013). "Innovation and spatial inequality in Europe and USA." *Journal of Economic Geography, 13*(1), 1-22.

Luthans, F., Luthans, K. W. & Luthans, B. C. (2004). "Positive psychological capital: Beyond human and social capital." *Business horizons, 47*(1), 45-50.

Luthans F., Youssef, C.M., & Avolio, B. J. (2007). *Psychological capital.* New York, NY: Oxford University Press.

Martinidis, G. (2017). "The Importance of Man Within the System: Defining and Measuring the Human Factor in Innovation, a Review." *Journal of the Knowledge Economy, 8*(2), 638-652.

McCann, P., & Ortega-Argilés, R. (2013). "Modern regional innovation policy." *Cambridge Journal of Regions, Economy and Society, 6*(2), 187-216.

Milbergs, E., & Vonortas, N. (2004). "Innovation metrics: Measurement to insight." *Center for Accelerating Innovation and George Washington University, National Innovation Initiative 21st Century Working Group, 22.*

Nicholas, T. (2014). "Are patents creative or destructive?." *Antitrust Law Journal, 79*(2), 405.

Patterson, F. (2002). "Great minds don"t think alike? Person-level predictors of innovation at work." *International review of industrial and organizational psychology, 17,* 115-144.

Peiró-Palomino, J. (2017). "The geography of social capital and innovation in the European Union." *Papers in Regional Science.*

Pinto, H. (2009). "The diversity of innovation in the European Union: Mapping latent dimensions and regional profiles." *European planning studies, 17*(2), 303-326.

Porter, M. E. (2008). *Competitive strategy: Techniques for analyzing industries and competitors.* New York: Simon and Schuster.

Putnam, R. D. (1995). "Bowling alone: America"s declining social capital." *Journal of democracy, 6*(1), 65-78.

Schultz, T. W. (1971). *Investment in Human Capital: The Role of Education and of Research,* New York: Free Press.

Schwab, K. (ed.) (2017). *The Global Human Capital Report 2017.* Cologny, Switzerland: World Economic Forum.

Severijns, J. (ed.) (2017). *Solving contradictions by connectivity: reflections on regional innovation and research policy. A Limburg initiative.* Limburg, Netherlands: the Province of Limburg.

Sleuwaegen, L., & Boiardi, P. (2014). "Creativity and regional innovation: Evidence from EU regions." *Research Policy, 43*(9), 1508-1522.

Spady, W. G. (1994). *Outcome-Based Education: Critical Issues and Answers.* Arlington, VA: American Association of School Administrators.

Sternberg, R. J. & Lubart, T. I. (1999). "The concept of creativity: prospects and paradigms." In R. J. Sternberg (Ed.), *Handbook of Creativity* (ch. 1). New York: Cambridge University Press.

The European Commission (2018). *Equal opportunities and access to the labour market.* Retrieved, January 12, 2018 from: https://ec.europa.eu/commission/equal-opportunities-and-access-labour-market_en

Thomas, M. (2017). *Regional Innovation Strategies.* KnowHub Article. Retrieved, December 18, 2017, from: http://www.know-hub.eu/knowledge-base/encyclopaedia/regional-innovation-strategies.html

Tötdling, F. & Trippl, M. (2005). "One size fits all? Towards a differentiated regional innovation policy approach." *Research Policy, 34(8),* 1203–1219.

Varsakelis, N. C. (2006). "Education, political institutions and innovative activity: A cross-country empirical investigation." *Research Policy, 35*(7), 1083-1090.

World Bank (2010) *Innovation Policy: A Guide for Developing Countries.* Washington, DC: World Bank.

Chapter 8

# Managing Organizational Learning Ambidexterity: An Exploratory Study of Australian Large Service Organizations

Agung N.L.I. Fahrudi

*Universitas Brawijaya, Indonesia*

**Abstract:** Leaders should provide internal contextual support for organizational learning to happen in response to the dynamic changes in the external contexts. This chapter applies Crossan et al.'s (1999) 4I framework examining the effects of external and internal forces on an organization's learning process and the extent of its innovation. The findings of multiple-case studies of four Australian large service organizations demonstrate that leaders strive to achieve simultaneous ambidexterity but they tend to focus on efficiency (exploitation) than on product differentiation (exploration) strategy in a resource-constrained environment. This study offers further insights for both academic and practitioners about what leaders actually do to facilitate organizational learning ambidexterity.

**Keywords:** organizational learning; ambidexterity; innovation; service; large organizations; leadership; strategy; Australia.

## 8.1. Introduction

Large successful organizations may fail to respond to emerging markets and technology. Levinthal and March (1993) argue that refinement of existing knowledge can lead to a 'success' trap in which an organization exploits its existing knowledge to enhance its core capabilities in existing market or technology, but it fails to develop new competencies required by the changing business requirements. A well-known example is the case of Blockbuster in which this large movie rental company was unable to survive in the competition. Blockbuster was too late in anticipating a new innovation of online movie services introduced by its competitor, Netflix. Che-Ha et al. (2014) argue that service organizations need to continuously explore new approaches to provide better service to their customers. While larger organizations, including those in the service industry, are more likely to be innovative because they tend to have more resources allocated for innovation and can benefit from economies of scale in exploring new opportunities (Desmet and Parente, 2010, Hashi and Stojcic, 2013), some still find it difficult to pursue exploratory innovation (Hashi and Stojcic, 2013) as their complex structures and bureaucracies lead them to exploit existing knowledge (Eisenhardt et al., 2010, Vaccaro et al., 2012).

In this study, exploratory innovation refers to radical changes to existing products or services to meet the needs of new customers or markets using new channel distributions or new technologies (Jansen et al., 2006). Exploitative innovation, on the other hand, is described as involving incremental changes to existing products or services to satisfy existing customers, and/or incremental improvements to existing processes and distribution channels (Jansen et al., 2006). According to March (1991), exploratory innovation can be associated with the search for entirely new knowledge, whereas exploitative innovation is linked to the refinement of existing knowledge.

Ideally, organizations need to pursue exploratory and exploitative learning simultaneously (ambidexterity) to enable them to both compete in existing markets and to develop the required new capabilities to compete in new markets and use new technologies in order to survive in ever-changing and dynamic business environments (O'Reilly III and Tushman, 2013, Raisch and Birkinshaw, 2008). While research on ambidexterity has highlighted the focal role of organizations' senior team and leadership behaviors in balancing exploration and exploitation, exactly how these leaders actually manage the interfaces of exploration and exploitation and the inevitable difficulties that come from these two conflicting activities has not been well documented (O'Reilly III and Tushman, 2013). This study tries to answer this question by using an organizational learning lens to examine what leaders actually do to achieve ambidexterity. The 4I organizational learning framework (Crossan et al., 1999) is used in this study to analyze how leaders manage organizational learning in terms of the tension between exploration and exploitation. This highlights the importance of leadership in influencing organizational learning (Berson et al., 2006).

The 4I framework of intuiting, interpreting, integrating and institutionalizing (Crossan et al., 1999) needs to be extended to include the all-important elements of both external and internal context in organizational learning for innovation. External forces are often interrelated in affecting the pursuit of exploratory and exploitative innovation. For example, changes in customer and technical concerns can influence the nature of competition which affects the leaders' decision to either deploy existing competencies (exploitation) or redefine new competencies (exploration) (Floyd and Lane, 2000). Leaders need to provide internal contextual support for learning to occur in the organization in order to pursue innovation in response to changes in the external context

(Berson et al., 2006). In addition, leaders should be able to foster both exploratory and exploitative learning in the process of innovation and are expected to flexibly switch between them as required (Rosing et al., 2011). Research has shown that no universal best practices should be sought to resolve the dilemma of exploration and exploitation but instead leaders need to understand the situational context to enable them to develop the capability to effectively adjust the internal contexts of their organizations to demands of the dynamic external environment or context (Almahendra and Ambos, 2015, Benner and Tushman, 2015).

Benner and Tushman (2015) in looking back over the ten years in which their original article 'Exploitation, Exploration, and Process Management: The Productivity Dilemma Revisited' was published and in looking towards the future, suggest that the process and nature of innovation needs to be revisited. This is because of the implications of decreasing costs of communication and information processing, the increasing modularity of products and services and production of innovation beyond the organization's boundary (i.e. open innovation) on innovation research. In this study, the innovation phenomena in four large service organizations is examined to determine if organizational learning ambidexterity remains relevant in the contexts they face.

## 8.2. Background

Literature suggests that the three major, high-level mechanisms to balance exploration and exploitation are temporal (or sequential), structural, and contextual ambidexterity (Turner et al., 2013). In sequential ambidexterity, Burgelman (2002) proposes that an organization pursues short bursts of exploration followed by long periods of exploitation. Conversely, to enable the simultaneous pursuit of exploration and exploitation, structural ambidexterity physically separates organizational units focusing on exploratory learning (e.g. R&D) from those focusing on exploitative learning (Tushman and O'Reilly III, 1996). In contextual ambidexterity, an organization designs business unit contexts that enable every individual in the organization to pursue both exploitation and exploration activities (Birkinshaw and Gibson, 2004). None of the above mechanisms for achieving ambidexterity is inherently superior and as such managers need to understand the situational contexts and adopt the most appropriate mechanism that is suitable for that particular contexts (Almahendra and Ambos, 2015). While Geerts, Blindenbach-Driessen and Gemmel's (2010) quantitative longitudinal study on ambidexterity found that service firms preferred sequential ambidexterity (not simultaneously pursuing both explorative and exploitative learning or innovation), more research is needed to determine if this is still valid and exactly how the pursuit of ambidexterity in service organizations is influenced by their external environment and how their leaders respond to the external environment or context.

With the underlying assumption that leaders are the focal actors who facilitate organizational learning, this study tries to identify how these leaders provide internal contextual support to facilitate organizational learning ambidexterity in the Crossan et al.'s (1999) 4I learning phases, similar to Berson et al.'s (2006) framework. However, this study differs from Berson et al.'s framework as it strives to incorporate the role of both external and internal contexts in facilitating organizational learning ambidexterity. Leaders' perception of their business environment (or external context) influences organizational learning orientations and innovation (Garcia-Morales et al., 2006). The development of new ideas or exploration of new knowledge may be influenced by external contexts, such as competition (e.g. Desmet and Parente, 2010), customer demands (e.g. Godin and Lane, 2013), technology development (e.g. Danneels and Sethi, 2011), strategic partners (e.g. Schamberger et al., 2013), and regulatory environment (e.g. Patanakul and Pinto, 2014). Not only do leaders need to be able to look outward to identify the external forces, they also need to be able to look inward to create an internal context for organizational learning that enables organizational members to respond to these external forces (Lin and McDonough III, 2011). The elements of the internal context for facilitating organizational learning examined in this study include strategy (e.g. Santos-Vijande et al., 2012), structure (e.g. Raisch, 2008), organizational culture (e.g. Wang and Rafiq, 2014), and organizational resources (e.g. Jansen et al., 2012).

In the intuiting and interpreting of 4I organizational learning phases which emphasize the exploration of new knowledge, leaders need to provide internal contextual support that can stimulate organizational members' creativity and sharing of knowledge to develop new initiatives (Berson et al., 2006). Intuiting focuses on an individual's thinking process of developing ideas, whereas interpreting focuses on understanding the process of meaning that enables individuals to communicate their ideas to their peers or group members (Crossan et al., 1999). In these intuiting and interpreting phases, leaders can develop organizational members' competences or expertise and motivate them to innovate through various human resource management practices, such as training and compensation (Lin and Sanders, 2017). In addition, leaders may also establish dedicated units for exploration (i.e. structural ambidexterity) to provide space and resources for a new initiative to get started (O'Reilly III and Tushman, 2011).

In the integrating phase, leaders need to provide a common purpose and shared understanding to integrate learning at the group and organizational levels (Berson et al., 2006). A shared understanding among individuals and groups needs to be achieved to allow for coherent and collective action within the organization (Crossan et al., 1999). Leaders can facilitate teamwork or collaboration among organizational members to encourage them to work collectively to achieve the organization's goals (Lin and Sanders, 2017). In organizations with separate exploratory and exploitative units, the integration between exploratory and exploitative activities takes place at the senior management team level (Benner and Tushman, 2003). Nevertheless, the integration of separated units at senior management team level is not sufficient - lower-level integration mechanisms are also required to promote the lateral knowledge flow across units (Gilbert, 2006, Raisch et al., 2009). Cross-functional interfaces (such as liaison personnel, task forces, and teams) can help the integration of exploratory and exploitative activities at the lower levels of management by enabling knowledge exchange across exploratory and exploitative units (Jansen et al., 2009). In addition, the integration of exploratory and exploitative learning need also take place at the individual employee level (using contextual ambidexterity) to minimize the coordination problems between exploration and exploitation (Birkinshaw and Gibson, 2004, Kang and Snell, 2009).

In the institutionalizing phase, leaders need to make knowledge available for exploitation (Berson et al., 2006). In other words, institutionalization enables organizations to retain lessons learned and transfer these lessons or knowledge to all organization members, and thereby facilitate the exploitation of what they have already learned. Institutionalizing can include the implementation of changes in the organizational systems, structures, strategy, routines, and infrastructures (Crossan et al., 1999). Leaders can create an organization culture that is conducive for innovation and develop organizational capabilities to configure and reconfigure resources and operational routines to respond to a changing business environment (Lin and Sanders, 2017). Leaders need to be able to institutionalize new learning in such a way that enables the organization to pursue exploration and exploitation simultaneously (Lengnick-Hall and Inocencio-Gray, 2013).

## 8.3. Research design

In this study, a qualitative approach within the interpretivist paradigm was undertaken as it could offer greater clarity in explaining what leaders actually did to manage exploitation and exploration and how they managed the inevitable conflicts that arose from these two conflicting activities. This is in line with O'Reilly III and Tushman's (2013) argument that more qualitative research is required to answer how the senior team and leadership behaviors address the conflicting demands of exploration and exploitation. In addition, a qualitative approach enables researchers to know what "exploration" and "exploitation" actually mean in the contexts of the organization under investigation (O'Reilly III & Tushman, 2013). This is important because this study used four service organizations in different sectors and what exploration and exploitation meant for each could be different given the context of the sector. Furthermore, the type of innovation and how the researched organization pursued these innovations could differ due to the idiosyncratic nature of the underlying phenomena in each of these organizations.

The case study methodology was adopted in this study because the research question was 'how' leaders facilitated organizational learning ambidexterity for innovation in order to respond to external challenges, and at the same time, the researcher had no control over behavioral events being investigated (Yin, 2009). Multiple-case studies of four large Australian service organizations were undertaken in an exploratory analysis of the complex phenomenon of organizational learning ambidexterity to account for contextual differences. In this study, a large organization refers to an organization has more than 49 employees and has assets of at least AUD12.5 million at the end of the financial year of the 30$^{th}$ of June (Australian Securities & Investments Commision, 2016). The reason for choosing large service large organizations is that service organizations need to continuously explore new approaches to provide better service to their customer, but being large, these organizations often find it difficult to pursue innovation due to the complexity of their structures and bureaucracies. For the purpose of the study, innovation does not refer to new services or practices in the industry but it can refer to something new to the organization being observed.

The selected four organizations in this study were a regional bank, a public university, a police academy, and a private hospital located in an Australian state. These organizations had engaged, or are engaged, in innovation. The sample selection was dictated by several reasons. First, the bank had demonstrated strong financial performance and had won industry awards for outstanding work in delivering quality services for its customers. Second, the university had undertaken significant structural reforms and had been recognized for its teaching quality and support for students. Third, the police academy had a high-tech training facility and had also undergone structural reforms for better efficiency and effectiveness. Lastly, the hospital had grown tremendously in the last few years and had succeeded in building a public-private partnership to serve its stakeholders.

Semi-structured interviews were conducted with 29 organization members from four organizations, mostly with top and middle managerial levels due to the significant importance of leadership role in ambidextrous organizations. The semi-structured interviews allowed for any new or emerging themes to be considered. Interview questions were adapted from Crossan and Berdrow's

(2003) interview protocol by incorporating explicit questions related to external and internal contexts that might influence organizational learning and innovation. These interviews were complemented by the use of documentary sources, such as the organization's official website, annual reports, and press releases. Interview data was classified thematically based on the predetermined framework of factors in the external and internal contexts and compared to the corresponding documentary sources to build interpretation for the within and cross-case analyses.

## 8.4. Conclusion

Findings emerging from this study indicate that a resource-constrained environment has compelled the four service organizations to focus on higher efficiency. Such pursuit of efficiency can be linked to mostly exploitation activities as suggested by March (1991). Since Australia has been facing slow economic growth since the 2008 global financial crisis (Uren, 2015), these large service organizations have experienced relatively similar resource-constrained environments despite the differences of industry-specific environment they faced. While the private sectors had to deal with intensified domestic competition, most of the public sector had to anticipate the gradual reduction of government funding due to the political pressures to decrease the Commonwealth Budget deficit in an environment of falling tax revenues. Interestingly, for the researched organizations, exploration in a resource-constrained environment can also mean significant or radical process improvements to increase efficiency and not merely about developing new products or services. For instance, the researched organizations tried to achieve increased efficiency by adopting radical technological-based innovation and/or administrative innovation, i.e. structural reform. This is in line with the argument of Davenport (1993) that some process improvements may result in radical changes and therefore can also relate to the exploration of new knowledge.

In order to compete more competitively, organizations need to pursue both cost-leadership and differentiation strategies simultaneously to create flexibility to adapt to a dynamic environment (Santos-Vijande et al., 2012). However, they need to avoid 'a stuck in the middle strategy' where they fail to successfully pursue either a differentiation or cost-leadership strategy (Porter, 1980). On the one hand, a cost-leadership strategy is used to achieve internal efficiency to provide a product and/or service at an acceptable standard but at a lower cost for customers. On the other hand, a differentiation strategy is implemented by organizations wanting to create unique products with added values and to offer greater benefits to customers (Porter, 1980). This differentiation strategy is closely related to variation and cost-leadership strategy is linked to efficiency. According to March (1991), variation can be associated with exploration, whereas efficiency can be related to exploitation.

The cases revealed that while these organizations tried to pursue both cost-leadership (efficiency) and differentiation strategies simultaneously, they tended to focus on efficiency (exploitation) rather than on product differentiation (exploration) in the face of a resource–constrained environment. These researched organizations found it difficult to compete merely based on lower prices (efficiency) and thus, they tried to differentiate their services, such as by introducing new products or services. Although Police Academy A was not in the competitive market, the academy also differentiated its services through the provision of updated education and training that enable frontline officers to give more focused and efficient policing services. This supports Cao et al.'s (2009) findings that resource-constrained organizations need to manage the trade-off between exploration and exploitation in achieving ambidexterity. However, the relative optimal levels of exploration and exploitation varied between these organizations due to their contextual differences. The tendency of focusing on cost-leadership or efficiency was higher among the public organizations (e.g. the public university) compared to their private counterparts (e.g. the regional private bank). Conversely, the competitive pressure for product innovation or differentiation was higher in private than public organizations. According to Wei et al. (2014), in order to achieve the appropriate balance between exploitation and exploration, an organization does not always pursue high exploitative learning and high exploratory learning but the organization can also pursue higher exploitative learning coupled with lower exploratory learning or have lower exploitative learning complemented with higher exploratory learning depending on the situational contexts.

While a previous longitudinal study found that service organizations preferred sequential to simultaneous ambidexterity (Geerts et al., 2010), the cases demonstrate that the service organizations being investigated also tried to pursue both exploitation and exploration simultaneously. In order to do this, the four researched organizations adopted structural and contextual approaches to ambidexterity. They used a structural separation approach to provide space and resources to enable the initiation of new ideas, particularly in the intuiting and interpreting phases of 4I organizational learning. To complement this structural separation, the researched organizations also adopted a contextual approach to enhance the integration between exploration and exploitation activities at the individual level (i.e. allowing individuals to both explore and exploit), as suggested by Birkinshaw and Gibson (2004).

### 8.5. Implications and future research

This exploratory study offers further insights for both academics and practitioners about how leaders manage organizational learning ambidexterity in large service organizations, particularly in a resource-constrained circumstance. This study makes the following contributions in terms of theoretical and practical implications. First, this study provides empirical evidence of how external and internal contexts can affect the simultaneous pursuit of exploration and exploitation. In a resource-constrained environment, leaders of the researched organizations tended to focus on efficiency or a cost-leadership (exploitation) strategy than on a differentiation (exploration) strategy. Senior leaders of the researched organizations formulated and communicated strategic priorities to inspire their members to pursue innovation aimed at increasing efficiency. In this way, this study contributes to expanding our understanding of the link between exploratory and exploitative learning and the strategy of the firm (i.e. cost-leadership and differentiation). Interestingly, the findings of this study show that exploitation and exploration in a resource-constrained environment cannot be strictly categorized in terms of efficiency and product differentiation. As mentioned above, exploration for the researched organizations could also mean radical process improvements aimed at increasing efficiency and was not limited to product differentiation. For example, they pursued exploratory innovations aimed at achieving higher efficiency, such as administration innovation like structural reforms to streamline business processes and the adoption of technological-based innovation that resulted in significant cost-saving. Since these organizations could not compete or survive merely based on cost efficiencies, they also strived to differentiate their services. They tried to produce customized or niche products by upgrading or recombining existing capabilities to target new customer groups. As such, the researched organizations strived to pursue both cost-leadership (exploitation) and differentiation (exploration) strategies simultaneously to achieve flexibility in order to respond to ever-changing business environments as suggested by Santos-Vijande et al. (2012).

Geerts et al. (2010) found that service organizations preferred sequential to simultaneous ambidexterity where the organizations tended to focus on increasing efficiency in service delivery and were more likely to invest in radically new capability only when an opportunity emerged. However, while the demand for new products was relatively stable for the researched organizations, technology development was growing rapidly and in turn significantly affected how service products were delivered (e.g. online banking, online learning, and robotic surgery). The significant changes of the underlying technologies in the product and production processes required these organizations to redefine their existing competencies and in turn led to the exploration of new knowledge as suggested by Floyd and Lane (2000). However, legacy systems and inadequate human resource capabilities could impede the adoption of new technology in the researched organizations. As such, these organizations had to invest in technology and human resources that could meet current and future business requirements and this required them to pursue a simultaneous approach to ambidexterity, i.e. pursuing both exploration and exploitation. Ideally, it should enable the introduction of new services with high efficiency and high differentiated value to the customer as recommended by Birkinshaw and Gupta (2013).

The second contribution this study makes is that it offers further insights into how organizational leaders achieve a simultaneous approach to ambidexterity. Leaders need to be able to foster both the exploration of new knowledge and exploitation of existing knowledge in order to innovate (e.g. Rosing et al., 2011). In line with this thought, leaders of the researched organizations encouraged their members to think in new directions and challenge institutionalized learning to promote more varieties of new exploratory ideas in the initiation phase of innovation. Conversely, these leaders narrowed innovation initiatives (through prioritization and integration of different views) and reinforced institutionalized learning in the implementation of the innovation process. Leaders can facilitate these learning processes in an organization through the development of a learning culture and human resource practices, as suggested by Berson et al. (2006). An organization's efforts to facilitate organizational learning through human resource management practices can be associated with a contextual ambidexterity because it assumes that as a whole the ambidexterity of an organization can result from specific actions of individuals (Kang and Snell, 2009). Leaders of the researched organizations have adopted contextual ambidexterity through the implementation of human resource practices (e.g. reward structures, more delegated decision-making, cross-functional teams etc.) that encouraged individuals to pursue both exploratory and exploitative learning.

However, the findings of this study demonstrate that the pursuit of a contextual approach alone is not adequate to promote radical changes, supporting the proposal of O'Reilly III and Tushman (2013). While individual members can have fantastic exploratory ideas, the decisions about significant resource allocation are made by senior management and not individual organization members. Interview respondents indicated that senior leaders would only support radical bottom-up ideas as long as these ideas did not require additional resources or could be implemented using available resources at hand. As such, the researched organizations also used a structural approach to provide space and resources to enable the initiation of new exploratory ideas. The establishment of dedicated units for exploration (e.g. the Segment Business Development team in the case of Bank A) could also develop appropriate contexts for exploration in particular areas as dictated by the organization's strategic priorities. In this way, this study contributes to expanding our understanding of the complementariness of contextual and structural ambidexterity.

Lastly, this study offers a better understanding of the innovation process through an extension of the 4I organizational learning lens to include the elements of the external and internal contexts of an organization on organizational learning for innovation. The process of exploratory innovation requires relatively high exploratory learning in the phase of idea generation and needs relatively high exploitative learning in the phase of idea implementation. Leaders across the four cases provided internal contextual support to facilitate both exploratory and exploitative learning for innovation. These leaders adjusted the internal context (i.e. strategy, structure, organizational culture, and organizational resources) in response to ever-changing external challenges. This study expands Berson et al.'s (2006) framework on how leaders provide internal contextual support to facilitate organizational learning for innovation in each of Crossan et al.'s (1999) 4I learning phases by incorporating the role of internal and external context.

While this study has offered several contributions as explained above, it also has some limitations and thus future research avenues are recommended. First, leaders or managers should contextualize the lessons learnt from this research to fit their organization-specific contexts. The importance of various external and internal forces may vary within different industrial sectors, among firms within the same industrial sectors, and over time within the same organization. As a result, certain situations may require different approaches with distinct configurations to support both exploratory and exploitative learning for innovation. Future research could focus on one industry or cross-industry with a larger number of organizations to obtain a deeper understanding of the effects of industry-specific contexts on the process of innovation and ambidexterity. Another recommendation for future research is cross-country research to determine the importance of issues like culture and regulatory environments on the process of ambidexterity and innovation.

Second, a broader approach can be taken in considering the benefits of organizational learning ambidexterity on innovation and in turn, competitive advantage. Innovation can lead to superior performance providing slack resources that can be invested in future innovation to sustain competitive advantage. However, inappropriate investments may also impede innovation resulting in future performance declines. Future research may look further at the detailed operational mechanisms and linkages between ambidextrous innovation and financial performance.

Another limitation is this study cannot explain the strategic importance of a particular common innovation (resulted from its underlying organization learning) in response to external challenges. Since the organizational learning process for innovation in an organization is bounded by its context, the investigation of the interplay of all external and internal factors as a whole in influencing this learning process is critical in understanding the complexity of the process. Exploring four large service organizations in different industries or sectors could highlight the contextual differences (particularly external contexts) among the researched organizations. How the ambidexterity challenge could be handled may be dependent upon the industry. For example, public institutions have a high reliance on the government funding framework that can influence the pursuit of exploration and exploitation. Interestingly, exploration for these public institutions could mean mostly significant business process improvements and may not be confined to product differentiation only. Conversely, private institutions like Bank A with no public contracts could have more exploration in terms of product differentiation since the pressures for product innovation was higher than its public counterparts. Nevertheless, the choice of four different sectors does not enable the clear observation of the strategic importance of a particular common innovation in response to external challenges. To do so would have required observation of all major players in the same sector exposed to similar strategic constraints. Further research can look at how the pursuit of innovation can affect performance differences among organizations in the same sector facing similar external challenges.

## References

Almahendra, R. & Ambos, B. (2015). "Exploration and exploitation: a 20-year review of evolution and reconceptualisation." *International Journal of Innovation Management,* 19, 15500081 - 155000831.

Australian Securities & Investments Commision. (2016). *Are you a large or small proprietary company* [Online]. Available: http://asic.gov.au/regulatory-resources/financial-reporting-and-audit/preparers-of-financial-reports/are-you-a-large-or-small-proprietary-company/ [Accessed April 16 2016].

Benner, M. J. & Tushman, M. L. (2003). "Exploitation, exploration, and process management: the productivity dilemma revisited." *Academy of Management Review,* 28, 238-256.

Benner, M. J. & Tushman, M. L. (2015). "Reflections on the 2013 decade award: 'exploitation, exploration, and process management: the productivity dilemma revisited' ten years later." *Academy of Management Review,* 40, 1-18.

Berson, Y., Nemanich, L. A., Waldman, D. A., Galvin, B. M. & Keller, R. T. (2006). "Leadership and organizational learning: A multiple levels perspective." *The Leadership Quarterly,* 17, 577-594.

Birkinshaw, J. & Gibson, C. (2004). "Building ambidexterity into an organization." *MIT Sloan Management Review,* 45, 47-55.

Birkinshaw, J. & Gupta, K. (2013). "Clarifying the distinctive contribution of ambidexterity to the field of organization studies." *The Academy of Management Perspectives,* 27, 287-298.

Burgelman, R. A. (2002). "Strategy as vector and the inertia of coevolutionary lock-in." *Administrative Science Quarterly,* 47, 325-357.

Cao, Q., Gedajlovic, E. & Zhang, H. (2009). "Unpacking organizational ambidexterity: Dimensions, contingencies, and synergistic effects." *Organization Science,* 20, 781-796.

Che-Ha, N., Mavondo, F. T. & Mohd-Said, S. (2014). "Performance or learning goal orientation: Implications for business performance." *Journal of Business Research,* 67, 2811-2820.

Crossan, M. M. & Berdrow, I. (2003). "Organizational learning and strategic renewal." *Strategic Management Journal,* 24, 1087-1105.

Crossan, M. M., Lane, H. W. & White, R. E. (1999). "An organizational learning framework: from intuition to institution." *Academy of Management Review,* 24, 522-537.

Danneels, E. & Sethi, R. (2011). "New product exploration under environmental turbulence." *Organization Science,* 22, 1026-1039.

Davenport, T. H. (1993). "Need radical innovation and continuous improvement? Integrate process reengineering and TQM." *Strategy & Leadership,* 21, 6-12.

Desmet, K. & Parente, S. (2010). "Bigger is better: Market size, demand elasticity, and innovation." *International Economic Review,* 51, 319-333.

Eisenhardt, K. M., Furr, N. R. & Bingham, C. B. (2010). "Microfoundations of performance: balancing efficiency and flexibility in dynamic environments." *Organization Science,* 21, 1263-1273.

Floyd, S. W. & Lane, P. J. (2000). "Strategizing throughout the organization: Managing role conflict in strategic renewal." *Academy of Management Review,* 25, 154-177.

Garcia-Morales, V. J., Llorens-Montes, F. J. & Verdu-Jover, A. J. (2006). "Antecedents and consequences of organizational innovation and organizational learning in entrepreneurship." *Industrial Management & Data Systems,* 106, 21-42.

Geerts, A., Blindenbach-Driessen, F. & Gemmel, P. (2010). "Achieving a balance between exploration and exploitation in service firms: a longitudinal study." *annual meetings of the Academy of Management.*

Gilbert, C. G. (2006). "Change in the presence of residual fit: Can competing frames coexist?" *Organization Science,* 17, 150-167.

Godin, B. & Lane, J. P. (2013). "Pushes and pulls: Hi(S)tory of demand pull model of innovation." *Science, Technology, & Human Values,* 38, 621-654.

Hashi, I. & Stojcic, N. (2013). "The impact of innovation activities on firm performance using a multi-stage model: Evidence from the Community Innovation Survey 4" *Research Policy,* 42, 353-366.

Jansen, J. J. P., Simsek, Z. & Cao, Q. (2012). "Ambidexterity and performance in multiunit contexts: Cross-level moderating effects of structural and resource attributes." *Strategic Management Journal,* 33, 1286-1303.

Jansen, J. J. P., Tempelaar, M. P., Van Den Bosch, F. A. J. & Volberda, H. W. (2009). "Structural differentiation and ambidexterity: The mediating role of integration mechanisms." *Organization Science,* 20, 797-811.

Jansen, J. J. P., Van Den Bosch, F. A. J. & Volberda, H. W. (2006). "Exploratory innvation, exploitative innovation, and performance: Effects of organizational antecedents and environmental moderators." *Management Science,* 52, 1661-1674.

Kang, S.-C. & Snell, S. A. (2009). "Intellectual capital architectures and ambidextrous learning: A framework for human resource management." *Journal of Management Studies,* 46, 65-92.

Lengnick-Hall, C. A. & Inocencio-Gray, J. L. (2013). "Institutionalized organizational learning and strategic renewal: The benefits and liabilities of prevailing wisdom." *Journal of Leadership & Organizational Studies,* 20, 420-435.

Levinthal, D. A. & March, J. (1993). "The myopia of learning." *Strategic Management Journal,* 14, 95-112.

Lin, C.-H. & Sanders, K. (2017). "HRM and innovation: a multi-level organizational learning perspective." *Human Resource Management Journal,* 27, 300-317.

Lin, H.-E. & Mcdonough III, E. F. (2011). "Investigating the role of leadership and organizational culture in fostering innovation ambidexterity." *IEEE Transactions on Engineering Management,* 58, 497-509.

March, J. G. (1991). "Exploration and exploitation in organizational learning." *Organization Science,* 2, 71-87.

O"Reilly III, C. A. & Tushman, M. L. (2011). "Organizational ambidexterity in action: How managers explore and exploit." *California Management Review,* 53, 5-22.

O"Reilly III, C. A. & Tushman, M. L. (2013). "Organizational ambidexterity: past, present, and future." *Academy of Management Perspectives,* 27, 324-338.

Patanakul, P. & Pinto, J. K. (2014). "Examining the roles of government policy on innovation." *Journal of High Technology Management Research,* 25, 97-107.

Porter, M. E. (1980). *Competitive Strategy: Techniques for Analysing Industries and Competitors,* New York, The Free Press.

Raisch, S. (2008). "Balanced structures: Designing organizations for profitable growth." *Long Range Planning,* 41, 483-508.

Raisch, S. & Birkinshaw, J. (2008). "Organizational ambidexterity: antecedents, outcomes, and moderators." *Journal of Management,* 34, 375-409.

Raisch, S., Birkinshaw, J., Probst, G. & Tushman, M. L. (2009). "Organizational ambidexterity: Balancing exploitation and exploration for sustained performance." *Organization Science,* 20, 685-695.

Rosing, K., Frese, M. & Bausch, A. (2011). "Explaining the heterogeneity of the leadership-innovation relationship: Ambidextrous leadership." *The Leadership Quarterly,* 22, 956-974.

Santos-Vijande, M. L., Lopez-Sanchez, J. A. & Trespalacios, J. A. (2012). "How organizational learning affects a firm"s flexibility, competitive strategy, and performance." *Journal of Business Research,* 65, 1079-1089.

Schamberger, D. K., Cleven, N. J. & Brettel, M. (2013). "Performance effects of exploratory and exploitative innovation strategies and the moderating role of external innovation partners." *Industry and Innovation,* 20, 336-356.

Turner, N., Swart, J. & Maylor, H. (2013). "Mechanisms for managing ambidexterity: a review and research agenda." *International Journal of Management Reviews,* 15, 317-332.

Tushman, M. L. & O"Reilly III, C. A. (1996). "Ambidextrous organizations: managing evolutionary and revolutionary change." *California Management Review,* 38, 8-30.

Uren, D. (2015). *Sustained slow growth post-GFC challenges economic minds* [Online]. Canberra: The Australian. Available: http://www.theaustralian.com.au/business/opinion/david-uren-economics/sustained-slow-growth-postgfc-challenges-economic-minds/news-story/a816dc04d4e99acb55c983d339ea7760 [Accessed April 12 2017].

Vaccaro, I. G., Jansen, J. J. P., Van Den Bosch, F. A. J. & Volberda, H. W. (2012). "Management innovation and leadership: The moderating role of organizational size." *Journal of Management Studies,* 49, 28-51.

Wang, C. L. & Rafiq, M. (2014). "Ambidextrous organizational culture, contextual ambidexterity and new product innovation: a comparative study of UK and Chinese high-tech firms." *British Journal of Management,* 25, 58-76.

Wei, Z., Yi, Y. & Guo, H. (2014). "Organizational learning ambidexterity, strategic flexibility, and new product development." *Journal of Product Innovation Management,* 31, 832-847.

Yin, R. K. (2009). *Case Study Research: Design and Methods.,* California, SAGE Publications.

Chapter 9

# Assessing Factors that Influence Employees' Creativity in Public-Sector Organisations: The case of Dubai Government Organisations

Mardeya D. Alblooshi

*University of Wollongong in Dubai, United Arab Emirates*

**Abstract:** The current study aimed to examine the mediating influence of organisational motivation to innovate between three antecedent factors—a) individual creativity components factors, b) determinants of work context factors and c) government regulation and incentives—on employees' creativity in Dubai government organisations.

A mixed-method approach was used, comprising a qualitative cycle, followed by a quantitative design, including structural equation modelling with data collected through a questionnaire.

The findings extended Amabile's (1988) model by examining the impact of government regulation and incentives as a factor external to the organisational context on employees' creativity. Also, organisational motivation to innovate acted as a mediator in most relationships between different factors and employees' creativity.

Moreover, this study is foundational research for other researchers in this field, especially in Dubai. Further, these findings will deepen the understanding decision-makers of the holistic role of organisational motivation to innovate to nurture employees' creativity.

**Keywords:** Creativity; public sector; Dubai government organisations.

## 9.1. Introduction

This research employed Amabile's (1988) componential theory of creativity and innovation in organisations. Amabile (1997) demonstrated that the theory incorporates individual and organisational factors that influence employees' creativity at work. However, Amabile and Pratt (2016) stated that one limitation of the componential theory of Amabile (1988), is that it concentrates exclusively on internal features within individual and organisation. It fails to contain external features outside the organisation. Thus, Amabile and Pratt (2016) added external factors to the new model.

There is a dearth of creativity literature that investigates factors external to organisations, such as family and friends (Madjar, Oldham & Pratt, 2002; Horng & Lee, 2009). Therefore, there is a need to identify whether government regulation and incentives, as an external variable of the organisational context, influence employees' creativity.

Moreover, in terms of the mediating role of organisational motivation to innovate, the integration of motivation and creativity began during the 1990s (Ambrose & Kulik, 1999). Hartmann (2006) considered motivation a major force through which employees' allocate effort efforts to introduce and execute fresh ideas. Indeed, both intrinsic and extrinsic motivational states have dominated scholarly concentration (Gong et al., 2017). According to Amabile and Pratt (2016), individual intrinsic task motivation is analogous to organisational motivation to innovate. However, prior studies have focused only on intrinsic task motivation. Thus, this research aims to empirically examine the latest changes in the model, as no studies were found that examined the role of organisational motivation to innovate as a summated variable on employees' creativity.

Since the current study focuses on public sector organisations, the literature shows that public-sector organisations are influenced by both internal and external factors. Perry and Porter (1982) categorised the factors that influence motivation in public organisation: individual, job, work environment and external environment characteristics. The authors clarified that the external environment could be divided into numerous categories such as socionormative, political, demographic, economic and technological.

Berman and Kim (2010) illustrated that although the significance of creativity is commonly acknowledged, the current literature does not comprise much mention of strategies to harness this potential in public administration. Most studies into creativity were conducted in the private sector (e.g., Amabile, 1988, 1997; Oldham & Cummings, 1996; Amabile & Gryskiewicz, 1989; George & Zhou, 2001; Foss, Woll & Moilanen, 2013; Eder & Sawyer, 2008), whereas few studies focused on the public sector (e.g., West & Berman, 1997; Rangarajan, 2008; Park et al., 2014). Consequently, additional empirical research is desperately required in the public sector. Thus, this study aims to examine if creativity practices adopted by public sector organisations that apply NPM principles show similar results as in private sector organisations or not.

Niu and Kaufman (2013) illustrated that most creativity theories have been developed in Western countries, particularly in the US. Lubart (1990) asserted that the Oriental and Western perspectives on creativity are different. Thus, Shalley, Zhou and Oldham (2004) clarified that findings from Western literature might not be applicable to Asia because based on current theories, employees' creativity is related to social–contextual factors that vary according to the organisational context. Hence, some studies have compared the impact of cultural difference on creativity. For instance, Yamada's (1991) conceptual research aimed to illuminate creativity barriers in Japan. The author agreed that sociocultural aspects related to creativity in Japan differ from those in Western countries, particularly in terms of language, education system and human resources management practices. Thus, all these factors are considered creativity obstacles in Japan. Moreover, Rice (2006) argued that research into creativity-building practices in countries other than the US usually focuses on advanced economies such as Europe and Japan.

Also, in terms of Arab countries, Mostafa (2005) stated that limited studies have investigated creativity and innovativeness in Arab countries. Creativity literature features just a few studies conducted in Arabic countries, such as the UAE (Zayed & Shaheen, 1995; Politis, 2005; Politis & Politis, 2010), Egypt (Rice, 2003, 2006; Mostafa, 2005; Mostafa & El-Masry, 2008), and the Kingdom of Saudi Arabia (Iqbal, 2011; ElMelegy et al., 2016).

Currently, all Dubai government organisations focus on creativity but few studies have investigated creativity in the UAE context (e.g., Politis, 2005, 2015; Politis & Politis, 2010; Dayan, Zacca & Di Benedetto, 2013).

Therefore, this study will contribute to the creativity research literature through the investigation of the influence of government regulations and incentives on employees' creativity as a variable that has never been examined in creativity studies. It will also examine whether organisational motivation to innovate has a mediation role between various factors and employees' creativity. Finally, the study will be conducted in Asia, specifically in Dubai, in which public sector organisations adopt several principles from private organisation such as focusing on creativity. As few studies in non-Western countries have examined the NPM execution in their public sector organisations (Jingjit & Fotaki, 2010).

## 9.2. Background

Numerous creativity theories and models have been developed to identify factors influencing individuals' and teams' creative behaviour. Key contributors include the componential theory of creativity and innovation in the organisational context (Amabile, 1988) and the interactionist theory (Woodman, Sawyer & Griffin, 1993). However, these theories focus only on the impact of individual and organisational factors on employees' creative outcomes. Building on the dimensions of the above theories and models, a large body of literature has examined the conditions required to enable employees' creativity within the workplace. The results indicate that employees' creativity is affected by individual characteristics (e.g., Amabile, 1989, 1996; Ganesan & Weitz, 1996;

Tierney, 1997; Eisenberger & Rhoades, 2001; Shin & Zhou, 2003; Eder & Sawyer, 2008) and organisational characteristics (e.g., Redmond, Mumford & Teach, 1993; Oldham & Cummings, 1996; Cummings & Oldham, 1997; Ekvall & Ryhammar, 1999; Zhou & George, 2001; Farmer, Tierney & Kung-McIntyre, 2003; Zhou, 2003; Politis, 2005; Hauksdóttir, 2011). Few studies have attempted to extend the early theories by examining factors outside the organisations that may influence employees' creative abilities. For example, other factors identified include family and friends (Madjar, Oldham & Pratt, 2002) and supportive family (Horng & Lee, 2009).

Rice (2003) stated that most studies related to business creativity, innovation and knowledge management concentrated on US management practices. The theories, models and suggestions are consequently culturally bound, according to the standpoints of the researchers and the cultural settings of the organisations investigated. Moreover, researchers who have studied practices in other countries usually focus on the developed economies of Japan and Europe. Unsurprisingly, literature showed that most studies were conducted in the US and Western countries (e.g., Axtell et al., 2000; Bommer & Jalajas, 2002; Haner, 2005; Zdunczyk & Blenkinsopp, 2007; Rasulzada & Dackert, 2009; Larson, 2011; Foss, Woll & Moilanen, 2013). Few studies were conducted in Asia (e.g., Politis, 2005, Gumusluoglu & Ilsev, 2009; Berman & Kim, 2010; Kalyar, 2011; Jiang, Wang & Zhao, 2012; Tseng & Liu, 2011; Lin & Liu, 2012; Peng et al., 2014).

Thus, several authors agreed that there was inconsistency in the results of research into factors that affect employees' creativity (e.g., Shalley, Zhou & Oldham, 2004; Foss, Woll & Moilanen, 2013; Sonenshein, 2014; Zhang et al., 2017). These authors suggested further research, particularly when testing the same theory or instrument in various places produced different results.

In terms of organisational motivation to innovate, according to Amabile et al. (1996), organisational motivation to innovate is a summated variable that contains organisational encouragement and a lack of organisational impediments. Prior research has examined the effect of each component of organisational motivation to innovate separately on employees' creativity: organisational encouragement (e.g., Chang et al., 2014; Birdi, Leach & Magadley, 2016) and lack of organisational impediments (e.g., ElMelegy et al., 2016). As mentioned earlier, Amabile and Pratt (2016) prioritised organisational motivation to innovate. Thus, there is a need to empirically examine the direct and indirect effects of organisational motivation to innovate as summated variable on employees' creativity.

Currently, creativity plays a vital role in public-sector organisations (McLean, 2005) Rangarajan (2008) stated that unlike private-sector organisations, investigating creativity has been ignored in the public sector for some time.

Compared to the private sector (e.g., Amabile & Gryskiewicz, 1989; Oldham & Cummings, 1996; Amabile, 1988, 1997; George & Zhou, 2001; Eder & Sawyer, 2008; Foss, Woll & Moilanen, 2013), few studies have examined creativity in public-sector organisations (e.g., Heinzen, 1990; West & Berman, 1997; Coveney, 2008; Benito, Montesinos & Bastida, 2008; Berman & Kim, 2010; Hui & Lau, 2010; Lauring & Selmer, 2013; Anne Loewenberger, Newton & Wick, 2014).

New Public Management (NPM) is kind of reform movement in public-sector organisations (Groot & Budding, 2008) which is applied to diverse degrees and with diverse emphases in public sector organisations (Van der Sluis, Reezigt & Borghans, 2017) and different private-sector practices and concepts were introduced to public-sector organisations across the world ( Jas & Skelcher, 2014).

Currently, the Dubai government implements (NPM) as several principles of private-sector organisations have been adopted by its entities. However, there is a lack of studies that examined the impact of adopting NPM principles in Dubai government organisations. Therefore, there is a need to recognise how this reform affects outcomes such as employee creativity.

Limited studies examined the impact of adopting NPM principles in non-Western counties (Jingjit & Fotaki, 2010). Hence, further empirical studies are required to clarify that adopting NPM principles (such as creativity) in public-sector organisations would lead to the same results as it has in the private sector. Most creativity studies have been conducted in private-sector organisations (e.g., Axtell et al., 2000; Bommer & Jalajas, 2002; Rasulzada & Dackert, 2009; Gumusluoglu & Ilsev, 2009; Tseng & Liu, 2011; Larson, 2011; Lin, 2011; Jiang, Wang & Zhao, 2012); fewer examined the public sector (e.g., Berman & Kim, 2010).

### 9.3. Research design

A mixed-method approach was used to conduct this study, which has an exploratory/qualitative cycle followed by quantitative design with data collected through a questionnaire.

The site for the study was three Dubai government organisations. Although the organisations are different in nature, they provided an appropriate setting to achieve research objectives for several reasons. First, creativity is part of these organisations' visions, missions and strategic plans. Second, creativity is among the behavioural competencies by which all employees must be evaluated in annual performance appraisals (e.g., a number of generated ideas annually). Finally, the three organisations won several internal and external awards for which creativity was a main criterion.

### Cycle 1: Qualitative phase of the research design

Interviews were conducted with key decision-makers to create a comprehensive summary of Dubai government organisational motivations related to: 1) Identifying how creativity and innovation are defined and if both concepts are related to each other. 2) Highlighting the adaptation of creativity and innovation in public-sector organisations, and 3) Recognising factors that influence employees' creativity in Dubai government organisations.

The population for this cycle included local and expatriate key decision-makers who are involved with creativity in Dubai government organisations. Consequently, the sample of this cycle for the study was narrowed down to nine local and expatriate employees working in three Dubai government organisations that focus on creativity.

NVivo 11 was used to analyse the qualitative data.

### Cycle 2: Quantitative phase of the research design

The objective of this cycle was to investigate the following research question:

What is the impact of 'organisational motivation to innovate' on the relationship between three antecedent factors—a) individual creativity components b) determinants of work context and c) government regulation and incentives—on the outcome, 'creativity among employees' in Dubai government organisations?

A self-administered questionnaire was used for the quantitative strand to answer the research question.

The population included local and expatriate employees working in Dubai government organisations. The sample for the study was 668 employees working in one of three Dubai government organisations. They were selected randomly. The sample included employees who hold various job designations to ensure a range of jobs were available to cover different work-related activities.

The quantitative data collection process comprised two parts: the pilot study and the main study.

### Pilot study process

The researcher conducted the pilot study to collect data from employees. The questionnaire required the participants to rank their opinion on several important issues related to the specific work environment factors that influence employees in the public sector.

Some minor necessary changes had been made to the Arabic questionnaire before conducting the main study. Also, additional questions related to respondents' age groups were added to the demographic information section.

### Administration of the main study

The data collection was then proceeded as follows: Participants were then contacted by the researcher by email and telephone and provided with information related to the study. Participants were asked to complete a paper copy of the emailed questionnaire. They needed to print and complete the questionnaire with the attached Main Study Participant Information Sheet. Participants were requested to complete the hard copy of the questionnaire at their place of work (or any convenient location), at a time convenient to them. Once completed, the survey was to be dropped (in a sealed envelope) into a locked drop box located at a designated place within the organisation. No identifying data were asked from participants. The researcher collected the completed questionnaires from the locked drop boxes on a previously agreed date.

Once the initial emails were sent to participants, and due to the lack of identifying data, a second, third and fourth reminder email was sent to the entire group with a notice for those who had already sent the questionnaire to ignore the reminders.

Factor analysis and structural equation modelling were used to analyse gathered data.

SPSS (version 23) was used for coding, editing, checking missing data, assumptions of normality, linearity, multicollinearity, outliers and factor analysis. While AMOS (version 23) was used for confirmatory factor analysis (measurement model) and structural equation modelling.

## 9.4. Conclusion

### Cycle 1: Qualitative phase of the research design

The findings of this cycle support the applicability of Amabile's (1988) componential theory of creativity and innovation: individual factors and work environment factors enable employees' creativity.

The contribution of the interviews was that factors outside the organisations, such as government regulation and incentives, also influence employees' creativity. This contribution overcomes the limitation of Amabile's (1988) theory, which does not consider the influence of factors outside the organisation on employees' creativity.

Also, the finding has highlighted that public-sector organisations in Dubai are categorised as NPM (i.e., they implements private-sector practices and concepts) (Jas & Skelcher, 2014).

**Cycle 2: Quantitative phase of the research design**

The following hypotheses were tested using SEM.

*H1: Organisational motivation to innovate mediates the relationship between individual creativity components—a) domain-relevant skills and b) creativity-relevant skills—and employees' creativity.*

*H2: Organisational motivation to innovate mediates the relationship between work context determinants— a) sufficient resources, b) managerial encouragement, c) work group supports, d) freedom, e) challenging work and f) realistic workload pressure—and employees' creativity.*

*H3: Organisational motivation to innovate mediates the relationship between government regulation and incentives, and employees' creativity.*

**The result of H1**

(a) The result of mediating effects showed positive indirect effects of domain-relevant skills via organisational motivation to innovate on employee creativity (b = -0.277, p = 0.001); the 95 per cent bootstrap CIs lower (-0. 582) and upper (-0.052) the indirect effects did not contain zero.

(b) The result showed no indirect effects of creativity-relevant skills via organisational motivation to innovate on creativity (b = 0.076, p = 0.115); the 95 per cent bootstrap CIs lower (-0.032) and upper (0.284) the indirect effects contained zero.

Note: The factor loading of intrinsic task motivation was too low, therefore after a careful consideration the decision was made to remove it from the model.

**The result of H2**

There was a direct relationship between organisational motivation to innovate and employees' creativity (β = .825, p = .020). Also, five full mediation effects were supported as follows;

(a) The result showed positive indirect effects of sufficient resources via organisational motivation to innovate on creativity (b = 0.217, p = 0.010); the 95 per cent bootstrap CIs lower (0.088) and upper (0.746) the indirect effects did not contain zero.

(b) The result showed positive indirect effects of managerial encouragement via organisational motivation to innovate on creativity (b = 0.237, p =

0.001); the 95 per cent bootstrap CIs lower (0.095) and upper (0.924.) the indirect effects did not contain zero.

(c) The result showed positive indirect effects of work group supports via organisational motivation to innovate on employees' creativity (b = 0.124, p = 0.024); the 95 per cent bootstrap CIs lower (0.011) and upper (0.392.) the indirect effects did not contain zero.

(d) The result showed positive indirect effects of freedom via organisational motivation to innovate on creativity (b = 0.263, p = 0.001); the 95 per cent bootstrap CIs lower (0.065) and upper (0.797) the indirect effects did not contain zero.

(e) The result showed positive indirect effects of challenging work via organisational motivation to innovate on creativity (b = 191, p = 0.001); the 95 per cent bootstrap CIs lower (0.051) and upper (0.743) the indirect effects did not contain zero.

(f) The result showed no indirect effects of realistic workload pressure via organisational motivation to innovate on creativity (b = 113, p = 0.095); the 95 per cent bootstrap CIs lower (- 0.012) and upper (0.531), the indirect effects contained zero.

**The result of H3**

The result showed positive indirect effects of government regulation and incentives via organisational motivation to innovate on creativity (b = 177, p = 0.001); the 95 per cent bootstrap CIs lower (0.055) and upper (0.628) the indirect effects did not contain zero.

## 9.5. Implications and future research

### Theoretical and empirical contributions

First, the current chapter has extended the componential theory of creativity and innovation in organisations (Amabile, 1988) by: 1)Overcoming the theory's limitation and examining the impact of new external variables (government regulation and incentives) on employees' creativity. 2) Examining empirically the direct and indirect impact of organisational motivation to innovate as a summated variable. Organisational motivation to innovate was studied as a summated variable, including both organisational encouragement and lack of organisational impediments (Amabile et al., 1996), in response to calls for further research (Amabile & Pratt, 2016).

Thus, the findings indicated good support for the revised model of Amabile and Pratt (2016) and provided support for the critical role played by the organisational motivation to innovate in influencing employees' creativity.

Second, the current study has contributed to public-sector literature, as most previous studies that examined factors that influence employees' creativity have focused on the private-sector, few studies have examined creativity in the public sector (e.g., West & Berman, 1997; Rangarajan, 2008; Park et al., 2014).

Indeed, one of the gaps identified in the literature is that although public-sector reforms have been applied to diverse degrees and with diverse emphasis in recent years (Van der Sluis et al., 2017), no studies have examined how public-sector reforms, such as NPM, have affected organisational outcomes.

Further, several studies (e.g., Jingjit & Fotaki, 2010; Trotta et al., 2011) have recently called for more research to examine if the nature of the relationship between key management principles, as proposed by New Public Management (NPM) principles, is evident in public sector. This study confirms that regulatory reforms affect creativity positively, only when combined with an enabling organisational context that encourages creativity (as measured in this study through: the fair, constructive judgment of ideas, reward and recognition for creative work, mechanisms for developing new ideas and an active flow of ideas and a shared vision) and lack of organisational impediments (as measured by an organisational culture that does not impede creativity through internal political problems, harsh criticism of new ideas, destructive internal competition, and avoidance of risk, and an overemphasis on the status quo (Amabile et al., 1996).

Third, this chapter had empirical contributions that helped to answer several calls for further research related to creativity literature:1) About how the indirect relationship between creativity and different wok context can be explained (e.g., Coelho, Augusto & Lages, 2011). Also, Coelho, Augusto and Lages (2011) called for further research on how an employee's association with colleagues affects creativity, both directly and indirectly.2) Examine the role of contextual, structural and other creativity-relevant factors that can be gathered using established survey instruments such as KEYS for evaluating the creative output of organisations that would be useful in public- sector organisations as suggested by Rangarajan (2008).

### Practical contributions

The findings of this chapter have significant contextual, managerial and policy implications.

### Contextual implications

First, most creativity theories have been established in Western countries, particularly in the US (Niu & Kaufman, 2013). Thus, several authors agreed that Oriental and Western creativity points of view are different (e.g., Lubart, 1990; Yamada, 1991; Shalley, Zhou & Oldham, 200). The current chapter indicates that Western creativity theories, such as the componential model of creativity and innovation in organisations (Amabile, 1988) cannot be used in Asian countries, such as the UAE, specifically in the public-sector context. The results of the direct relationships between individual and work context factors with employees' creativity in this study were different than those of studies conducted in Western countries. Thus, this study examined the theory in a new context with regards to employees' creativity.

Second, limited creativity studies have been conducted in the UAE context. Thus, this study has filled this contextual gap and is considered among one of the first studies to be conducted in UAE, particularly in the context of the Dubai government. Moreover, previous studies have investigated only work climate factors (Politis, 2005; Politis & Politis, 2010), while another study examined the impact of self-leadership on the dimensions of entrepreneurial orientation, creativity and productivity (Politis, 2015). Therefore, this chapter examined three groups of factors: individual, work and external factors. Thus, a comprehensive understanding on the mediating impact of organisational motivation to innovate on the relationship between three different kinds of different factors and employees' creativity was provided. Finally, this chapter can be considered a foundation for other researchers interested in the creativity field, especially in the UAE context. Therefore, managers must conduct the best benchmark with some pioneer organisations to update the current work context factors.

Third, the existing literature has shown mixed results regarding the relationship between different factors and employees' creativity. The results of the current study are significant because they provide further evidence for the nature of the relationship in the Dubai government context.

### Managerial implications

This chapter provided useful implications for managers who prioritise enhancing employees' creativity in the workplace.

First, organisational motivation to innovate was perceived as a significant mediating factor. This finding provides an impetus for further studies to provide conclusive evidence regarding how the cultural/regional context interacts with key organisational processes, such as organisational motivation to innovate to affect employees' creativity and other related outcomes at the individual and organisational level. Hence, managers should realise that without sufficient organisational motivation to innovate, enhancing individuals' creativity cannot happen. Therefore, managers need to ensure that they inculcate a constructive, creative climate through strategies and obtain maximum potential advantages by adopting an organisational policy that enhances creativity.

Second, managers must consider changes that should be involved when considering employees' creativity. According to Cumming and Oldham (1997), individual preferences, main concerns and problem-solving styles might change over time, which necessitates adjustments to guarantee the appropriate fit between employees' creative potential and their work climate.

Third, managers and decision-makers should consider creativity expenditure as a long-term investment that will benefit the organisations. As a result, they should search for the means to create a creative climate in which employees develop and grow their creative competencies. Additionally, there is a need to establish strategies that value candidates who possess creativity skills and abilities and who are fully involved in their work-related tasks and regard them as a part of their human capital.

Fourth, the achieved results suggest that managers must realise that it is not sufficient for the organisations to employ creative people and expect creative performance. One of the manager's main roles is encouraging the availability of different mechanisms related to organisational motivation to innovate. These results showed the significant role of organisational motivation to innovate on the relationship between different factors in promoting employees' creativity.

Thus, organisations that aim to develop employees' creativity should consider these points when planning for creative projects because employee characteristics and work context factors will not fulfil the required goals unless organisational motivation to innovate is present.

## Policy implications

First, Berman and Kim (2010, p. 641) defined creativity management as a new management concept in public administration, which increases creativity and initiative. Therefore, to develop more creative employees, local and federal governments in the UAE should establish creativity management mechanisms in their public organisations to develop and monitor all employee creativity issues. A mechanism that can be assessed by key performance indicators and survey questionnaires related to creativity to assess the current situation and provide solutions to overcome existing limitations on creativity.

Second, there is a need to generate and maintain a good fit between government regulation and incentives issued by both federal and local governments with organisational mechanisms related to motivating employees' creativity in public-sector organisations. The results showed organisational motivation to innovate mediated the relationship between government regulation and incentives and employees' creativity. Therefore, both federal and local governments in the UAE, while issuing government regulation and incentives related to creativity, should ensure that they develop the current creativity mechanisms in public-sector organisations to improve employees' creativity.

## References

Amabile T.M. (1998). "How to kill creativity", *Harvard Business Review*, vol. 76, pp. 77-89.

Amabile, T.M. & Gryskiewicz, N.D. (1989). "The creative environment scales: Work environment inventory", *Creativity research journal*, vol. 2. no. (4), pp.231-253.

Amabile, T.M. (1979). "Effects of external evaluation on artistic creativity", *Journal of personality and Social Psychology*, vol. 37, no. 2, pp.221- 233.

Amabile, T.M. (1988). "A model of creativity and innovation in organizations", *Research in organisational behavior*, vol. 10, no. 1, pp.123-167.

Amabile, T.M. & Conti, R. (1999). "Changes in the work environment for creativity during downsizing", *Academy of Management Journal*, vol. 42, no. 6, pp.630-640.

Amabile, T.M. & Pratt, M.G. (2016). "The dynamic componential model of creativity and innovation in organisations: Making progress, making meaning", *Research in Organisational Behavior*, vol. 36, pp.157-183.

Amabile, T.M., Conti, R., Coon, H., Lazenby, J., & Herron, M. (1996). "Assessing the work environment for creativity", *Academy of management. journal*, vol.39, no. 5, pp.1154-1184.

Amabile, T.M. (1996). "Creativity and innovation in organization", *Harvard Business School, Mass*, pp. 1-15.

Amabile, T.M. (1997). "Motivating creativity in organisations; on doing what you love and loving what you do", *California Management Review*, vol.40, no.1, pp. 39-58.

Ambrose, M.L. & Kulik, C.T. (1999). "Old friends, new faces: Motivation research in the 1990s", *Journal of management*, vol.25, no. 3, pp. 231-292.

Anne Loewenberger, P., Newton, M. & Wick, K. (2014). "Developing creative leadership in a public sector organisation." *International Journal of Public Sector Management*, vol. 27, no. 3, pp.190-200.

Axtell, C.M., Holman, D.J., Unsworth, K.L., Wall, T.D., Waterson, P.E. & Harrington, E. (2000). "Shopfloor innovation: Facilitating the suggestion and implementation of ideas", *Journal of occupational and organizational psychology*, vol. 73, no. 3, pp.265-285.

Berman, E.M. & Kim, C. (2010). "Creativity Management in Public Organisations Jump-Starting Innovation", *Public Performance & Management Review*, vol. 33, no.4, pp. 619-652.

Coelho, F., Augusto, M. & Lages, L.F. (2011). "Contextual factors and the creativity of frontline employees: The mediating effects of role stress and intrinsic motivation", *Journal of Retailing*, vol. 87, no. 1, pp.31-45.

Dayan, M., Zacca, R. & Di Benedetto, A. (2013). "An exploratory study of entrepreneurial creativity: Its antecedents and mediators in the context of UAE firms", *Creativity and Innovation Management*, vol. 22, no.3, pp.223-240.

Eisenberger, R. & Rhoades, L. (2001). "Incremental effects of reward on creativity", *Journal of personality and social psychology*, vol. 81, no. 4, pp.728-741.

Foss, L., Woll, K. & Moilanen, M. (2013). "Creativity and implementations of new ideas: do organisational structure, work environment and gender matter? ", *International Journal of Gender and Entrepreneurship*, vol. 5, no. 3, pp.298-322.

George, J.M. & Zhou, J. (2001). "When openness to experience and conscientiousness are related to creative behavior: an interactional approach", *Journal of applied psychology*, vol. 86, no. 3, pp.513-524.

Gong, Y, Wu, J, Song, L J & Zhang, Z. (2017). "Dual tuning in creative processes: Joint contributions of intrinsic and extrinsic motivational orientations", *Journal of Applied Psychology*, vol.102, no.5, pp.829-84.

Groot, T. & Budding, T. (2008). "New public management"s current issues and future prospects", *Financial Accountability & Management*, vol. 24, no.1, pp.1-13.

Hartmann, A. (2006). "The role of organisational culture in motivating innovative behaviour in construction firms", *Construction innovation*, vol. 6, no.3, pp.159-172.

Iqbal, A. (2011). "Creativity and innovation in Saudi Arabia: An overview, Innovation Management", *Policy & practice*, vol. 13, pp. 376-390.

Jas, P. & Skelcher, C. (2014). "Different regulatory regimes in different parts of the UK? A comparison of narrative and practice in relation to poor performance in local government", *Local Government Studies*, vol. 40, no.1, pp.121-140.

Larson, M. (2011). "Innovation and creativity in festival organisations", *Journal of Hospitality Marketing & Management*, vol.20, no.3-4, pp.287-310.

Lin, C.Y. & Liu, F. (2012). "A cross-level analysis of organisational creativity climate and perceived innovation: The mediating effect of work motivation", *European Journal of Innovation Management*, vol.15, no.1, pp. 55-76.

Mathisen, G.E. & Einarsen, S. (2004). "A review of instruments assessing creative and innovative environments within organizations", *Creativity Research Journal*, vol.16, no. 1, pp.119-140.

Niu, W. & Kaufman, J.C. (2013). "Creativity of Chinese and American cultures: A synthetic analysis", *The Journal of Creative Behavior*, vol. 47, no. 1, pp.77-87.

Park, C.H., Song, J.H., Lim, D.H. & Kim, J.W. (2014). "The influences of openness to change, knowledge sharing intention and knowledge creation practice on employees' creativity in the Korean public sector context", *Human Resource Development International*, vol. 17, no. 2, pp. 203-221.

Politis, J.D. (2005). "Dispersed leadership predictor of the work environment for creativity and productivity", *European Journal of Innovation Management*, vol. 8, no. 2, pp.182-204.

Rangarajan, N. (2008). "Evidence of different types of creativity in government A multimethod assessment", *Public Performance & Management Review*, vol. 32, no.1, pp.132–163.

Rasulzada, F. & Dackert, I. (2009). "Organisational creativity and innovation in relation to psychological well-being and organizational factors", *Creativity Research Journal*, vol. 21, no. 2-3, pp.191-198.

Shalley, C.E. (1995). "Effects of coaction, expected evaluation, and goal setting on creativity and productivity", *Academy of Management Journal*, vol. 38, pp. 483–503.

Woodman, R.W., Sawyer, J.E. & Griffin, R.W. (1993). "Toward a theory of organizational creativity", *Academy of management review*, vol. 18, no. 2. pp. 293-321.

Zhou, J. (2003). "When the presence of creative co-workers is related to creativity: Role of supervisor close monitoring, developmental feedback, and creative personality", *Journal of Applied Psychology*, vol. 88, no. 3, pp. 413–422.

Zhang, W., Jex, S.M., Peng, Y. & Wang, D. (2017). "Exploring the effects of job autonomy on engagement and creativity: The moderating role of performance pressure and learning goal orientation", *Journal of Business and Psychology*, vol. 32, no. 3, pp. 235-251.

Chapter 10

# Patterns of Service Innovation: An Empirical Study of Automotive Engineering Services in Germany

Florian Müller

*University of Bremen, Germany*

**Abstract:** This chapter contributes a qualitative study, from the German automotive engineering service industry, to the growing body of scholarly work that studies how service innovation emerges from interactions and collaborative activities that take place among a network of actors. In doing so, this chapter employs a qualitative research design that is informed by different sources of empirical data, mostly in-depth interviews. The theoretical viewpoint taken in this study is informed by the service-dominant logic, which entails a broader and systemic view of service innovation. This view emphasizes the centrality of interactions and considers innovation as a process of reconfiguring the institutionalized rules of resource integration in service ecosystems. Based on this perspective, the key finding is an empirically developed process typology that distinguishes five patterns of service innovation.

**Keywords:** Service Innovation; Innovation Pattern; Service Ecosystem; Automotive Engineering; Automotive Industry; Digital Transformation; Service-Dominant Logic; S-D Logic; Business-to-Business Services; Service Networks and Systems

## 10.1. Introduction

In today's rapidly changing and increasingly networked business environment, organizations are becoming ever more reliant on their capacity to continually develop new and more compelling value propositions (Lusch and Vargo, 2006). In this regard, a growing number of organizations recognize service as a primary driver of economic prosperity and growth. At the same time, organizations are frequently operating and competing in complex service networks (Vargo and Lusch, 2011). Contemporary thinking suggests that in such a setting, service innovation can no longer evolve from within the organization but instead requires collaboration and engagement among multiple actors of a service network, including customers and suppliers (Lusch and Nambisan, 2015).

However, the growing recognition of service innovation in networks stands in sharp contrast to the firm-centric focus of the innovation literature that considers innovations as the outcome of systematic processes of research and development (R&D) that end with market diffusion (Godin, 2006, p. 639). Furthermore, the literature on service innovation is highly fragmented, and a common understanding as to what service innovation is and how it should be studied has not yet emerged (Carlborg et al., 2014). Complexity in service innovation arises especially from the fact that the innovation behavior of firms varies between industries and economies (e.g., Metcalfe and Miles, 2000). More industry-specific research is thus necessary that observes the emergence of innovations in networked settings and shows how different actors participate in such processes.

More recently, the interest in service innovation has been further elevated by the growing popularity of the service-dominant logic (S-D logic) (Vargo and Lusch, 2008, 2004). S-D logic describes an alternative world-view, in which service is the fundamental basis of economic exchange and the central logic needed to explain value creation. From this view, all economic and social actors (e.g., organizations, departments, and employees) are resource integrators that are connected with other actors through value co-creation and service exchange and, thus, form wider actor-to-actor (A2A) structures (Vargo and Lusch, 2011, 2016). An institutional view of innovation aims for a more realistic and complete understanding of how service innovation emerges from interactions and collaborative activities that take place among a network of actors in a service ecosystem (Lusch and Nambisan, 2015). Vargo and Lusch (2014, p. 161) define service ecosystems as *"relatively self-contained, self-adjusting systems of resource integrating actors connected by shared institutional logics and mutual value creation through service exchange."* The connection between institutionalization and service innovation is thereby twofold: First, the service ecosystem perspective emphasizes innovation as a collaborative process that involves interactions among a network of actors whose resource integration practices are enabled, guided and constrained by *institutions* and their interdependent assemblages (institutional arrangements) (Vargo et al. 2015; Vargo and Lusch 2016). Scholars argue that, for service innovation to occur, some of the existing institutions (i.e., rules, practices, and norms) have to be disrupted and renewed (Vargo et al., 2015). Second, institutions determine how actors interact with one another and how resources are integrated, which makes them crucial to the understanding of the complex and interconnected processes through which service innovations emerge in real world-contexts. However, as yet, most literature on service ecosystems is purely conceptual work, and there is a paucity of empirical studies that employ S-D logic to study innovation in service ecosystems based on real-world settings (Carlborg et al., 2014).

Service innovation processes are by no means homogeneous, and significant differences exist in the innovation behavior among industries or firms (Evangelista, 2006). One specific stream of the innovation literature focuses on knowledge-intensive business services (KIBS). KIBS involve complex problem solving, invoke a value creation process that is characterized by intense interaction between customer and provider, and rely upon professional knowledge in service provision (Muller and Doloreux, 2007). The innovativeness of KIBS firms has been widely acknowledged in the literature (e.g., Muller and Doloreux, 2007). For instance, den Hertog (2000) highlights the vital role of KIBS in regional innovation systems as facilitators, carriers, and sources of innovation. Nevertheless, KIBS industries have seldom been the focus of empirical examinations from the viewpoint of service innovation. More research is thus required to understand the processes that lead to the innovation of KIBS themselves.

One of the most significant KIBS domains in Germany is the automotive engineering service (AES) industry. Engineering services are provided in the form of engineering projects by highly-specialized professional service firms, so-called engineering service providers (ESPs). Their primary customers are large German original equipment manufacturers (OEMs) of automobiles, such as BMW, VW or Daimler. In recent years, the AES industry has entered a phase of accelerated change. Formerly dominated by pyramid-like supplier-hierarchies, service provision and interactions between ESPs and other actors are now increasingly taking place in more complex networked constellations and are based on varying modes of collaboration (Schneider, 2011, pp. 44–46). For the ESPs, this shift entails an elevation of their role towards more responsibility and autonomy during service provision (Blöcker, 2016). This development is, however, accompanied by growing competition and cost-pressure among the incumbent ESPs (cf. Blöcker, 2016). There is a growing need for ESPs to engage more actively in service innovation, which requires interactions and collaborative efforts with other actors from their network. The current innovation literature provides little orientation for ESPs with respect to how innovation processes should take place in networked constellations and which interactions and activities they involve, which underscores the practical relevance of innovation research in this industry.

This chapter addresses the outlined research gaps by employing the S-D logic and the service ecosystem perspective in the study of service innovation processes in the empirical domain of the AES industry in Germany. The outlined research gaps reflect the need to make service innovation processes in the AES industry more explicit and comprehensible. In this regard, typologies are an effective means of reducing the complexity of a research phenomenon by conceptualizing different types (Bailey, 1994, pp. 5–8).

Previous studies have especially encouraged the development of industry-specific typologies that use qualitative data to conceptualize different types (i.e., categories) of service innovation processes (e.g., Hipp and Grupp, 2005; Carlborg et al., 2014). In the development of such a typology, this chapter addresses the following question:

> How can service innovation processes in the German AES industry be categorized?

Typologies that describe specific types of innovation processes in networks can help both researchers and practitioners to understand how the activities of different actors are interdependent. Especially for the management of ESPs, understanding these network interdependencies is essential in order to participate in, and benefit from, innovation processes (e.g., related to new technologies) that will transform their business environment and are typically not completely under their own control.

## 10.2. Background

The innovation literature proposes classification schemes that characterize types of innovation processes or conceptualize actor behavior within such processes (Hipp, 2000). Bailey (1994, p. v) suggests these classification schemes can be distinguished into two research approaches: typologies and taxonomies. While typologies are primarily based on conceptual or qualitative research, taxonomies are based on quantitative research and typically use cluster analysis to classify cases according to their differences and similarities. Table 10.1 provides an overview of relevant innovation taxonomies and typologies.

Innovation patterns proposed in the literature vary as to their approach and conceptual logic. Innovation taxonomies typically highlight characteristics of service firms that identify reasons for different industry-specific innovation activities, whereas innovation typologies are more concerned with the processes through which innovations in services emerge and the conceptualization of types of service innovation processes. A further distinction can be made between typologies examining KIBS-specific innovation processes and those employing S-D logic to classify service innovation processes based on categories not limited to certain types of innovations, such as technical innovations, but are more broadly applicable in different innovation contexts.

**Table 10.1:** An Overview of Innovation Taxonomies and Innovation Typologies

| *Type* | *Approach* | *Conceptual Logic* | *Sources* |
|---|---|---|---|
| Innovation Taxonomies | Quantitative empirical research that characterizes group- or industry-specific innovation behaviors | Innovation in services as distinct from innovation in products. Service innovation as an innovation pattern on its own. | Pavitt et al. (1989), Evangelista (2000), Miozzo and Soete (2001), De Jong and Marsili (2006), Camacho and Rodriguez (2008) |
| Innovation Typologies | Qualitative empirical or conceptual research that distinguishes and describes types of innovation processes | Innovation processes in KIBS industries are distinct from other industries. | den Hertog (2000), Toivonen and Tuominen (2009) |
| | | Service innovation as all-encompassing and as a process of institutional change (S-D logic) | Koskela-Huotari et al. (2016) |

## Innovation Taxonomies

Many studies attempting to identify innovation patterns assume the existence of significant differences in the innovation behavior between firms or industry sectors; however, they also assume a similarity in the patterns taken to innovate by some groups of firms. Studies that follow this assumption, typically draw on quantitative sector-level or firm-level data and use factor analysis to classify firms into different clusters or groups, distinguished by a specific characteristic innovation pattern (Hipp, 2000). The taxonomies resulting from this deductive approach divide companies into different classes, whose characteristics correspond to specific types of innovation outcome or innovation.

Taxonomies have significantly contributed to innovation research; however, they have also been criticized for various reasons. For example, Hipp (cf. 2000, p. 136) argued that many taxonomies limit the scope of their analysis to organizational factors and neglect other equally important contextual variables, such as those related to technology or a firm's social and economic environment. Another problematic point is that quantitative studies assume that service innovations are necessarily the outcome of well-managed innovation activities, starting with the identification and analysis of a problem or need and ending with the development and marketing of a service. However, more recent studies have shown that service innovations also tend to arise in an unplanned and sometimes chaotic fashion (e.g., Gallouj and Weinstein, 1997; Toivonen and Tuominen, 2009). Finally, a growing number of scholars argue that there is no standard or unique pattern of innovation for specific firms or industries and that taxonomies do not adequately reflect that the individual ways that firms innovate (Camacho and Rodriguez, 2008; de Jong and Marsili, 2006).

**Innovation Typologies**

Innovation typologies have produced another stream of the literature that conceptualizes specific types of innovation processes, based on the commonalities and differences in the innovation behavior of firms or industries. Innovation typologies are distinct from innovation taxonomies, in that they are the result of qualitative empirical studies or conceptual research (Bailey, 1994; cf. Hipp, 2000, pp. 115–117). In comparison to taxonomies, innovation typologies are underrepresented in the innovation literature. Scholars widely agree that the innovation behavior of KIBS firms does not adhere to many traditional innovation models that were developed in manufacturing industries (Camacho and Rodriguez, 2008; Muller and Doloreux, 2007). One reason is that the innovation activities of KIBS firms (more than in other industries) rely on intense collaboration with local customers (Miles, 2008). Scholars have thus attempted to address these peculiarities by proposing KIBS-specific innovation typologies. A frequently cited KIBS-specific innovation typology has been proposed by den Hertog (2000). He conducted conceptual research and developed a multi-dimensional model that frames service innovation along four dimensions of novelty: service concept, client-interface, service delivery system, technological options. Den Hertog asserted that innovation often requires changes in multiple dimensions simultaneously and relies heavily on knowledge and creativity.

Despite the increasing interest in a service ecosystem perspective, there has been little empirical analysis of innovation processes in service ecosystems. As one of the few exceptions, Koskela-Huotari et al. (2016), studied the innovation behavior of four different enterprises (two manufacturing companies, a food marketplace, and a retailer) and describe patterns in the way these firms reconfigure the logic in their service ecosystems by making, breaking and maintaining institutional rules. An essential finding of Koskela-Huotari et al. (2016) is that the emergence of innovation in service ecosystems requires some rules to be broken, while others must be maintained. The authors explain this by virtue of the fact that actors (in most institutionalized practices) need a certain degree of orientation based on established routines and practices, so that changing too many rules simultaneously may be counterproductive.

## 10.3. Research design

This chapter employs a research design that combines qualitative-empirical techniques with an abductive case study methodology. This research design enables an in-depth investigation of service innovation processes and an exploration of service innovation patterns.

### Data Sources and Analysis

The qualitative research design was chosen in alignment with definitions and conceptual views from existing S-D logic literature. More specifically, this study adopts the S-D logic interpretation of service innovation as an interactive process that leads to the institutionalization of new resource integration practices (Vargo et al., 2015). Furthermore, S-D logic invokes a systemic view of service innovation that suggests analyzing changes and interactions in service innovation processes on different systemic levels, i.e., micro-, meso-, and macro-level. As suggested in the S-D logic literature (Chandler and Vargo, 2011; Wieland et al., 2016), the collection, and ensuing analysis, of the empirical data concentrates on ESPs as focal actors (i.e., micro level). Additionally, their interactions with other actors in service networks and service ecosystems are investigated and aggregated to a meso and macro systemic view of their business environment (Barile et al., 2016). Data were collected from the ecosystem in which ESPs operate and interact with other actors, in particular, with large OEMs, who are primary customers of their services. To extend the analytical scope beyond individual actors (micro-level) and to gain a meso- and macro-understanding of service ecosystems, insights were aggregated across interviewees and firms.

The qualitative research design that is employed in this chapter is informed by four different sources of empirical data: preliminary and in-depth interviews, as well as archival data and field observations. The primary source of data is in-depth interviews with 37 experts from the automotive industry, which comprised 32 telephone interviews with individuals, three face-to-face interviews with individuals and two telephone group interviews with two respondents each. Interviews lasted between 25 and 94 minutes, totalling more than 30 hours of interviews. All interviews, except two (which were declined by the interviewees), were audio-recorded and transcribed.

This research has employed the MaxQDA software for qualitative data analysis; specifically to manage the amount and complexity of data and the respective links between codes and text-passages (cf. Gibbs, 2014). The management of data and code structures with MaxQDA supported the goal of establishing a *"chain of evidence"* and maintaining it over the course of the research (Yin, 2014, p. 127). This chain begins with the documentation of the data (audio files, interview transcripts, and notes) and their entry into the database of the research project in MaxQDA. The chain continues via data coding up to the linking of the codes with the concepts developed in this research.

## Course of the Research

The research process employed in this study followed an abductive approach to case study research based on the guidelines provided by Dubois and Gadde (2014, 2002). In accordance with the abductive research process, primary research activities, such as data collection, literature research, and theory development were carried out mainly in parallel and were closely interlinked (Dubois and Gadde, 2002). In the course of the research process, the research aims, the scope of the data, the focus of the analysis, and the considered theoretical knowledge were subject to significant reorientations resulted in the division of the research process into multiple consecutive phases. The analysis of the empirical data was an iterative process that involved multiple rounds of interview screening for relevant text passages, continuous comparisons between interviewee statements and theoretical concepts, as well as with knowledge from the literature (cf. Gibbs, 2014). This was a constant process throughout different phases of this research, beginning with a broad range of topics and eventually narrowing the analysis down to service innovation. During the analysis, the scope of the considered interviews was gradually refined, such that the analysis was extended to additional interviews and other firms.

In the final phase of the research, the detection and conceptualization of service innovation patterns happened in two interrelated cycles of selecting and managing the data and their analysis and interpretation. Related activities included assessing interviews according to relevance and prioritizing them for analysis. The interviews were screened for information, which enabled the differentiation of service innovation processes, both with a focus on individual organizations, as well as across organizations (i.e., cases). The aim was to identify variables in service innovation processes that would allow the classification and distinguishing of specific types, based on their similarities and differences. Findings were synthesized into an analytical framework with several dimensions and characteristics. The application of the analytical framework to the interview data supported the detection and differentiation of service innovation patterns and informed the construction of the service innovation typology. The choice of concepts for the dimensions and characteristics of the analytical framework was made in close alignment with the S-D logic, so that existing concepts, which helped to distinguish service innovation processes, were incorporated. Dimensions and characteristics of the analytical framework were mapped to text passages, which described similar behaviors and activities in service innovation processes. The application of dimensions and characteristics to the data led to the analytical framework itself being modified and adapted in several iterations; thereby providing a better match to the service innovation processes reflected in the data. Over time, this resulted in the conceptualization of several tentative types of service innovation processes. In the course of further analysis, relevant contextual information was then assigned to these types, with the goal of gaining a more comprehensive understanding. Initially, more than ten different patterns were detected in the empirical data. However, the large number of patterns reduced the usefulness and manageability of the typology and led to a considerable overlap between process types. As suggested by Bailey (1994), the number of types was reduced by continuously comparing and matching the patterns with each other and the empirical data; this process eventually led to five patterns remaining.

## 10.4. Conclusion

The central concept developed in this study is a service innovation process typology (Table 10.2). The typology is based on an analytical framework with three dimensions and several characteristics that allow to differentiate five service innovation patterns. Patterns are characterized by a specific combination of dimensions and characteristics and can be distinguished from other types by this combination. The typology provides a common structure for the description and discussion of service innovation processes in the AES industry, which also illustrates differences in the innovation behavior of ESPs.

The typology comprises the following five innovation patterns as reflected in the empirical data:

*The Lifecycle Pattern* refers to the interrelation between changes on three different systemic levels of a service ecosystem, which originate on the macro-level and drive cyclic configuration processes on the meso- and micro-levels. The pattern highlights that innovation in AES is fundamentally driven and constrained by the manner in which the markets change and evolve (*Adapting along Evolutionary Pathways*). From this broader perspective, the role of ESPs, in the renewal of institutions, is characterized by ongoing attempts to keep managerial attitudes and behaviors of the organization in alignment with changing institutions. This includes, among other things, a regular adaptation of internal rules and norms (*Synchronizer*). Furthermore, the Lifecycle Pattern examines the long-term development of engineering services and competencies in the AES industry. The Lifecycle Pattern makes apparent that the foundation of engineering services is knowledge and skills, which over more extended periods are repeatedly reconfigured and recombined (*Combinational evolution*).

**Table 10.2**: Typology of Service Innovation Processes in the AES Industry

| *Patterns* | *Interaction Mode* | *Roles in the Renewal of Institutions* | *Recombinant Practices* |
|---|---|---|---|
| Lifecycle | Adapting along Evolutionary Pathways | Synchronizer | Evolutionary Combining |
| Association | Adapting along Evolutionary Pathways / Outlining Value Co-Creation Possibilities | Synchronizer / Stimulator | Associating Value Propositions |
| Copycat | Outlining Value Co-Creation Possibilities | Stimulator | Transferring and Adapting Resources / Associating Value Propositions |
| Co-Innovation | Moderating Co-Creation Processes | Co-Designer | Evolutionary Combining |
| Exploration | Outlining Value Co-Creation Possibilities / Brokering Knowledge | Stimulator | Evolutionary Combining |

*The Association Pattern* describes the association of value propositions and competencies in the creation of more comprehensive service offerings. The pattern reflects two interaction modes: The first derives from the fact that the association of value propositions and competencies is driven by a reformation of traditional market structures that exerts pressure on ESPs to adapt (*Adapting along Evolutionary pathways*). The second shows how ESPs assume a more active role in the market in which they bring further comprehensive service offerings to other customers (*Outlining Value Co-Creation Possibilities*). The Association Pattern shows in many respects how ESPs need to remain in synchronicity with changing institutional arrangements (*Synchronizer*). New institutional rules put pressure on ESPs to assume more responsibility for their services than they did in the past. With the development of ESPs into a more autonomous role in the market, there are more opportunities for them to encourage OEMs to enact rules and norms in ways that are beneficial for both OEMs and ESPs (*Stimulator*). As the name of the pattern implies, the service innovation process is primarily characterized by the recombinant practice of *Associating Value Propositions* (and competencies).

*The Copycat Pattern* refers to the specific case of an ESP whose service offerings draw on a particular combination of competencies, some of which are provided from within their own organization, and others are purchased and integrated from an external subcontractor. In this specific context, the Copycat Pattern describes a series of interrelated steps and mechanisms, which enable the contracting ESP to replicate the competence of the external ESP. The pattern reflects two different practices of recombination. First, it draws on a transfer and adaptation of resources to a new application context (*Transferring and Adapting Resources*). Also, in the specific cases that are reflected in the data, the newly developed competence becomes part of a service package that increases the chance of the ESP being awarded an initial project and thereby entering the market (*Associating Value Propositions*). The underlying service innovation processes are characterized by interactions between the ESPs and other actors from their networks, so that external resources are integrated into the competence development activities. Before the ESP can offer the copied competence in the market, it is first necessary to stimulate changes in the way the customer tenders and outsources services (*Stimulator*). To achieve this, the ESP must show the OEM the advantages of a bundled order placement (*Outlining Value Co-Creation Possibilities*).

*The Co-Innovation Pattern* is a result of an ongoing shift in traditional roles between OEMs and ESPs in the provision of services, which opens up new opportunities for both parties to innovate in close collaboration. The interaction modes between ESPs and OEMs are characterized by a moderating role of the ESP. Instead of dictating the steps or driving their own ideas in the innovation process, the role of the ESP is to carefully assist the customers in becoming innovative themselves (*Moderating Co-Creation Processes*). Trust in the ESPs helps customers in the renewal of rules and practices in ways that create beneficial boundary conditions for subsequent service provision (*Co-Designer*). This approach does often involve a more extended phase of recombinant steps in which the outcome of the process is iteratively refined in search for more compelling results (*Evolutionary Combining*).

*The Exploration Pattern* describes how ESPs innovate in an open and exploratory way by searching for innovation and value co-creation opportunities in networks without being driven by the predetermined needs or interests of a specific customer. In such networks, ESPs take on a role as knowledge brokers, for example, by using their knowledge of technical problems, solutions, processes, institutions or networks in the automotive sector. They bring together resources and actors in new constellations that are beneficial for the actors involved and for the ESP personally (*Brokering Knowledge*). For example, ESPs integrate external resources and collaborate with different suppliers and ESPs in the development of new technological solutions and prototypes that then become the foundation of new service offerings. The customer is usually not initially involved in such activities, but instead joins the process at a later stage after some preparatory work has already been completed. Subsequently, the ESPs need to outline the respective value of their solution (*Outlining Value Co-Creation Possibilities*). Before a new service or solution can be implemented, it is, therefore, necessary to encourage the customer to deviate from existing rules and practices (*Stimulator*). As to the reflected recombinant practices, the underlying service innovation processes of the Exploration Pattern are often linear and may proceed over a longer period of time, during which a nascent solution is often refined in multiple iterations (*Evolutionary Combining*).

The five patterns emphasize the diverse and often complex pathways in which engineering services are innovated. Rather than innovating in a specific way, ESPs engage in a variety of innovation processes in parallel, which can be interrelated and mutually dependent.

## 10.5. Implications and future research

The results of this chapter contribute to a better understanding of service innovation processes in the specific AES domain, but additionally, they expand and complement the recent theoretical discussions of a service ecosystem perspective on innovation, providing new concepts and opinions, and, most importantly, new empirical insights.

### Theoretical Implications

The study extends recent conceptualizations of innovation as a collaborative process in service ecosystems (Vargo et al., 2015), by demonstrating that the innovation behavior of ESPs in the German AES industry relies fundamentally on interactions and collaborative activities with other actors from their network. The roles of ESPs and their interactions with other actors that were identified in this study underline the need for a more decentralized understanding of service innovation. In fact, the processes that lead to innovation in the AES industry are not entirely controlled by individual parties. Instead, control and influence over critical innovation activities are often distributed amongst several actors and may change in the course of the service innovation process. The five patterns that were identified in this study show that the role of ESPs in these processes varies, with respect to the activity level and the extent of control. Furthermore, the five service innovation patterns reflect actor constellations and role configurations of varying complexity, ranging from dyadic relationships (i.e., ESP-OEM) to more complex formations in which entire networks of actors are involved. The research showed that the setting of an innovator and an innovation-adopter is only one specific constellation (i.e., the role of the firm is active, the customer is passive) among several other possibilities. Hence, scholars should approach service innovation processes with an open mind that neither overemphasizes nor neglects specific actor constellations.

Recent conceptualizations of innovation processes in service ecosystems emphasize that the interactions between actors are essential because they allow actors to engage in processes of institutional change and renewal, which enable service innovation (Vargo et al., 2015). The five patterns that were identified in this study confirm this link by showing that differences in the way ESPs interact with other actors in service innovation processes also influences the role of ESPs in the renewal and change of institutions. ESPs interact with various actors, such as universities, start-ups, but most critical for their innovation activities are the interactions between the ESPs and the OEMs. These interactions often take place during the provision of engineering services. In this respect, the selection of customers and the engagement with other actors during service provision are important variables that influence the innovation capabilities of ESPs. Changing the mode of collaboration during service provision or the constellation of actors involved can, therefore, exert a significant influence on their innovation capabilities. In this regard, recent changes in the reconfiguration of work modes in engineering projects have, on the one hand, reduced the intensity of interactions, but, on the other, they have expanded the capacity of ESPs to recombine resources and competencies. These findings extend recent academic thoughts on innovation in service ecosystems as a process of changing and renewing institutions and institutional arrangements (Vargo et al., 2015; Vargo and Lusch, 2014), by offering insights into the different roles of actors in such processes.

The principle tenet of S-D logic is that for innovations to occur, at least some actors need to work towards the disruption and renewal of institutions and institutional arrangements (e.g., Koskela-Huotari et al., 2016; Vargo et al., 2015), by enacting and enforcing rules that encourage other actors to change their behavior. So far, the literature on service ecosystems has paid little attention to asymmetries in institutional power and control. Recent studies that employ S-D logic and an institutional view of service innovation have focused solely on actors in dominant positions, who can orchestrate the roles and resource integration activities of other actors by enacting new rules or switching to a new role in the interaction (e.g., Aal et al., 2016). By contrast, this study has analyzed how ESPs can innovate and influence institutional rules as a group of actors who are in a less dominant position than their customers. Findings show that ESPs additionally contribute to the disruption and renewal of institutions, but more subtly and indirectly than described by previous studies (e.g., Koskela-Huotari et al., 2016). They rely on a close collaboration with their customer, who is much more influential. Changes in resource integration practices and value propositions can thus only be made with consent between the ESP and the OEM. In contrast, the findings indicate that actors might be able to extend their institutional influence when they establish and maintain relationships of trust with other actors (who are more powerful) from their service ecosystem. The restricted direct institutional influence of ESPs suggests the importance of embracing the individual roles of actors in service ecosystems and acknowledging the existence of asymmetries in institutional power and control.

## Practical Implications

Radical technological progress in the areas of mobility services, autonomous driving, and electric mobility are far from being fully implemented and will continue to transform the automotive industry in the coming decades. OEMs become more reliant on the innovation impulses of the ESPs, as they reduce their own involvement in several of the traditional engineering activities, which they have previously carried out. It would be advisable for them to design the rules and practices in their service ecosystems in ways that not only lead to a high-cost pressure on their suppliers, but also encourages competition among ESPs and suppliers, based on the value and innovativeness of their service offerings. For the ESPs, it becomes more significant to assume a more active role in the market, in which they not only adapt to their environment but make active contributions to the development of more compelling value propositions. The five conceptual elaborations of roles, interactions, and activities in service innovation processes that are presented in this study offer managers a basic orientation regarding possible suggestions, as to how to engage in service innovation and how to cope with a high degree of uncertainty, regarding the course and outcome of service innovation processes.

The recent trend in the AES industry towards a model of service provision, in which OEMs are less involved, gives ESPs more freedom in the organization and management of engineering activities during service provision. However, it also limits the exchange of information and knowledge between the two sides, thus potentially preventing ESPs from engaging in service innovation. Given this trend, it becomes crucial for ESPs to create additional interaction possibilities and to open up new lines of communication that allow them to exchange information and knowledge with customers beyond the daily project business. In this regard, recent attempts by ESPs to facilitate dynamic interactions with various actors via community meetings already reflect such an approach.

Finally, the findings of this study have implications for OEM managers and policymakers. They should be aware that changing the institutionalized mode of collaboration in service ecosystems has an extensive impact on the innovation capabilities of the different groups of actors. While the S-D logic emphasizes that service innovation means that organizations strive for better ways to serve their customers, some OEMs seem to make it extremely difficult for their ESPs to actually find better ways to serve them. Given the fact that OEMs seem increasingly dependent on external innovation impulses, it would be advisable for them to design the rules and practices in their service ecosystems in ways that not only lead to a high-cost pressure on their suppliers, but also encourages competition among ESPs and suppliers, based on the value and innovativeness of their service offerings.

### Future Research

With the conceptualization of innovation patterns in the AES industry, this study takes a first step towards an empirically grounded and S-D logic-based understanding of service innovation processes in the AES industry. Given the complexity of the subject, however, it cannot be claimed that this phenomenon is now fully understood. This study has drawn attention to the fact that actors, who operate in different roles, vary regarding their institutional influence. Hence, the assumption that all actors can instigate new institutional rules would be oversimplified. In this regard, this research has outlined some general differences in the ways ESPs interact with OEMs to stimulate institutional change. Future research can examine the influence of asymmetries in power and control on the innovation behavior of different actors in service ecosystems. Service innovation in the AES industry typically takes place in multi-actor constellations, in which changes in the role of ESPs require consent and close coordination with assorted other parties, e.g., with the purchasing and the specialist department of the OEM. Future studies should focus even more specifically on the interactions and the evolution of roles in such multi-actor constellations and consider the differences in the institutional power of different actors. In the AES industry, for example, future work could study the interactions between ESPs and OEMs on the level of departments and project teams, and, in this way, complement the findings of the present study. Modelling interactions and role changes among specific constellations of actors could be a fruitful approach to better understand how actors participate in institutionalization processes and how their institutional influence evolves.

## References

Aal, K., Di Pietro, L., Edvardsson, B., Renzi, M.F., Mugion, R.G. (2016). "Innovation in Service Ecosystems: An Empirical Study of the Integration of Values, Brands, Service Systems and Experience Rooms." *J. Serv. Manag.* 27, 619–651.

Bailey, K.D. (1994). *Typologies and Taxonomies: An Introduction to Classification Techniques.* SAGE, Thousand Oaks.

Barile, S., Lusch, R., Reynoso, J., Saviano, M., Spohrer, J. (2016). "Systems, Networks, and Ecosystems in Service Research." *J. Serv. Manag.* 27, 652–674.

Blöcker, A. (2016). "Branchenanalyse Entwicklungsdienstleister" (Working Paper No. 17). Hans-Böckler-Stiftung, Duesseldorf.

Camacho, J.A., Rodriguez, M. (2008). "Patterns of Innovation in the Service Sector: Some Insights from the Spanish Innovation Survey." *Econ. Innov. New Technol.* 17, 459–471.

Carlborg, P., Kindström, D., Kowalkowski, C. (2014). "The Evolution of Service Innovation Research: A Critical Review and Synthesis." *Serv. Ind. J.* 34, 373–398.

Chandler, J.D., Vargo, S.L. (2011). "Contextualization and Value-in-Context: How Context Frames Exchange." *Mark. Theory* 11, 35–49.

de Jong, J.P.J., Marsili, O. (2006). "The Fruit Flies of Innovations: A Taxonomy of Innovative Small Firms." *Res. Policy* 35, 213–229.

den Hertog, P. (2000). "Knowledge-Intensive Business Services as Co-producers of Innovation." *Int. J. Innov. Manag.* 04, 491–528.

Dubois, A., Gadde, L.-E. (2014). ""Systematic combining" - A Decade Later." *J. Bus. Res.* 67, 1277–1284.

Dubois, A., Gadde, L.-E. (2002). "Systematic Combining: an Abductive Approach to Case Research." *J. Bus. Res.* 55, 553–560.

Evangelista, R. (2006). "Innovation in the European Service Industries." *Sci. Public Policy* 33, 653–668.

Evangelista, R. (2000). "Sectoral Patterns of Technological Change in Services." *Econ. Innov. New Technol.* 9, 183–222.

Gallouj, F., Weinstein, O. (1997). "Innovation in Services." *Res. Policy* 26, 537–556.

Gibbs, G.R. (2014). "Using Software in Qualitative Data Analysis" in: *The SAGE Handbook of Qualitative Data Analysis.* SAGE, Los Angeles, pp. 277–294.

Godin, B. (2006). "The Linear Model of Innovation: The Historical Construction of an Analytical Framework." *Sci. Technol. Hum. Values* 31, 639–667.

Hipp, C. (2000). *Innovationsprozesse im Dienstleistungssektor: Eine Theoretisch und Empirisch Basierte Innovationstypologie, Technik, Wirtschaft und Politik.* Physica-Verlag, Heidelberg.

Hipp, C., Grupp, H. (2005). "Innovation in the Service Sector: The Demand for Service-Specific Innovation Measurement Concepts and Typologies." *Res. Policy* 34, 517–535.

Koskela-Huotari, K., Edvardsson, B., Jonas, J.M., Sörhammar, D., Witell, L. (2016). "Innovation in Service Ecosystems - Breaking, Making, and Maintaining Institutionalized Rules of Resource Integration." *J. Bus. Res.* 8, 2964–2971.

Lusch, R.F., Nambisan, S. (2015). "Service Innovation: A Service-Dominant Logic Perspective." *MIS Q.* 39, 155–175.

Lusch, R.F., Vargo, S.L. (2006). "Service-Dominant Logic: Reactions, Reflections and Refinements." *Mark. Theory* 6, 281–288.

Metcalfe, J.S., Miles, I. (2000). *Innovation Systems in the Service Economy, Economics of Science, Technology and Innovation.* Springer, Boston.

Miles, I. (2008). "Patterns of Innovation in Service Industries." *IBM Syst. J.* 47, 115–128.

Miozzo, M., Soete, L. (2001). "Internationalization of Services: a Technological Perspective." *Technol. Forecast. Soc. Change* 67, 159–185.

Muller, E., Doloreux, D. (2007). T*he Key Dimensions of Knowledge-Intensive Business Services (KIBS) Analysis: A Decade of Evolution.* Fraunhofer ISI, Karlsruhe.

Pavitt, K., Robson, M., Townsend, J. (1989). "Technological Accumulation, Diversification and Organisation in UK Companies, 1945–1983." *Manag. Sci.* 35, 81–99.

Schneider, K. (2011). *Modernes Sourcing in der Automobilindustrie, 1st ed, Gabler Research Informationsmanagement und Computer Aided Team.* Gabler Verlag, Wiesbaden.

Toivonen, M., Tuominen, T. (2009). "Emergence of Innovations in Services." *Serv. Ind. J.* 29, 887–902.

Vargo, S.L., Lusch, R.F. (2016). "Institutions and Axioms: an Extension and Update of Service-Dominant Logic." *J. Acad. Mark. Sci.* 44, 5–23.

Vargo, S.L., Lusch, R.F. (2014). "Inversions of Service-Dominant Logic." *Mark. Theory* 14, 239–248.

Vargo, S.L., Lusch, R.F. (2011). "It's all B2B…and Beyond: Toward a Systems Perspective of the Market." *Ind. Mark. Manag.* 40, 181–187.

Vargo, S.L., Lusch, R.F. (2008). "Service-Dominant Logic: Continuing the Evolution." *J. Acad. Mark. Sci.* 36, 1–10.

Vargo, S.L., Lusch, R.F. (2004). "Evolving to a New Dominant Logic for Marketing." *J. Mark.* 68, 1–17.

Vargo, S.L., Wieland, H., Akaka, M.A. (2015). "Innovation through Institutionalization: A Service Ecosystems Perspective." *Ind. Mark. Manag.* 44, 63–72.

Wieland, H., Vargo, S.L., Akaka, M.A. (2016). "Zooming Out and Zooming In: Service Ecosystems as Venues for Collaborative Innovation." in: *Service Innovation: Novel Ways of Creating Value in Actor Systems.* Springer, Tokyo, pp. 35–50.

Yin, R.K. (2014). *Case Study Research: Design and Methods,* 5th ed. SAGE, Los Angeles.

Chapter 11

# The Insect Economy: Sustainable Business Opportunities based on Insects as Biological Resources

Maria Real Perdomo

*Heilbronn University of Applied Sciences, Germany*

**Abstract:** This work studied the 'Insect Economy' – the group of business opportunities related to insects as biological resources - and its potential to contribute to the sustainable development of the world. It is embedded in the research fields of sustainable entrepreneurship, innovation and sustainable business models. The concept of 'Insect Economy' is created through this research. For this reason, business opportunities related to insects were initially identified and described. They were structured in the form of the statistical classification of products by activity in the European Economic Community. In total, more than 7 classes of products and 25 subcategories could be covered. Secondly, a selected field of insect-based business models were assessed regarding its sustainability. The data originated from interviews with entrepreneurs and analysis indicated multiple sustainability characteristics associated to every analyzed business model. The best tool for this assessment consisted of mechanisms for sustainable business model innovation. It was also used to classify the data, which resulted in a typology of four types of *sustainable* business opportunities. In the future, the 'Insect Economy' can be used as a context for creating sustainable goods and services, while being suitable for quantitative (and qualitative) research in the field of sustainable entrepreneurship, innovation and business models.

**Keywords:** Bio-Economy; Insects; Sustainable Entrepreneurship; Innovation; Business Models; Business Opportunities; Sustainable Business Model Patterns; Sustainable Development Goals; Food Production Systems; Biological Resources

## 11.1. Introduction

With the world facing numerous societal challenges, conventional business logic has been identified as their major driver. The conventional logic produces business practices powered by monetary outcomes as the foremost indicator of value creation (Beckmann and Schaltegger, 2014). This approach has led to a lack of connection between the society and the environment whose harm is now tangible at a global scale.

The dominant logic influences the way companies perceive business opportunities and the way these opportunities are then depicted in business models. The latter is a tool describing the way a firm creates, delivers and captures value (Osterwalder et al., 2005), along with the way it materializes in business practices. Thus, conventional business logic needs to reconnect with society as well as the environment, while also reflecting this realignment in business models and ultimately, in the business practice.

Such a paradigm shift can emerge from 'sustainable entrepreneurs,' namely individuals or groups eager to take proactive decisions to achieve sustainability through market innovation. Ideally, in so doing, they reach mass markets. As a result, they can contribute to the necessary large-scale transformation (Schaltegger and Wagner, 2010).

The policy concept of the Bio-Economy attempts to provide favouring conditions for such a transformation. It envisions the development of a sustainable 'market economy' combining knowledge from life sciences, biotechnology, and renewable bio-based resources to address the societal challenges. Hence, the Bio-Economy holds clear guidelines in terms of providing innovative and sustainable products, processes and services based on bio-resources (BioÖkonomieRat, 2015).

Insects as a bioresource can become of particular interest with regards to sustainable business practices. This animal class plays a central role in all terrestrial ecosystems. As part of its extensive array of adaptations, from social behaviors and complex communication to metamorphic cycles, it provides fundamental benefits to the environment and society (*ecosystem services*). Some characteristics and behaviors of insects are already used in business including insects as pollinators in agricultural fields, carminic acid from scale insects as a natural dye for both clothing and food etc.

Thus, under the umbrella of the concept of Bio-Economy, business opportunities around insects as biological resources are already flourishing in strategic sectors, such as the food and textile industry. Since the release of the report "Edible Insects" (Van Huis et al., 2013), insects have been promoted explicitly as a source of feed and food in an effort to alleviate food insecurity. This report resonated especially across western countries and is leading to the development of businesses in this field (Taponen, 2019).

Thus, there is a sound argument that using insects as bioresources can open a broad spectrum of business opportunities with intriguing sustainability potential in a number of business sectors. Using the full potential of insect-based business opportunities requires a systematic exploration, description and characterization. However, such analysis is lacking.

If insects are to contribute to the necessary paradigm shift in business, they should no longer be seen as an isolated bio-resource for value creation. Instead, it is important to adopt a holistic point of view and gain a comprehensive understanding of the business opportunities and their sustainability potential, such as the one based on the model of the ecosystem services. A consistent assessment and classification of the sustainability potential of insect-based business models does not yet exist.

In the endeavour to understand the scope of business opportunities related to insects and their sustainability potential, this work explored, described and characterized business opportunities related to insects as biological resources (research objective 1), while also assessing and classifying their potential to foster sustainable development (research objective 2). The group of business opportunities based on insects is termed the *Insect Economy*. More precisely, *this concept is defined as a subset of innovative and sustainable products, processes, and services resulting from the Bio-Economy, which is based on the use of insects as biological resources.*

The development and validation of the concept "Insect Economy" is based on the following academic frameworks: (a) sustainable entrepreneurship (Fichter and Tiemann, 2018) and (b) sustainable business models (Tiemann and Fichter, 2014), and on the policy framework: Bio-Economy (OECD, 2009). Both frameworks are influenced by the Sustainable Development Goals. Therefore, it builds the fundament of this work.

## 11.2. Background

Our world is faced with societal challenges such as biodiversity loss, poverty and hunger. The Sustainable Development Goals (SDGs) provide a solution approach to it. The SDGs consist of 17 goals and 169 "action-oriented [targets are] global in nature and universally applicable, taking into account different national realities, capacities and levels of development" (United Nations, 2016; p. 10). They consider the holistic nature of development, including a sustainable economic system, thereby reflecting an in-depth understanding of the interconnectedness of social, ecological and economic systems (Foxon et al., 2013).

The Bio-Economy holds the potential to contribute to reaching the SDGs. It represents a structural framework that consists of well-grounded economic ideas supported by not only the scientific research in life sciences, but also enabling technologies related to bio-based resources. These 'ingredients' shall lead to products, services or processes based on solid business cases and industrial leadership that produce significant profit margins while creating new markets and contributing to solving the great societal challenges.

However, to achieve the desired sustainable impact of its products, services and processes have to become competitive under the consideration of the costs of negative externalities (International Advisory Committee, 2015). This means that the attained environmental savings or burden relief effects must outweigh the 'investment' of resources, energy, or other ecological costs incurred by the introduction of innovation.

**Figure 11.1:** Context of Business Opportunities based on Insects as biological resources

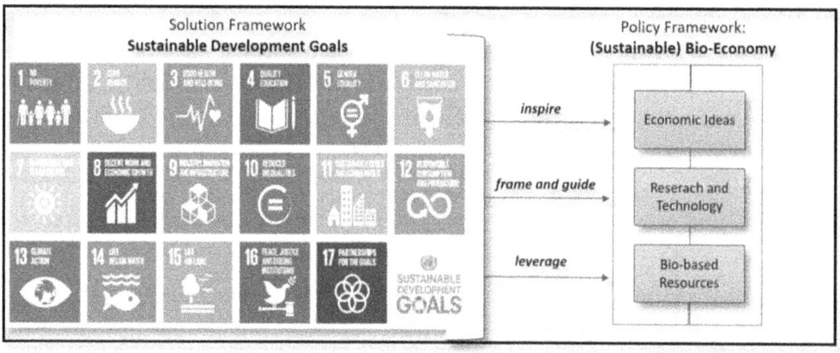


Source: Own based on (United Nations, 2016) and (BioÖkonomieRat, 2015)

The transition towards a *Sustainable* Bio-Economy is likely to require radical shifts in the way goods and services are designed, produced and used. To make these far-reaching shifts, the status quo demands a profound rethinking – a process requiring entrepreneurial spirit and disruptive innovation. The SDGs can be used as an orientation for companies to align their strategies and contribution to sustainable development as a way of making the necessary transition.

The nexus between sustainable development and business opportunities are at the heart of sustainable entrepreneurship. Fichter and Tiemann (2018) define this field of research "as the discovery, creation, evaluation, and exploitation of opportunities to create innovative goods and services that are consistent with Sustainable Development Goals". Thus, sustainable entrepreneurship research can serve as a lens to identify *sustainable* business opportunities based on insects. These can be understood as situations, where new goods, services, raw materials, and business models can be introduced and sold at greater than their cost of production, which are consistent with the Sustainable Development Goals.

In sum, the Sustainable Development Goals and the (Sustainable) Bio-Economy provide a rich context for business opportunities based on insects (see Figure 11.1). These opportunities, in turn, can be identified through the research lens of sustainable entrepreneurship. Therefore, these concepts build the fundament to explore and describe business opportunities.

The aim of this work is to *assess and classify* business opportunities once they have been identified. A straightforward approach for this is to articulate the business logic of the opportunity and the way it materializes in business practices using a business model. A prominent example of a business model template is the Business Model Canvas developed by Osterwalder and Pigneur (2010). It breaks down the value creation process into building blocks, namely the profit formulae, the value proposition, and value delivery and thereby, establishes a shared language and mental model simplifying description and assessment of business models (and business opportunities).

Business models consistent with the Sustainable Development Goals also strive to establish a business case for sustainability. The latter enables the creation of measurable ecological and social value on top of the economic value and goes beyond the aim of gaining a 'license to operate.' Specific associated tools to business models can inspire entrepreneurs to make their businesses more sustainable. One of the examples of this would be the sustainable business model patterns. (Bocken et al., 2013)

Another such tool is the *Business Model Innovation Grid*. The Grid aims to inspire businesses to make their business model more sustainable. It is an evolving tool, which consists of three dimensions, eight strategies and 52 mechanisms for sustainable business model innovation (see Figure 11.2). (Bocken et al., 2014, Centre for Industrial Sustainability, 2014)

**Figure 11.2:** Business Model Innovation Grid

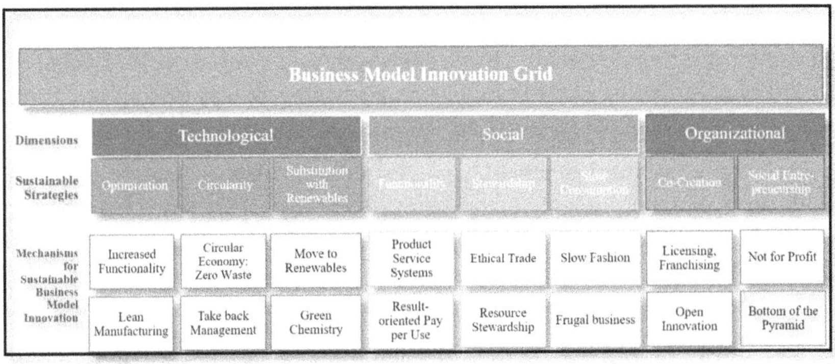


Source: Own based on Centre for Industrial Sustainability (2014)

The tool is suitable for assessing existing business models regarding their sustainability as well as classification adopted to the Insect Economy because of the structured format in the form of mechanisms. There are at least three sustainability indicators emerging from the tool.:

- The number of mechanisms of sustainable business model innovation combined in a single business model.
- The mechanisms stretching across multiple sustainable strategies, and
- Stretching across more than a single dimension.

Thus, the number and diversity of mechanisms used in a business model can be deemed indicators of sustainability.

## 11.3. Research design

This chapter followed two mayor research objectives: (1) identifying, describing and characterizing emergent business opportunities around insects; and (2) assessing and classifying them. To achieve these objectives, this chapter adopts a qualitative research approach for the thorough exploitation of data related to business opportunities based on insects as biological resources.

To answer research question (1), insects were initially studied through the lens of the Bio-Economy framework. This includes (a) synthesizing the beings of insects from a biological point of view, the way they contribute to the resilience of ecosystems, and the evolution of (human) perception about insects over time. It then explores insects in the context of academic research (b). Based on these fundaments, further data sources were explored to identify specific business opportunities (c). They stemmed from multiple types of media, including academic and grey literature, conferences and company websites.

The discovered opportunities were listed in a database and structured according to the statistical classification of products by activity in the European Economic Community (CPA). Each opportunity was assigned to a CPA, e.g. Products of Agriculture and Fishing, and a subcategory, e.g. 01.4 _Live animals and animal products. Once assigned, each opportunity was described.

The findings set the fundament to characterize the Insect Economy as a whole in the form of a morphology. A morphology is appropriate to study more general structural interrelations of concepts such as the 'Insect Economy.' In the present context, it builds on the academic and policy framework described previously as well as extensive literature research about insects as biological resources.

Once the overall set of business opportunities of the Insect Economy and the morphology were determined, a subset of the business opportunities was selected for assessment and classification. The focus was put on insect as feed, food, pet food, and waste converters, since these are currently the most dynamically developing opportunities (Taponen, 2016). The data for the assessment and classification were collected through 20 qualitative interviews with (co-) founders and CEOs.

The interview questions focused on eight selected dimensions extracted from the morphology to assess sustainable business opportunities. Three of them are the Business Model Canvas, Business Model Innovation Grid, and the Sustainable Development Goals (SDGs).[1] For the data analysis, a computer-aided approach was applied, using MAXQDA software. As a result of the analysis, not only were deeper insights gained into the Insect Economy, but the morphology was also reviewed and updated.

Out of the eight dimensions, the Grid turned out to be the most insightful dimension with respect to the sustainability assessment. Therefore, the mechanisms for sustainable business model innovation were used to classify the analysed business models. To do so, the responses of the entrepreneurs related to each mechanism were matched.

Subsequently, central commonalities among those responses were identified with the purpose of classification. As a result of an iterative process in the analysis, four features resonated, namely (1) 'Product' and (2) 'Process and Technology', and (3) 'Producer' and (4) 'Consumer'. Once the features were identified, the typology was structured in the form of a table, where the mechanisms were grouped to types, described and named.

## 11.4. Results

This paper creates the concept 'Insect Economy' and introduces it to sustainable entrepreneurship and innovation research. It studies this concept from both the sectoral level (meso level), and the business model level (micro level). The results of both levels are as following:

At the sectoral level, an extensive number of business opportunities based on insects emerging worldwide were explored. The identified opportunities are structured by using the statistical classification of products by activity in the European Economic Community (acronym CPA). In total, 7 CPA sections and 25 subcategories could be covered (see Figure 11.3). The most noticeable CPA sections are Products of Agriculture and Fishing, Manufactured Products and Water Supply, Sewage; Waste Management and Remediation Services. The scope and scale of these opportunities justifies the introduction of the term Insect Economy.

---

[1] The other five dimensions are: (1) Global challenges, (2) Sustainability from the Business Case Perspective, (3) Sustainable Business Drivers, (4) Factors of Diffusion Dynamics, and (5) Risk factors.

**Figure 11.3**: Overview of CPAs in the Insect Economy

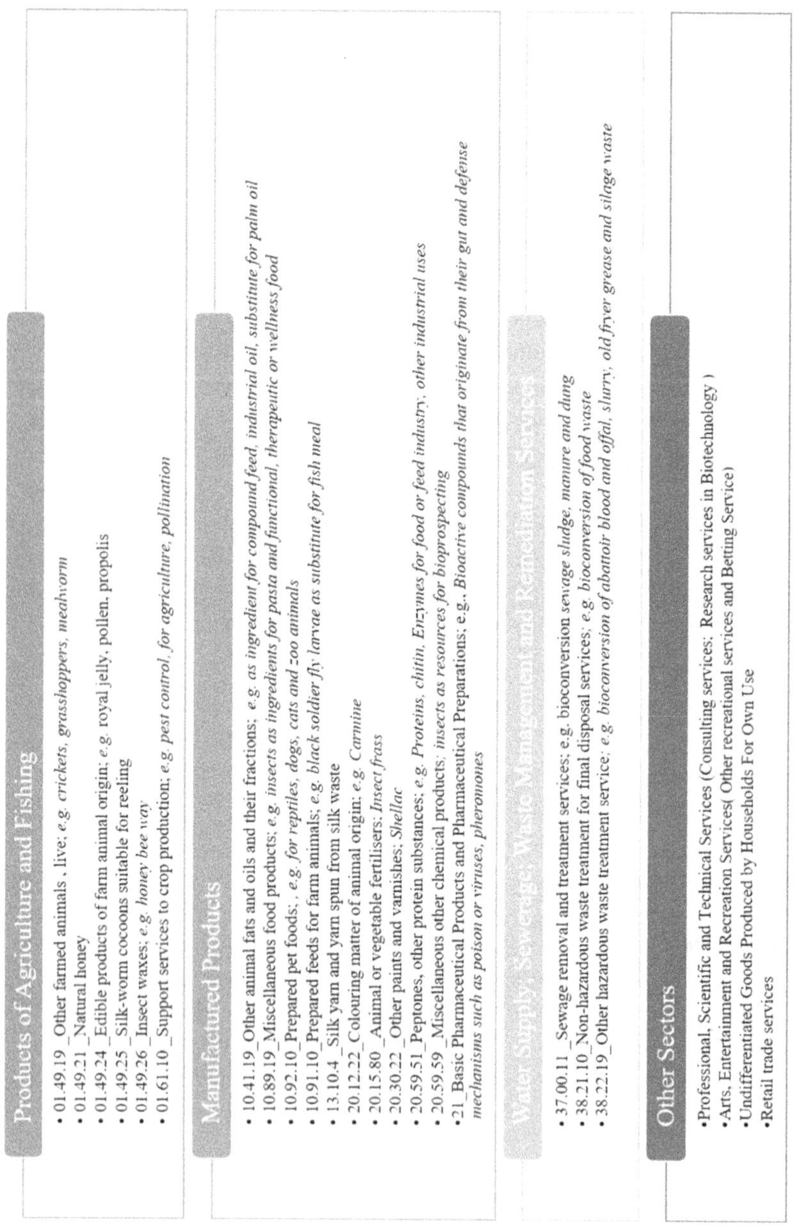


Another result at the sectoral level is the morphology characterizing the Insect Economy and reducing the complexity and number of variables to make it tangible and describable. The morphology is divided into three overall categories: the *insect* as a novel resource, *economy*, and *sustainability*. Each category comprises of multiple *dimensions*, which in turn are further broken down into *features*. The morphology of the Insect Economy comprises of 21 dimensions and 141 features. Thereof, four dimensions and 23 features refer to the overall category *insects*, nine dimensions and 48 features to the overall category *economy*, and eight dimensions and 69 features to the overall category *sustainability*.

To gain a deeper understanding of the Insect Economy, the sector level description was broken down to specific business models in the scope of 'insects as' food, feed, pet food, and organic waste converters. Key findings from the interviews with entrepreneurs in these fields show that:

1. They diversify their business model by creating multiple value propositions created throughout the value chain. For example: while rearing insects as feed, insects are used as organic waste converters by feeding them on organic side-streams and selling insect frass as fertilizer or compost.
2. The analyzed business models hold great potential to contribute to sustainability. Among others, this is reflected in the fact that they can contribute to 13 out of 17 Sustainable Development Goals.
3. Through the lens of the Business Model Innovation Grid, 20 - out of 52 currently identified - mechanisms for sustainable business model innovation were recognized. This indicates that sustainability is directly linked to the business model of the ventures.

The Grid itself produced two principal results relevant both for the tool and the understanding of the Insect Economy. Before naming them, it is important to know that the elements of the Grid were identified and categorized mainly from the literature. Thus, they still lack empirical rigor.

The data analysis of the interviews contributes to the academic development of the Grid, since it identified all of its hierarchical levels: It could recognize all dimensions, and seven out of eight sustainable. In addition, 17 out of 52 mechanisms for sustainable business model innovation could be identified.

The empirical evidence detected shortcomings because the mechanisms did not entirely fit the empirical evidence. To overcome these shortcomings, three new mechanisms were introduced. Those were termed (1) Empowerment, (2) Circular Economy: Modularity and (3) Producer Education, Communication & Awareness. Thus, in total, 20 mechanisms for sustainable business model innovation could be identified among the 20 business models described by the interviewed entrepreneurs.

**Table 11.1:** Typology of Sustainable Business Opportunities in the Insect Economy.

| Dimensions/Title | Insects as Enablers for Business Opportunities that Create… | | | |
|---|---|---|---|---|
| Label of the Types | Insects as Enablers for Naturally More Sustainable Food Products | Insects as Enablers for Sustainable Food Productions Systems | Insects as Enablers for Empowerments of Producers | Insects as Enablers for Cultural Change in Consumer Behavior |
| Description | Insects as Food and Feed and Fertilizer | Technology and processes to produce insects or to use them as a waste management tool | Accesible technology and processes for (low-income) producers to rear insects | Awareness raising in the context of promoting insects as food |
| Central Commonality (Morphology Dim.): Innovation Object | Product | Technology and Process | Mixed | Mixed |
| Central Commonality (Morphology Dim.): Type of Customer | Mixed | Mixed | Producers (B2B) | Final Consumer (B2C) |
| Business Model Innovation Grid: Mechanisms for Sustainable Business Model Innovation | Circular Economy: Zero Waste | Circular Economy: Modularity | Empowerment | Radical Transparency about Societal Impacts |
| | | Reuse, Recycle, Remanufacture | Bottom of the Pyramid | *Consumer* Education, Communication and Awareness |
| | | Industrial Simbiosis | *Producer* Education, Communication and Awareness | |
| | | Product Longevity | Frugal Business | |
| | | Open Innovation | Incubators and Entrepreneur Support Models | |
| | | | Licensing, Franchising | |

The number and the structured format of the mechanisms allowed grouping them. This grouping led to a typology of ideal types of business opportunities in the Insect Economy (see Table 11.1). Four types of sustainable business opportunities were identified and described. Those are:

| | |
|---|---|
| Type (1) | Insects are Enablers for *Naturally* More Sustainable Food Products |
| Type (2) | Insects are Enablers for Sustainable Food Production Systems |
| Type (3) | Insects are Enablers for Empowerment of Producers |
| Type (4) | Insects are Enablers for Cultural Change in Consumer Behavior |

The titles of the types show that insects are able to become enablers for more sustainability related to the food production system. Business models related to insects as biological resources address sustainability on multiple dimensions: as a product (type 1), through technology and production processes (type 2), by being economically accessible to (low income) producers, and informing consumers and thereby, raising awareness about the sustainability character of insect-based production systems.

Six out of 20 mechanisms for sustainable business model innovation did not fit one of the four types. The exceptions are (1) 'Move to Renewables,' (2) 'Green Chemistry', (3) 'Product Service Systems,' (4) 'Collaborative Approaches: Institutional Entrepreneurship,' (5) 'Hybrid Businesses & Social Businesses,' and (6) 'Localization.' Thus, further analysis is required to bundle these mechanisms.

## 11.5. Implications and future research

### Research Implications

This work created and justified the concept 'Insect Economy' and introduced it to sustainable entrepreneurship and innovation research. It studied the concept from sectoral (outcome: list of CPAs and morphology), and business model level (outcome: typology). Both levels indicated that the Insect Economy – and particularly, the field of insects as food, feed, pet food, and organic waste converters - are contexts for creating innovative goods and services consistent with Sustainable Development Goals. Thus, this work identified and developed a relevant context for sustainable innovation, sustainable entrepreneurship, and business model research.

Furthermore, this work advanced research about the Business Model Innovation Grid. Yip and Bocken (2018) addressed this gap by assessing sustainable business model archetypes for the banking industry. This work addressed the gap by laying a sectoral focus on the food production system related to insects. In this regard, the work validated the Grid itself and demonstrated that the tool is useful for assessing and classifying business models. In the context of Insect Economy, it enabled a fine-grained assessment regarding the sustainability of ventures in the specific field.

**Practical Implications**

This work holds strong practical value. One the one hand, it can be seen as a source of inspiration to identify business opportunities. There are at least three sources of inspiration:

1. The first source is the list of CPA sections and subcategories shown in Figure 11.3.
2. The second source is the morphology of the Insect Economy. As a configuration of an extensive set of characteristics, it may motivate entrepreneurs to configure their own business solutions.
3. The third source is the Typology of Sustainable Business Opportunities showing the way a business model may be configured by using mechanisms for sustainable business model innovation.

These three sources of inspiration can also help entrepreneurs make their ideas more concrete. While the first source is specific and draws on concrete solutions, the second one - the morphology - takes an abstract approach to recognizing business opportunities and configuring a solution. The last source - the typology - may help from the conceptual phase of the innovation process onwards.

Furthermore, this work shows entrepreneurs the potential to strategically align economic arguments and sustainability. These dimensions can be derived from different sources: (1) The morphology - which contains eight dimensions[2] and 69 features related to the category sustainability; (2) the SDGs, and (3) the Business Model Innovation Grid. Thus, it helps entrepreneurs view that contributing to sustainability does not need to be a philanthropic ambition, but societal goals and business goals can be tied together. Moreover, the typology can serve as a benchmark for entrepreneurs to compare themselves to peers.

---

[2] The eight features are: (1) The strategic dimension of the Business Model Innovatin Grid; (2) The mechanisms of sustainable business model innovation of the Grid; (3) SDGs; (4) Global Challenges; (5) Sustainability from the business case perspective; (6) Factors of Diffusion Dynamics; (7) Sustainable Business Drivers; and (8) Risk Factors.

### Future Research

It was mentioned earlier that the Insect Economy, and particularly sustainable ventures related to insect-based food production systems ('insects as' food, feed, pet food, and organic waste converters), offer a relevant *context* for sustainable innovation, sustainable entrepreneurship, and business model research. The overall advantage of using this context is it consisting of a broad set of commonalities shared by the ventures such as the industry sectors, biological resource (insect), and support system. This allows for comparability as well as conducting quantitative and long-term studies, lacking among these emerging fields of research.

Researchers interested in using this context can draw on the 'Entomology Company Database' (Taponen, 2019). Other than the Insect Economy, which comprises of a broad number of business opportunities, this database is limited to four business sectors. It, however, is periodically updated and comprises of an extensive list of companies in the field of insects as feed, food, waste conversion, and biological pest control. Therefore, it is an ideal source to study insect-based food production systems. Taponen created the database in January 2016, and only two years later, version 76 contains 417 companies of which 267 are active.

## References

Beckmann, M. & Schaltegger, S. (2014). *Unternehmerische Nachhaltigkeit. In:* Heinrichs, H. (ed.) *Nachhaltigkeitswissenschaften.* Berlin; Heidelberg: Springer Spektrum.

Bioökonomierat. (2015). *What is Bioeconomy?* [Online]. Available: http://biooekonomierat.de/home-en/bioeconomy.html [07.01.2015].

Bocken, N., Short, S., Rana, P. & Evans, S. (2013). *A value mapping tool for sustainable business modelling.* Corporate Governance, 13, 482-497. http://dx.doi.org/10.1108/cg-06-2013-0078

Bocken, N. M. P., Short, S. W., Rana, P. & Evans, S. (2014). *A literature and practice review to develop sustainable business model archetypes.* Journal of Cleaner Production, 65, 42-56. http://dx.doi.org/10.1016/j.jclepro.2013.11.039

Centre For Industrial Sustainability. (2014). *A literature and practice review to develop sustainable business model archetypes, Wikipedia, The Blue Economy, Ask Nature, McKinsey: The Resource Revolution, The Ellen MacArthur Foundation, SUSTAINIA100* [Online]. Available: http://vlaanderen-circulair.be/bmix/index.php [24.03.2017].

Fichter, K. & Tiemann, I. (2018). *Factors influencing university support for sustainable entrepreneurship: Insights from explorative case studies.* Journal of Cleaner Production, 175, 512-524. https://doi.org/10.1016/j.jclepro.2017.12.031

Foxon, T. J., Köhler, J., Michie, J. & Oughton, C. (2013). *Towards a new complexity economics for sustainability.* Cambridge Journal of Economics, 37, 187-208. http://dx.doi.org/10.1093/cje/bes057

International Advisory Commitee. *Communiqué of the Global Bioeconomy Summit 2015.* Global Bioeconomy Summit 2015, Version: 26.11.2015 2015 Berlin.

OECD. (2009). *The Bioeconomy to 2030: designing a policy agenda.* Available: http://www.oecd.org/futures/bioeconomy/2030 [08.02.2016].

Osterwalder, A. & Pigneur, Y. (2010). *Business model generation: a handbook for visionaries, game changers, and challengers,* Hoboken, NJ, Wiley-VCH. ISBN: 978-047-090-103-8 (elektronische Ausgabe)

Osterwalder, A., Pigneur, Y. & Tucci, C. L. (2005). *Clarifying Business Models: Origins, Present, and Future of the Concept.* Communications of the Association for Information Systems, 16, 1-25.

Schaltegger, S. & Wagner, M. (2010). *Sustainable Entrepreneurship and Sustainability Innovation: Categories and Interactions.* Business Strategy and Environment. 10.1002/bse

Taponen, I. (2016). *Database Analysis: The Chosen Species.* Available: https://ilkkataponen.com/2016/01/14/database-analysis-the-chosen-species/ [14.1.2016].

Taponen, I. (2019). *Entomology Company Database.* Webpage. Available: https://ilkkataponen.com/entomology-company-database/ [29.03.2019].

Tiemann, I. & Fichter, K. (2014). *Übersicht der Konzepte und Instrumente nachhaltiger Geschäftsmodellentwicklung: Analysen im Rahmen der StartUp4Climate Initiative AP 3.1.* Carl von Ossietzky Universität Oldenburg, Borderstep Institut, StartUp4Climat Initiative. Oldenburg/ Berlin.

United Nations. (2016). *Sustainable Development Goals* [Online]. Available: http://www.un.org/sustainabledevelopment/sustainable-development-goals/ [14.04.2016].

Van Huis, A., Itterbeeck, J. V., Klunder, H., Mertens, E., Halloran, A., Muir, G. & Vantomme, P. (2013). *Edible insects: future prospects for food and feed security.* ISBN: 978-92-5-107595-1

Yip, A. W. H. & Bocken, N. M. P. (2018). *Sustainable business model archetypes for the banking industry.* Journal of Cleaner Production, 174, 150-169. https://doi.org/10.1016/j.jclepro.2017.10.190

Chapter 12

# A Developmental Perspective on Business Model Innovation: Exploring Sequences of Change in High-Performing IT Firms

Edgar Brea

*University of Queensland, Australia*

**Abstract:** Although business model innovation has emerged as a powerful competitive strategy, the lack of knowledge about the dynamics driving business model change limits our understanding of how established firms can innovate their business models continuously over time. To address this issue, this study proposes and operationalises the concept of business model development, and empirically explores the mechanisms of business model change over time in high-performing IT firms. To this end, sequences of business model change are identified from longitudinal financial data and examined in search of distinctive patterns, using a combination of data mining methods and traditional statistical analyses. Results indicate an association between business model change patterns and firm performance, as well as insights on the drivers, magnitude, order and frequency of business model development.

**Keywords:** Business model innovation; business model change; business model development; business model evolution; business models; innovation; organisational change; firm performance; data mining; IT sector

## 12.1. Introduction

Altering and enhancing existing business models through business model innovation has emerged as a powerful competitive strategy that can provide an advantage over extended periods of time (Zott and Amit, 2013). Success stories of firms disrupting markets and sustaining financial rewards over competitors through business model innovation can be found in virtually any industry. A key success factor for long-term competitiveness lies in the implementation of multiple, rather than punctual, business model innovations over time.

The concept of business model innovation is appealing for practitioners because it facilitates identification of new ways to generate profit through exploiting unmet customer needs and detecting new and alternative sources of value creation (Johnson et al., 2008). The concept is also attractive because it considers external actors as a key part of the value creation process, which responds to the corporate need for an instrument that reflects the networked nature of modern businesses (Allee, 2000). However, business model innovation is an underused source of competitive advantage (Zott and Amit, 2009), and only one in every four firms worldwide actively pursue it (Lindgardt and Ayers, 2014). Also, the business model frameworks available for practitioners are not designed to understand how particular changes affect each of the model components and how a change stimulates successive changes over time. Insights on these dynamic factors may allow managers to keep their business models flexible and adaptable (De Reuver et al., 2013).

In the research domain, the number of academic articles on business model innovation has increased steadily since the late 1990s (Wirtz et al., 2016). The topic can be traced back to seminal business theories such as disruptive innovation, open innovation, organisational ambidexterity and dynamic capabilities. In recent studies, the business model has been treated as independent, dependent and moderator variable to investigate value creation, competitive advantage and organisational change, among others (Foss and Saebi, 2017). It is then a new unit of analysis to explore other organisational phenomena (Gassmann et al., 2016). Although important, the theory supporting further business model innovation research is limited (Massa et al., 2017). To develop a much-needed body of knowledge about business models and business model innovation, we must not only concentrate our research efforts on defining and classifying business models, but on assessing the mechanisms under which firms change and innovate their business models over time (Morris et al., 2015).

As seen above, despite the relevance of business model innovation for practitioners and academics, significant knowledge gaps hinder the realisation of the full potential of business model innovation for both groups. The main concern for the former is the uncertainties and challenges faced by managers when changing their business models. For the latter, the challenges centre on the lack of a dynamic-rich theory explaining business model change, hindering the advancement of the field. These challenges are the direct result of four main issues, which represent the key problems addressed by this study.

Firstly, there is a lack of methodological and theoretical tools designed for the examination of change in business models across time (Schneider and Spieth, 2013). These tools are required to build dynamic models of change, and without them, it remains difficult to produce actionable knowledge on the mechanisms driving business model innovation and development (Ginsberg, 1988). Secondly, there is a limited focus on the patterns of change as the main unit of analysis in business model research. There is also limited empirical research studying business model innovation as a long-term process comprising multiple instances of change, a perspective that can potentially disclose new information on how firms implement change by identifying meaningful patterns in the data (Biemann and Datta, 2013).

Thirdly, there are little clues as to when a firm should change its business model, the type of change required and the sequence in which the change should be implemented. Timing is key for the success of strategic renewal and organisational change (Amburgey et al., 1990), but it has not been properly investigated in business model research. Fourthly, there is little certainty on what drives a firm to change its business model at an ongoing basis. Specifically, there is a knowledge gap on the nature of the actions required for repeated business model change, and on the role of the environment and the firm's internal condition as drivers of change.

This dissertation responds to these research problems by exploring the dynamic mechanisms enabling business model development in successful, high-performing firms. It examines the distinctive properties of business model development to understand what determines success in business model change processes. The research specifically asks: (1) To what extent are there distinguishable patterns of change associated with business model development in established firms? (2) What are the characteristics of such patterns in terms of the magnitude, frequency and order of changes involved in the process? (3) What is the nature of the actions and factors driving business model development over time?

## 12.2. Background

The first research issue motivating this study relates to the theoretical and methodological tools available to understand the dynamics of business model change. The static aspects of business models covering conceptualisations, internal components and typologies, have dominated the literature, particularly between the late 1990s and late 2000s (Timmers, 1998, Afuah and Tucci, 2000, Osterwalder, 2004). However, the dynamic aspects of business models covering emergence, evolution and change, have gained traction in recent years (Demil and Lecocq, 2010). A rampant attention towards change has required the adoption of theories from other fields to counteract the lack of theory on business models and to help explain the dynamics associated with change.

Two of these theories are organisational ambidexterity and dynamic capabilities. It has been argued that the business model change process comprises an exploration phase in which the new model is created and implemented, and an exploitation phase in which the business model is stabilised (Winter and Szulanski, 2001). In the same vein, scholars have highlighted the risks of prolonged exploitation as it limits the firm's strategic agility during the next exploration phase (Doz and Kosonen, 2010). Dynamic capabilities have inspired concepts such as dynamic consistency to explain the firm's capacity to change its business model while also sustaining operational and financial performance (Demil and Lecocq, 2010). Similarly, it has been argued that the firm's recognition of the need for a change in the business model is hardly trivial and it requires dynamic capabilities (Leih et al., 2014). These two theories have promoted a much-needed focus on the resources and knowledge (and their particular allocation over time) needed to innovate a business model. However, it has left little room for dedicated attention to deep processual aspects such as sequences of elements changed and particular developmental patterns.

Regarding methodological approaches, most empirical studies on business model change and innovation are qualitative, case-based, and involving well-delimited time windows of typically three to five years (Wirtz et al., 2016). Thus, there has been a preference for in-depth analyses to understand what happens when a firm changes its business model, as well as a focus on change in particular instants within the life of the organisation. Although fundamental to the field, these dominant methodological choices have yet to be complemented with research designed to examine large samples of firms over prolonged periods of time (where changes may or may not occur), which will increase our ability to identify frequent and statistically meaningful patterns of change.

The second and third research issues relate to insights on how firms change their business models. Scholars have previously tackled the problem by proposing typologies to describe the business model change process from a lifecycle perspective (Zott and Amit, 2015). Business model change has also been classified by the extent to which the final model differs from the initial model (Saebi, 2015), and by the type of specific reconfiguration actions that a business model can be subjected to (Santos et al., 2009). Nevertheless, the deductive nature of these typologies prevents us from exploring additional, less frequent patterns. Furthermore, there is limited research assessing the time in which the change occurs. One of the few existing studies evidenced that high-performing firms are more likely to adjust their business models more frequently than low performers (Mitchell and Coles, 2003), although the size of the difference was not assessed. There is also limited research exploring what components are changed and in what order. Some of the few existing research have indicated that business model elements are changed through stages and that there is a linear progression across them (Christensen et al., 2016). Others have formulated business model change patterns in terms of the number of different business models implemented at the same time, without covering the particular sequences in which the firm's elements are altered (Andries et al., 2013). As it can be seen, the reliance on prescribed stages and types have not provided definitive insights on the frequency and order of business model change.

The fourth research issue concerns the drivers of continuous business model change over time. Previous studies have focused on either the antecedents of change or the behaviour of the organisation to provide clues on this regard. Evidence suggests that external antecedents, such as increased competition and economic recessions, are key drivers of change (Sosna et al., 2010). There is also evidence on the role of internal emotional factors like encouragement and playfulness in inducing business model innovation (Tankhiwale, 2009), as well as entrepreneurial orientation and opportunity recognition (Guo et al., 2015). These studies considered either external or internal antecedents, thus, comparisons of both sides in a single study are rare. On the other hand, some scholars have explored the behaviour associated with business model change, such as experimentation and discovery-driven learning. Some argue that implementing a novel business model involves prolonged experimentation periods where optimal business models are discovered (McGrath, 2010), suggesting that a purposeful trial-and-error learning behaviour drives business model development over time (Sosna et al., 2010). Nevertheless, the literature still has not tackled the questions of whether emergent, rather than predetermined actions drive change over time, and the joint role of internal and external agents in driving the process.

## 12.3. Research design

As part of the theoretical framework supporting this study, the business model is conceptualised as a system of firm's activities and resources that are interconnected under the same goal to create customer value, to deliver the value created to the targeted customer and to appropriate a portion of value back to the firm and its partners (Amit and Zott, 2010). Thus, the business model is deconstructed into three well-accepted dimensions of economic value: value creation, value delivery and value capture (Foss and Saebi, 2017). For its operationalisation, the business model is treated as a complex system in which the firm's dynamic equilibrium behaviour and complementarity mechanisms are the drivers of change. Then, principles from organisation studies, strategy and innovation management are integrated into the framework to describe the dynamic features of business model development.

By framing business model innovation as a developmental process involving sequences of change events unfolding over time, this study builds on firm-level historical data to identify fluctuations in the variables used to operationalise business model change, an uncommon approach in the field

(Massa et al., 2017). Quantitative variables are used to represent the three generic dimensions existing in any business model regardless of its type or firm characteristics, enabling a systematic comparison of business model changes within and between a large number of firms.

Specifically, this exploratory, longitudinal and quantitative research builds on a set of 12 financial ratios to examine fluctuations in a firm's value creation, delivery and capture dimensions that are attributable to business model transformations for a sample of 1,651 listed firms in the IT sector worldwide. The firms' yearly financial data, spanning up to 29 years, were collected from a large financial database and transformed into individual sequences of change events. The transformation involved the use of a density-based algorithm for outlier detection to identify change events. Data were imported, transformed, and analysed using a data and computational infrastructure comprised by a relational database and a series of scripts in R (statistical package), which were purposefully designed for this study.

A validation procedure assessed the accuracy of the identification process for business model change events through qualitative data and in-depth analysis for four firms from the larger sample. Then, the sequences of change events were used as inputs for clustering and data mining analysis, complemented by frequency domain analysis and traditional statistical tests, which revealed the patterns of business model development in high-performing firms. Figure 12.1 illustrates the research design and process.

The methodological approach supporting this study allowed the use of data mining techniques specifically designed to explore large datasets in search for commonalities that are generally unknown to the researcher (Aggarwal, 2015). In addition, the reliance of historical quantitative data presents a differentiated alternative to explore business model innovation from typical qualitative studies dominating the research field (Wirtz et al., 2016).

The methodology is supported by a number of check points to address key threats to validity. To ensure construct validity, this study incorporates a qualitative validation to confirm the existence of business model changes using alternative data sources and analytic tools. To ensure internal validity, dedicated tests have been performed to the data in order to actively assess validity threats, such as the test for cross-correlation and multicollinearity among the ratios used to measure business model changes, as well as the use of synthetic sequences of change to test the accuracy of the clustering methods. Lastly, to avoid risks associated with statistical conclusion validity, the research design builds not only on a large sample of firms (compared to other studies in the field), but on a large number of observations comprising a period of about three decades worth of data.

**Figure 12.1:** Research design and process, including data collection, transformation, validation and analysis

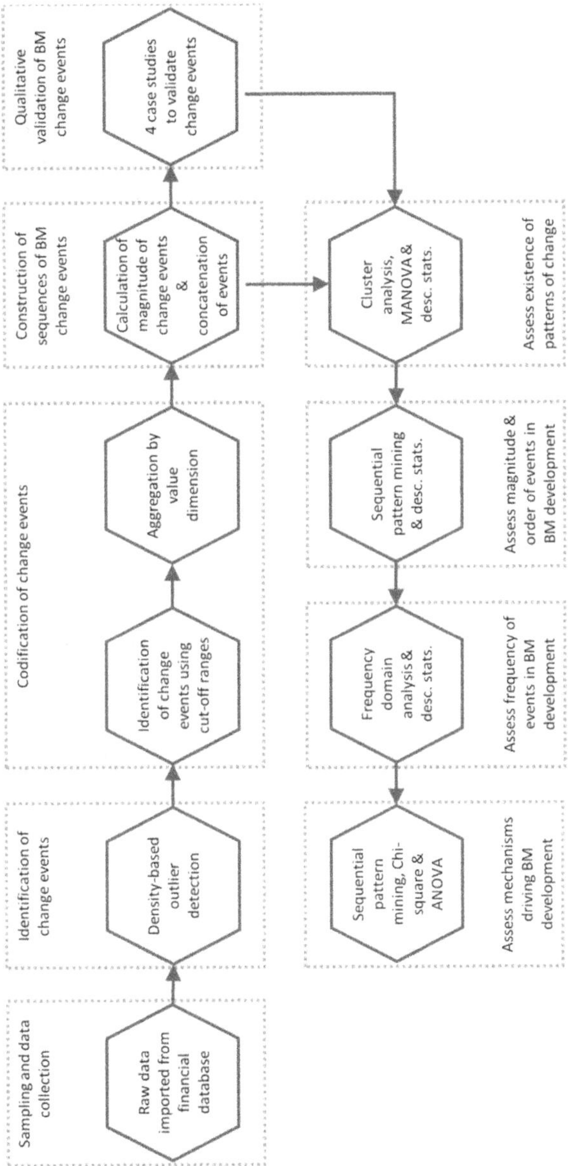

## 12.4. Conclusion

The results of this study provide insights on four key aspects of business model change. Firstly, the results indicate a significant association between the timing and intensity in which firms change their business models and their average performance over time. The results of the multivariate analysis of variance indicate that there are statistically significant differences in the performance means of firms when they are clustered by business model change pattern similarities. This means that the choice of the type, the timing and the sequence in which business models are changed matter for performance.

Secondly, sequential pattern mining analyses indicate that business model changes are more likely to culminate in events where the value delivery dimension is altered. Additionally, the analyses reveal that events where the three dimensions are simultaneously changed are more likely to be found in large firms than in small firms (regardless of their age). This suggests that in smaller firms, elements are changed one at a time as managers learn how the model is behaving, whereas large firms are more likely to rationalise the change plan upfront, resulting in more elements changed at the same time.

Thirdly, in terms of frequency and magnitude, high-performing firms are more likely to develop their business models through frequent and incremental alterations, except for high-performers in the mature-large group who, compared to high-performers in the young-small, young-large and mature-small groups, showed a preference for radical over incremental changes not seen in the rest of the firms in the same group. This suggests that age and size play a role in the way firms respond to competition by choosing incremental over radical, and frequent over sporadic business model change strategies.

Lastly, regarding drivers of change, both environmental and internal forces influence the intensity at which high-performing firms alter their business models. Similarly, both unconscious and deliberated actions influence business model development in high-performing firms. Insights on the drivers reflect the diversity of factors affecting change in the business model, and that, depending on the circumstance, emergent environmental response may drive decisions to alter the business model, whereas in others, conscious strategic decisions may drive the process. Table 12.1 presents the complete list of findings and insights from this study.

**Table 12.1:** Findings and corresponding research questions answered

| *Research question* | *Finding* |
|---|---|
| 1. What are the factors driving business model development? | 1. Both the collective action of the firms sharing an industry, as well as the firm's individual situation of age and size, influence the intensity at which high performers typically alter their business models |
| 2. What is the nature of the actions driving business model development? | 2. Evidence of both predetermined and unconscious actions driving business model development |
| 3. To what extent are there distinguishable patterns of change associated with business model development? | 3.1 Existence of relationship between business model change and performance over time<br>3.2 Existence of common patterns of business model change<br>3.3 Type, timing and order of business model change have performance implications |
| 4. What is the frequency of change characterising the business model development process? | 4.1 Business model change events occur at a slightly higher frequency in high-performing firms (except for mature-large firms)<br>4.2 There is a higher probability that a high-performing firm changes its business model at multiple (rather than a single) rates over time than that observed for the rest of the firms in each age-size group |
| 5. What is the magnitude of change characterising the business model development process? | 5.1 Evidence of a larger proportion of incremental alterations over radical changes (for the full sample of firms)<br>5.2 Young-large firms, regardless of their performance, are more likely to implement radical changes than young-small, mature-small and mature-large firms<br>5.3 High-performing mature-large firms is the only group with larger counts of radical changes over incremental (than that seen in the rest of firms in the group) |
| 6. What is the order of change characterising the business model development process? | 6.1 Although there is no dominant order, business model change in high-performing firms is likely to end in events where the value delivery dimension is altered<br>6.2 Events where the three dimensions are simultaneously changed are more likely to be found in large firms than in small firms |

## 12.5. Implications and future research

This dissertation contributes to theory on business model change and innovation in three ways. Firstly, it builds on the concept of business model innovation to propose the concept of business model development. It extends the approach characterising business model innovation research that focuses on the transition from one configuration to a novel version, to focus on the whole trajectory of business model development comprising multiple transitions. The data suggests that business models are in constant dynamism, implying the existence of a previously unexplored process in which the business model develops as the firm develops. Thus, the study examines a previously unexplored process, which may potentially "serve as the foundation for brand new theory" (Colquitt and Zapata-Phelan, 2007).

Secondly, by adopting the process-based approach, this study contributes to the foundation of new thinking and research in business model innovation that centres on analysing the flow of events leading to business model emergence and on identifying patterns of the process across multiple cases (Pettigrew, 1992). A well-established stream of process-based research will complement the more traditional variance-based studies that explain change in terms of cause-effect relationships, forming an comprehensive theoretical base to support the evolution of the business model innovation field of study (Van de Ven and Poole, 2005).

Thirdly, in satisfying the condition that a robust process theory should explore the time parameters associated with change as it facilitates the construction of process models (Monge, 1990), the study provides evidence of the existence of unique patterns of business model change in high-performing firms across three time parameters: magnitude, frequency and order of change. The parameterisation of change across these dimensions helps determine why and how the change processes generated by other organisational phenomena affect the development of business models (Tsoukas, 1989).

In terms of methodological contributions, the quantitative, longitudinal and multi-firm approaches in this study are a noticeable departure from the typical case study approach dominating the literature, in which a business model innovation is studied in isolation from the multitude of other instances of business model innovations. The agglomeration of individual time series into a single sequence of change is an approach that can be replicated in different research contexts in order to identify dynamic patterns of organisational change.

Furthermore, with its proposed set of parameters, this study offers a way to analyse change trajectories of multiple business models in a systematic and consistent manner, which may inspire further statistically-based studies, thereby increasing generalisation of research findings. The procedure for parameterisation of business model changes from a firm's financial data and the subsequent coding system presented here may serve as an example for future quantitative studies in the business model and business model innovation field. The implementation of data mining algorithms for data analysis is also a methodological novelty in social science research. Previous studies on life course trajectories are among the rare social science research examples using data mining techniques. This dissertation adds to this small group of empirical studies that uses knowledge discovery algorithms to mine meaningful patterns from the data.

From a managerial standpoint, this study may assist practitioners in adjusting established business models. In contrast to designing business models for start-ups, altering existing business models impose different challenges for managers (Massa and Tucci, 2014), which demands a deeper understanding of how a change in one business model element impacts other elements, and how to anticipate and develop strategic plans for business model innovation. As this study assesses two key issues facing practitioners pursuing innovation, namely the sequence of actions and timing of change (Christensen, 1997), the insights presented here could guide businesses in anticipating and developing innovation plans with a greater degree of certainty to transform their business models faster and more effectively. For instance, the evidence that high-performing firms are more likely to modify their business models more frequently than other firms suggests that a well-established capacity to respond to environmental fluctuations is key to success.

Apart from providing guidance on the rate, magnitude and order of change, this study encourages practitioners to use the ratios and methodology presented to build their own sequences of change and correlate past business model changes with financial performance to determine optimal pathways to superior performance. The analysis of past events of business model change could also help assess how efficient the firm is in responding to external and internal circumstances requiring an adjustment in its business model. Also, managers could estimate time series models that fit their historical trajectories of business model change to predict future changes, which would help them anticipate potential business model reconfiguration, and to decide whether to stay on track or change their course of business model development.

It is a key aspiration of this study to stimulate and encourage further research to increase our understanding of the dynamic mechanisms of business model innovation. The research model designed and developed in this study paves a new way for longitudinal examination of change events driving the emergence of business model innovation within a firm. An advantage of the methodology is that it can be replicated to other types of innovation, such as technological, process and product, as well as to other types of organisational processes that are not associated with a final tangible product such as emergence of new strategies. This can be done by replacing the financial ratios with a new set associated with the phenomenon under analysis.

There are considerable opportunities to expand the study conducted in this dissertation into other industries. Business model innovation is not limited to a particular sector; regardless of the economic activity conducted, every business entity has some form of business model in place (Chesbrough, 2007). It is interesting to observe whether the findings from IT firms diverge (or converge) with findings from sectors such as health care or financial services. A convergence might suggest a reduced influence of the type of goods produced on the process of business model innovation, whereas a divergence could be interpreted as strong influence of the rate of technological development, regulatory forces, and product lifecycles on the dynamics of business model innovation.

An additional avenue for further research on business model innovation is the use of more detailed data from the sample of firms, increasing the number of parameters to more than 12. Incorporating measures such as type and number of commercial partners, number of distribution channels used, and percentage of revenue from new products allows increased measurements of business model changes per unit of time. Future studies could incorporate qualitative information to either enrich or validate the patterns found from quantitative data. Lastly, research could develop predictive models to project how a business model could or should evolve over time, providing that the internal and external forces driving the development of a business model can be modelled as well.

Future studies could also seek ways to complement the theoretical and methodological propositions of this dissertation with additional principles and data to observe how other organisational aspects from the field of corporate strategy and innovation impact or are impacted by the trajectories of business model development. For instance, trajectories of technological development can be examined in combination with business model change trajectories in search of inflection points, where events demarcate a change in behaviour of one trajectory caused by the other, as well as degree of cross-correlation between the two trajectories. Juxtaposing trajectories of change of organisational capabilities with trajectories of business model change could also help understand the role of dynamic capabilities development on business model innovation.

## References

Afuah, A. & Tucci, C. L. (2000). *Internet business models and strategies: Text and cases*, McGraw-Hill Higher Education.

Aggarwal, C. C. (2015). *Data mining: The textbook*, Springer.

Allee, V. (2000). "Reconfiguring the value network." *The Journal of Business Strategy*, 21, 36-39.

Amburgey, T. L., Kelly, D. & Barnett, W. P. "Resetting the clock: The dynamics of organizational change and failure." Academy of Management Proceedings, 1990. Academy of Management, 160-164.

Amit, R. H. & Zott, C. (2010). "Business model innovation: Creating value in times of change." *IESE Business School Working Paper.*

Andries, P., Debackere, K. & Looy, B. (2013). "Simultaneous experimentation as a learning strategy: business model development under uncertainty." *Strategic Entrepreneurship Journal*, 7, 288-310.

Biemann, T. & Datta, D. K. (2013). "Analyzing sequence data optimal matching in management research." *Organizational Research Methods*, 1094428113499408.

Chesbrough, H. (2007). "Business model innovation: it"s not just about technology anymore." *Strategy & Leadership*, 35, 12-17.

Christensen, C. M. (1997). *The innovator"s dilemma*, New York, HarperCollins.

Christensen, C. M., Bartman, T. & Van Bever, D. (2016). "The hard truth about business model innovation." *MIT Sloan Management Review.*

Colquitt, J. A. & Zapata-Phelan, C. P. (2007). "Trends in theory building and theory testing: A five-decade study of the Academy of Management Journal." *Academy of Management Journal*, 50, 1281.

De Reuver, M., Bouwman, H. & Haaker, T. (2013). "Business model roadmapping: A practical approach to come from an existing to a desired business model." *International Journal of Innovation Management*, 17, 1340006.

Demil, B. & Lecocq, X. (2010). "Business model evolution: in search of dynamic consistency." *Long Range Planning*, 43, 227-246.

Doz, Y. L. & Kosonen, M. (2010). "Embedding strategic agility: A leadership agenda for accelerating business model renewal." *Long Range Planning*, 43, 370-382.

Foss, N. J. & Saebi, T. (2017). "Business models and business model innovation: Between wicked and paradigmatic problems." *Long Range Planning.*

Gassmann, O., Frankenberger, K. & Sauer, R. (2016). *Exploring the field of business model innovation: New theoretical perspectives*, Springer.

Ginsberg, A. (1988). "Measuring and modelling changes in strategy: Theoretical foundations and empirical directions." *Strategic Management Journal*, 9, 559-575.

Guo, H., Su, Z. & Ahlstrom, D. (2015). "Business model innovation: The effects of exploratory orientation, opportunity recognition, and entrepreneurial bricolage in an emerging economy." *Asia Pacific Journal of Management*, 1-17.

Johnson, M. W., Christensen, C. M. & Kagermann, H. (2008). "Reinventing your business model." *Harvard Business Review*, 86, 57-68.

Leih, S., Linden, G. & Teece, D. (2014). "Business model innovation and organizational design: A dynamic capabilities perspective." *Business model innovation: The organizational dimension.*

Lindgardt, Z. & Ayers, M. (2014). "Driving growth with business model innovation." Available: https://www.bcgperspectives.com/content/articles/growth_innovation_driving_growth_business_model_innovation/ [Accessed 01/11/2014].

Massa, L., Tucci, C. & Afuah, A. (2017). "A critical assessment of business model research." *Academy of Management Annals*, 11, 73-104.

Massa, L. & Tucci, C. L. (2014). "Business model innovation." *In:* Dodgson, M., Gann, D. M. & Phillips, N. (eds.) *The Oxford handbook of innovation management*. Oxford University Press.

Mcgrath, R. G. (2010). "Business models: a discovery driven approach." *Long Range Planning*, 43, 247-261.

Mitchell, D. & Coles, C. (2003). "The ultimate competitive advantage of continuing business model innovation." *Journal of Business Strategy*, 24, 15-21.

Monge, P. R. (1990). "Theoretical and analytical issues in studying organizational processes." *Organization Science*, 1, 406-430.

Morris, M., Schindehutte, M., Richardson, J. & Allen, J. (2015). "Is the business model a useful strategic concept? Conceptual, theoretical, and empirical insights." *Journal of Small Business Strategy*, 17, 27-50.

Osterwalder, A. (2004). *The business model ontology: A proposition in a design science approach*. Docteur en Informatique de Gestion, Universite de Lausanne.

Pettigrew, A. M. (1992). "The character and significance of strategy process research." *Strategic Management Journal*, 13, 5-16.

Saebi, T. (2015). "Business model evolution, adaptation or innovation? A contingency framework on business model dynamics, environmental change and dynamic capabilities." *In:* FOSS, N. J. & SAEBI, T. (eds.) *Business model innovation: The organizational dimension*. Oxford: Oxford University Press.

Santos, J., Spector, B. & Heyden, L. V. D. (2009). "Towards a Theory of Business Model Innovation within Incumbent Firms." *In:* INSEAD (ed.). INSEAD.

Schneider, S. & Spieth, P. (2013). "Business model innovation: Towards and integrated future research agenda." *International Journal of Innovation Management*, 17.

Sosna, M., Trevinyo-Rodriguez, R. N. & Velamuri, S. R. (2010). "Business model innovation through trial-and-error learning: The Naturhouse case." *Long Range Planning*, 43, 383-407.

Tankhiwale, S. (2009). "Exploring the interrelationship between telco business model innovation and the change in business process architecture." *Journal of Telecommunications Management*, 2.

Timmers, P. (1998). "Business models for electronic markets." *Electronic Markets*. CommerceNet.

Tsoukas, H. (1989). "The validity of idiographic research explanations." *Academy of Management Review*, 14, 551-561.

Van De Ven, A. H. & Poole, M. S. (2005). "Alternative approaches for studying organizational change." *Organization Studies*, 26, 1377-1404.

Winter, S. G. & Szulanski, G. (2001). “Replication as strategy.” *Organization Science,* 12, 730-743.

Wirtz, B. W., Pistoia, A., Ullrich, S. & Göttel, V. (2016). “Business models: Origin, development and future research perspectives.” *Long Range Planning,* 49, 36-54.

Zott, C. & Amit, R. (2009). “Business Model Innovation: Creating value in times of change.” *Universia Business Review.*

Zott, C. & Amit, R. (2013). “The business model: A theoretically anchored robust construct for strategic analysis.” *Strategic Organization,* 11, 403-411.

Zott, C. & Amit, R. (2015). “Business model innovation: Toward a process perspective.” *The Oxford handbook of creativity, innovation, and entrepreneurship.*

Chapter 13

# What the 3D Printing Community Teaches Us About Innovation

Marco Wirth

*University of Würzburg, Germany*

**Abstract:** The origin of innovations has been a central theme in management and innovation research for several decades. The dissertation investigates knowledge reuse in open online communities. Here, "remixing"—an established term in the music domain—is very often used to describe the phenomenon of repurposing existing things to create something new. Although examples of remixes are omnipresent in today's culture and economy, it is difficult to study or even quantify the phenomenon because designers, artists, innovators, and companies are usually reluctant or even unwilling to disclose their sources of inspiration. To overcome this problem, the dissertation uses publicly available data from Thingiverse, the largest open online community for printable 3D models. The dissertation investigates the phenomenon of remixing with the help of an extensive quantitative dataset on models and users as well as the qualitative findings from 78 interviews with designers of the platform.

**Keywords:** additive manufacturing; 3D printing; remix; knowledge reuse; maker movement; thingiverse; online community.

## 13.1. Introduction

Additive manufacturing—commonly known as 3D printing—denotes a manufacturing technology that facilitates the production of physical objects from digital, three-dimensional blueprints. The elementary difference to known, established processes, such as drilling, turning, or milling, is the way in which the object to be manufactured is created: In traditional, subtractive processes, material is removed, whereas in additive processes it is added. This generative, layer-wise production of real, physical objects on the basis of digital, three-dimensional models is the fundamental functional principle and the commonality of all additive manufacturing processes (Gebhardt, 2016). Major benefits of this technology are that it allows for the creation of very complex models and its flexibility for various design geometries.

The technology has existed for more than three decades and is primarily used in the professional, industrial context for the production of prototypes.

Technological progress, falling prices, and not least the expiry of the patent for a simple additive process have led to increased attention for 3D printing. Due to strong growth rates and a series of characteristics, above all the possibility to produce individual pieces economically, the technology was considered to have the potential to start the next industrial revolution (Anderson, 2012; Berman, 2012; Markillie, 2012).

The veritable hype and the associated enormous expectations of the technology were followed by a deep disappointment, which is also reflected in the share price performance of various companies in the industry sector. As a result, the previously announced industrial revolution was "postponed" (Holweg, 2015) or "blown off" altogether (Brandon, 2016; Dilawar, 2016).

Despite the fact that the technology will not completely replace traditional manufacturing, the market has already reached a volume of more than 6.5 billion euros in 2017. Double-digit growth rates in recent years have also led to optimistic prognoses. Analysts forecast a global market volume of 24.1 billion euros for the industry in 2023 (Wohlers et al., 2018). The European Union has also recognized the topicality and importance for its industry and has, therefore, declared additive manufacturing to be a "Key Enabling Technology." The experts involved assume that the technology will play a key role—both in terms of *industrial leadership* and *social change* (Vallés, 2014; Duchêne et al., 2016).

In addition to productive use in an industrial context, 3D printing has also reached consumers. The number of desktop 3D printers sold for *household use* rose from just 355 in 2008 to over 528,000 in 2017 (Wohlers et al., 2018). Hobbyists who own their own 3D printers and share their designs and innovations openly online are part of the so-called "maker movement" (Anderson, 2012; Dougherty, 2012; Gershenfeld, 2012; Richardson, 2012; Buxmann and Hinz, 2013). An integral part of this ecosystem is the online platform and community Thingiverse, which in October 2018 featured nearly 3 million models that have been downloaded over 340 million times (Jackson, 2018).

## The "holy grail" of innovation research

Despite the manifold questions arising from growth, media coverage, and the different application scenarios in industry and household, science and research have so far primarily dealt with questions of processes and materials (Gausemeier et al., 2013; Guo and Leu, 2013; Li et al., 2016). In particular, questions on *economic and social impacts* have received barely any attention (Baumers et al., 2016; Ford et al., 2016; Luchs et al., 2016; Jiang et al., 2017).

A major problem in assessing the technology is the undifferentiated viewing and evaluation of 3D printing in households within the media. In many cases, simple desktop 3D printers used by hobbyists and industrial additive manufacturing systems such as those used in industry have been equated in the media. In reality, however, these are two fundamentally different classes that must be considered separately. Recent publications show that 3D printing and associated innovations are relevant in private households (Oehlberg et al., 2015; Fordyce et al., 2016; Stanko, 2016; West and Kuk, 2016; Kyriakou et al., 2017). The decisive factor here is the focus of the research: These studies do not focus on manufacturing technology, but on the *insights* that this type of production enables. A large number of hobbyists publish and share their models within online platforms. Astonishing is the fact that many users mark their own designs and state that their ideas and innovations are based on the ideas of others. This concept of *innovation by recombination* can be traced back to Schumpeter (1942), who argues that every innovation is essentially a combination of existing factors. Since then, recognizing and understanding how such combinations lead to new insights and ideas has been considered "the 'holy grail' of innovation research" (Gruber et al., 2013, p. 837). Especially platforms and IT artifacts have great potential to support users during this innovation process (Markus, 2001; Huysman and Wulf, 2006; Müller-Wienbergen et al., 2011). However, there is still little research on information systems as drivers of knowledge reuse (Couger et al., 1993; Alavi and Leidner, 2001; Sambamurthy and Subramani, 2005). In addition, designers who carry and promote desktop 3D printing by publishing their models have also been largely neglected in the analysis to date. This stands in sharp contrast to the obvious potential offered by an analysis of these innovation processes.

## 13.2. Background

The *origin of innovations* has been a central theme in management and innovation research for several decades (Rosenberg, 1982; von Hippel, 1988; Van de Ven, 1999; Hargadon, 2003; Simonton, 2004; Usher, 2011). One of the main objectives of this research is to gain a better understanding of the innovation process and the influencing factors involved. The aim is to improve problem solving and idea generation in organizations in the hope that this will ultimately lead to successful products and services.

A research topic that has already attracted the attention of scientists and practitioners in this context is the role of existing knowledge in generating new innovations. The traditional understanding of innovation is usually associated with an "Aha! Moment" (Berkun, 2010; Birkinshaw et al., 2012)—that is, a spontaneous epiphany, as most famously captured in Isaac Newton's falling apple that led him to understand the concept of gravity. In contrast to this intuitive but also naïve view on innovation, there is a common understanding among scholars that innovations do not emerge in isolation but are at least to some extent recombinations of previously existing building blocks (Schumpeter, 1942; Van de Ven, 1986; Nelson and Winter, 1982; Scotchmer, 1991; Kasparek, 1994; Metcalfe, 1998; Weitzman, 1998; Murray and O'Mahony, 2007; Arthur, 2009; Uzzi et al., 2013; Salter and Alexy, 2014).

## Innovation through recombination: remixing

Driven by the emergence of various open platforms and communities on the Internet, the concept of *innovation through recombination* has once again received increased popularity and attention in recent years (Lessig, 2008; Tuite and Smith, 2012; Sapsed and Tschang, 2014; Yew and Monroy-Hernández, 2014; Oehlberg et al., 2015; Stanko, 2016; Kyriakou et al., 2017; Özkil, 2017). Here, *"remixing"*—an established term in the music domain—is very often used to describe the phenomenon of repurposing existing materials to create something new (Gunkel, 2016).

Online platforms, on which content and data are made available under open licenses, increasingly make it easier for users to publish and exchange a wealth of ideas (von Hippel, 2005; Hill and Monroy-Hernández, 2013). Thus, these platforms provide a promising starting point for innovators to transfer and remix existing ideas into new contexts. Often, existing solutions are combined in new ways or parts are taken to integrate them into their creations. The theoretical concept behind this process is referred to in the literature as "knowledge reuse" (Markus, 2001; Majchrzak et al., 2004). So far, the reuse of knowledge has been examined primarily in the context of open-source software (Haefliger et al., 2008; Sojer and Henkel, 2010) and crowdsourcing projects (Bayus, 2013). The corresponding studies and investigations provide valuable insights into the significance of reuse in practice and point to promoting and inhibiting factors. However, little is known about the emergence of the phenomenon, such as different forms of knowledge reuse or the existence of generalizable patterns. In addition, although previous work has already considered platform design in terms of generating ideas (Leimeister et al., 2009; Tanenbaum et al., 2013), little research exists to date on information systems as drivers of knowledge reuse (Couger et al., 1993; Alavi and Leidner, 2001; Sambamurthy and Subramani, 2005; Mitchell and Subramani, 2010). This is particularly surprising because the lack of scientific knowledge stands in sharp contrast to the obvious potential that IT artifacts possess to support user creativity (Markus, 2001; Huysman and Wulf, 2006; Müller-Wienbergen et al., 2011).

## 13.3. Research design

The conducted literature analysis suggests that more empirical research is needed to answer open questions about the importance of remixes for innovation, the remix process, the role of IT-based platforms, and the profile of remixing individuals. To this end, remixing is examined on the basis of real data collected on the Thingiverse platform. Due to the size and diversity of the dataset, a structured, analytical approach is necessary (Müller et al., 2016).

### Quantitative, exploratory study

Thingiverse supports two main file formats for 3D designs on its platform: STL and OpenSCAD. The STL format is characterized by its direct representation of the geometry of the object. OpenSCAD files describe models using a text-based modeling language and must be compiled accordingly to create the actual three-dimensional object. This programming approach allows designs to be parameterized, which in turn allows for easy customization and individualization by other users. Accordingly, such designs are referred to as "customizers."

In addition to the actual blueprints or model data, Thingiverse stores various metadata of designs, such as their names, a unique ID, the designer, the date of publication, a list of tags, or comments from users. A design also includes dynamic data, such as the number of views, downloads, likes, and confirmed makes. Remix relationships between designs are also visible. These are available on the platform in the form of lists that contain the direct "ancestors" and "descendants" for each model. This family analogy makes it possible to examine existing relationships between "parents" and "children" and moreover to create "family trees" which can be used for further analyses (see Figure 13.1).

**Figure 13.1:** Concept of remix relationships and generations.

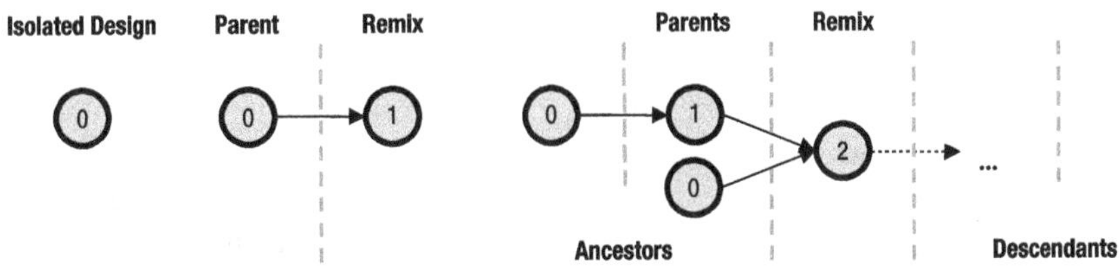


The data collection was performed using a web crawler implemented in C#. As part of the data collection process, information was extracted on a total of 216,541 designs published between the launch of the online platform in November 2008

and October 2014. 378 are excluded from this initial set as they violate the platform's terms of use (e.g. weapons) and a further 13 designs that are flagged within the platform for copyright infringement. A further 3,054 designs have been removed from the dataset because they have not been published under open licenses and, therefore, cannot be remixed. Since a change in the terms of use in February 2012, only open licenses are now available. The final dataset consists of a total of 213,096 designs, 116,659 of which are remixes.

For the preparation, processing, and analysis of the quantitative data, the free statistical programming language R is used in particular (Ihaka and Gentleman, 1996; R Core Team, 2016; Wickham and Grolemund, 2016). In addition, various extensions in the form of packages are being used. These include functionalities for manipulating data (Wickham and Francois, 2016), network analysis (Csárdi and Nepusz, 2006), and visualizing data and results (Gu et al., 2014; Wickham, 2009). In addition, the open-source software "Gephi" is used to create visualizations of the remix relationships in the form of "family trees" (Bastian et al., 2009).

### Qualitative study

In order to evaluate and extend the previous quantitative findings, a qualitative study was carried out. To this end, 78 semi-structured, open interviews were conducted with Thingiverse designers. All interviews were recorded and transcribed verbatim. For each of the 78 interviews, a detailed case was created that included for example quotes, timelines, designs, images of designs, technical details of the design, biographical information about the designer, and comments on the role of remixing. The data in these cases was encoded using the software NVivo (Bazeley and Jackson, 2013; QSR International, 2018). Then, a case-by-case analysis was performed, in which each of the interviews was sequentially coded in several revision cycles. Subsequently, a cross-case evaluation is possible in which interviews and coding are compared across all interviews. The aim of this overarching evaluation is to identify superordinate, generalizable patterns (Paré, 2004; Lune and Berg, 2017).

## 13.4. Conclusion

The results confirm the importance of remixes in terms of number, downloads, and makes of designs. The analysis of the remix relationships has shown that in addition to a simple linear evolution, there are eight other composite *remix patterns*. These can be divided into two fundamentally different classes: convergent remixes, which are characterized by remix relationships with several parents, and divergent remixes, which are characterized by relationships with several children (see Table 13.1). All patterns were visualized, described, formalized, and quantified.

**Table 13.1:** Convergent and divergent remix patterns.

| | *Pattern* | *Description* |
|---|---|---|
| Convergent remix patterns | Merge 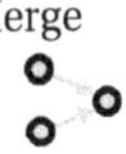 | Here, two different designs are merged or remixed into a new design. The resulting merge contains aspects of both previously independent designs. |
| | Compilation 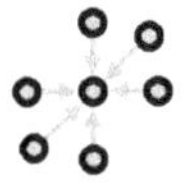 | A new design can be a best-of compilation of a variety of ideas that had no relation to each other before. For this, a large number of selected designs are put together into a new remix. The influence of individual parents is often difficult to recognize in large compilations. |
| | Siblings 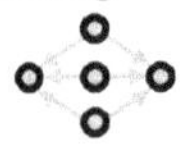 | In some cases, designers combine the same parents into new, different designs. These new remixes are not directly linked but share the same ancestors. This remix pattern can lead to simultaneous inventions—a situation in which very similar designs are created by different designers. |
| | Retrospect 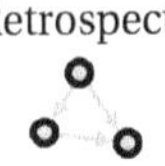 | A retrospect combines the ideas and solutions of different generations of ancestors. Consequently, it is not a remix of a single design, but a retrospect that reuses the best of different generations. To be considered a retrospect, the corresponding remix must be based on at least two previous generations. |
| Divergent remix patterns | Fork  | In this pattern, a concept or design reaches a point where it splits into two new designs. The original design evokes different associations and needs, which are the basis for remixes. |
| | Bouquet  | Some designs prove to be particularly suitable for remixing. Accordingly, such designs are reused relatively often. In this way, a large bouquet of diverse children is created, all based on the same parent. |
| | Customizer 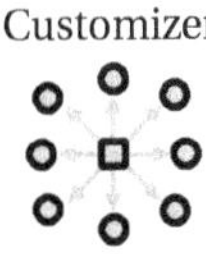 | A customizable design can be easily adapted by the user to his or her personal needs. The customizers on Thingiverse can be changed within a set of predefined parameters and are, therefore, predestined to be remixed. This circumstance leads to the fact that a relatively large number of individualized derivatives are created around customizers. |
| | Template Builder 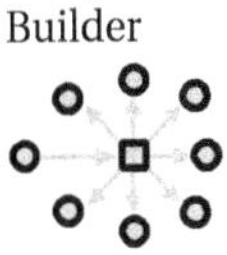 | In this pattern, a regular design is remixed to a customizer. In some cases, a designer may think that a particular design would be more useful to the user base if it could be easily customized. A template is, so to speak, the springboard that connects the original idea and its many descendants. |

The *knowledge transfer* from one category to another induced by remixing shows that the flow is not mutually balanced. On the one hand, there are donor categories that provide much inspiration for remixes in other categories but experience only limited inflows themselves. Absorbing categories, on the other hand, often draw on inspiration from other categories, but are themselves of little inspiration to others. Since supporting and promoting user activity is a core task of any online platform, features that foster remixing have been explored. Customizers are very likely to be remixed themselves, as they can be easily adapted within the platform. A remix of a customizer, on the other hand, is already too special to serve as a suitable input for further remixes. The *complexity* of each remix was determined using the dimensions "origin" and "parent category." The results, which are summarized in a complexity matrix, show that both very simple and extremely complex remixes can be found. The last aspect studied is the *user base* of the platform. Users can be assigned to different stereotypes: Never-remixers who do not make use of remixing and always-remixers who design all their designs on the basis of other designs. The user base can also be divided into two parts with regard to the use of the customizer feature: Some of the designers do not use any customizers at all, while others rely entirely on the available customization functionality. These findings are subsequently used to create a comprehensive taxonomy of the user population based on the criteria of experience, sophistication, and style.

In order to analyze the remix phenomenon qualitatively, interviews with 78 designers of the platform Thingiverse were carried out. The cross-case evaluation provides results that both support and extend the previous findings of the quantitative, exploratory study. The basic principle that characterizes open online communities is the free exchange of knowledge. The interviews show that designers who make their designs available under open licenses can be distinguished into three different types with regard to the use of these licenses: pragmatists, realists, and idealists. The interviews underline the importance of remixing in the creative process. Designers with low skills tend to attach great importance to remixing. It is noteworthy that numerous designers have already internalized the concept of remixing and use it in various contexts, even beyond the platform. Another contribution of the qualitative study is the identification, explanation, and illustration of six different remix processes: *inspiration, play, learning, speed, improvement,* and *empowerment.* Relevant for the differentiation are the skills of the designer, the trigger of the remix process, and the motivation that drives the designer. It has also been shown that three criteria play a role in the decision to remix: adaptability, relevance, and credibility. Only digital attention and success metrics, especially the number of likes, are relevant for the assessment of relevance. For the evaluation of practicality and feasibility, however, the designers tend towards "physical" metrics and rely on the number of registered makes and the comments of other users.

## 13.5. Implications and future research

So far, the *phenomenon of remixing* has received little attention. This lack of prior research stands in sharp contrast to the emergence and subsequent spread of open online platforms that provide a basis for the exchange and reuse of knowledge. In order to shed light on remixing as a source of innovation in these digital environments, an explorative approach was chosen that draws on quantitative and qualitative data collected on the world's largest 3D printing platform and community.

### Implications for theory

With regard to theory, various implications can be derived from the dissertation. The most important implications are explained in more detail below.

### Generalized research propositions

The results of the explorative study allow the final formulation of five generalized research propositions regarding *importance, patterns, category transitions, platform features,* and *user groups*:

1. Remixes pose a second major source of innovation in open online communities besides the emergence of isolated designs.
2. Remixes occur in the form of several different, clearly distinguishable paths, including convergent and divergent patterns.
3. The co-existence of different design categories allows for cross-category remixes, which are asymmetric, with categories tending to either donate or absorb ideas.
4. The effectiveness of remixing on online platforms and their attractiveness to different user groups is influenced by a variety of platform features for browsing and processing its contents.
5. To foster innovation in online communities, platforms need to address the needs and interests of different user groups, each characterized by distinct preferences regarding platform features.

A significant theoretical contribution is made by the formulation of these five generalized research propositions. Future explorative research can build on these propositions and complement them iteratively. In the long run, a coherent theoretical framework can be developed that explains the role of remixing in innovation processes. On the other hand, other research projects can use the hypotheses to develop testable hypotheses. In this way, the results presented here can also be tested and extended in other contexts.

**Different remix processes**

With the help of the cross-case analysis of the interviews, six different remix processes have been identified: *inspiration, play, learning, speed, improvement,* and *empowerment.* This stands in stark contrast to the previous theory, which only describes one multi-stage "knowledge reuse for innovation" process (Majchrzak et al., 2004). One reason for this discrepancy is to be found in the respective object of investigation. Majchrzak et al. (2004) consider extensive commercial research projects. Since these are strongly focused on the result to be achieved, action and subsequent consequences play no role in the motivation of the process. The designers interviewed in the present study deal voluntarily and out of non-commercial interests with the modeling of three-dimensional designs. Their motivation is more complex and includes not only the result but also the action and consequences. Due to the one-dimensional view of the motivation of a knowledge reuse for innovation process, only three of the identified processes can be traced back to previous theory. In the following, the connection between the results and the existing theory will be explained and why this theory needs to be extended, especially with regard to voluntary, non-commercial knowledge reuse for innovation processes—such as those found among makers and hobbyists.

The results of the qualitative study complement the existing research in that six different remix processes could be identified by interviewing the designers. Situation and circumstances are decisive when it comes to identifying the respective process. The interviews show that a process can be described using three different characteristics. These are the *skills* of the designer, the *trigger* of the remix process, and the *motivation* that drives the designer in the respective process. The results are consistent with the basic theoretical model of motivational psychology (Heckhausen and Heckhausen, 2018). Therefore, the relevant factors can be broken down into person- and situation-related factors. It is understandable that the abilities relate to the person of the designer, whereas the trigger of the process can be assigned to the respective situation. The interaction between person (skills) and situation (trigger) finally results in the motivation of the process. As described above, in previous studies, only the *result* was used as motivation. However, the findings of this study prove that the *action* and potential subsequent *consequences* can also represent the motivation for a process. In total, six independent process types have been identified: inspiration, play, learning, speed, improvement, and empowerment.

## Implications for practice

A deeper understanding of the phenomenon remix is necessary to design and maintain creative communities. Finally, ideas, solutions, and innovations can be generated this way. Against this background, the following aspects appear to be particularly relevant in practice.

Remix activity increased sharply as Thingiverse created the ability to customize existing designs by means of customizers. The new functionality allows designers with very little experience to remix designs and lowers the entry barrier accordingly. Such *tools for non-technical users* serve as a "gateway drug" for future designers. The simplicity and straightforwardness of the functionality allow anyone to quickly achieve success, which in the medium term motivates users to engage intensively with the technology.

The flow of knowledge resulting from the remixing of existing innovations is asymmetrical between the different categories of the platform. Thus, some categories benefit more from these category transitions than others. Because resulting unequal distributions can quickly lead to dissatisfaction, it is important to *assess asymmetric cooperation results* accordingly. It is desirable to correctly assess such situations, which can also occur during cooperation in other teams or companies, and to adapt incentives and reputation mechanisms in such a way that donors and recipients, to whom the results may be easier to attribute, are fairly assessed.

The majority of designers have already internalized the concept of remixing and actively utilize it—even beyond the platform. Especially for young people, remixing is a form of expressing own ideas (Koman, 2005; Knobel and Lankshear, 2008). In order to enable remixing in new contexts and to open up *new usage potentials*, it is important to create the necessary prerequisites. The basis for reuse are ideas, information, things, and knowledge—especially if these are available under free licenses. Here, in particular, science can set a good example by making more research results freely accessible. Studies that conclude that open access articles are cited more frequently than comparable, not freely accessible articles in the same journal show that not only potential re-users benefit from this (Antelman, 2004; Eysenbach, 2006).

## Limitations and further research

The results of the work have numerous implications for theory and practice. Nevertheless, the investigations carried out are subject to some limitations, which in turn open up perspectives for further research.

The explorative analysis is based on a snapshot of the Thingiverse platform. The chronological sequence and thus also the causal relationship between dynamic information, such as the number of downloads, makes, and remixes of a design, cannot be reconstructed with sufficient accuracy. As a result, for example, no far-reaching statements can be made about the success of designs or remixes. One way of countering this limitation of the current dataset is to record the data continuously. In this way, it can be reconstructed whether a design was remixed, for example, because it has many downloads, or whether the popularity of a remix is based on the respective parents' influence.

The determination of the complexity of a remix is based on metadata on origin and number of parents. Although this procedure allows an objective classification, it does not always accurately represent the actual threshold of originality of a design. In order to gain further insights into the relationship between parents and their remixes, manual coding of the remix relationships is indispensable. In order to encode the relationship or the degree of kinship, an examination of the differences in form or function, for instance, is useful. If, for example, a cup was remixed, it is important for the evaluation of originality whether the respective remix only has a larger handle (form) or whether the cup was adapted so that it can now be used as a flower vase (function). Another relationship that was addressed in the work is the respective remix process, from which a new design emerges. Future research projects can take up here and investigate what effects the process has on the respective remix.

Within the dissertation, an open online community was considered at first glance. The majority of the interviewed designers describe themselves as makers and identify themselves with the ideals of this movement, which also includes the free sharing of knowledge. Therefore, it makes sense to transfer the findings and results to other domains. In particular, the five research propositions developed have the potential to motivate further research and contribute to our understanding of creativity in the digital age.

**Acknowledgments**

The most important results, conclusions, and implications of the original dissertation (Wirth, 2018) and thus of this chapter were previously published in various scientific papers (Wirth and Thiesse, 2014; Flath et al., 2015; Thiesse et al., 2015; Wirth et al., 2015; Flath et al., 2017; Friesike et al., 2018). This would not have been possible without the help and support of Prof. Dr. Frédéric Thiesse, Prof. Dr. Sascha Friesike, and Prof. Dr. Christoph M. Flath. A special thanks also goes to the incredibly imaginative designers who make their designs available on Thingiverse under open licenses—it was them who made this research possible in the first place.

## References

Alavi, M. and Leidner, D. E. (2001). "Review: Knowledge Management and Knowledge Management Systems: Conceptual Foundations and Research Issues". *MIS Quarterly,* 25(1), pp. 107–136.

Anderson, C. (2012) *Makers: The New Industrial Revolution.* New York: Crown Business.

Antelman, K. (2004). "Do Open-Access Articles Have a Greater Research Impact?". College & Research Libraries, 65(5), pp. 372–382.

Arthur, W.B. (2009) *The Nature of Technology: What it is and How it Evolves.* London: Penguin Press.

Bastian, M., Heymann, S., and Jacomy, M. (2009). "Gephi: An Open Source Software for Exploring and Manipulating Networks", Proceedings of the 3rd International Conference on Weblogs and Social Media (ICWSM), San Jose.

Baumers, M., Dickens, P.M., Tuck, C.J., and Hague, R. (2016). "The cost of additive manufacturing: Machine productivity, economies of scale and technology-push". *Technological Forecasting and Social Change,* 102, pp. 193–201.

Bayus, B.L. (2013). "Crowdsourcing New Product Ideas over Time: An Analysis of the Dell IdeaStorm Community". *Management Science,* 59(1), pp. 226–244.

Bazeley, P. and Jackson, K. (2013) *Qualitative Data Analysis with NVivo.* 2nd edn. Los Angeles: SAGE Publications.

Berkun, S. (2010). *The Myths of Innovation.* Sebastopol: O"Reilly.

Berman, B. (2012). "3-D Printing: The New Industrial Revolution". *Business Horizons,* 55(2), pp. 155–162.

Birkinshaw, J., Bouquet, C., and Barsoux, J.-L. (2011). "The 5 Myths of Innovation". *MIT Sloan Management Review,* 52(2), pp. 43–50.

Brandon, J. (2016). "4 Important Lessons You Can Learn Now That 3-D Printing Is Dying". Inc. Available at: https://www.inc.com/john-brandon/the-slow-sad-and-ultimately-predictable-decline-of-3d-printing.html (Accessed: 4 May 2019).

Buxmann, P. and Hinz, O. (2013). "Makers". *Business & Information Systems Engineering,* 5(5), pp. 357–360.

Couger, J.D., Higgins, L.F., and McIntyre, S.C. (1993). "(Un)Structured Creativity in Information Systems Organizations". *MIS Quarterly,* 17(4), p. 375.

Csárdi, G. and Nepusz, T. (2006). "The igraph software package for complex network research". *InterJournal, Complex Systems,* 1695(5).

Dilawar, A. (2016). "The 3-D Printing Bubble May Have Burst". *Newsweek.* Available at: http://europe.newsweek.com/3d-printing-makerbot-stratasys-469704 (Accessed: 4 May 2019).

Dougherty, D. (2012). "The Maker Movement". *Innovations: Technology, Governance, Globalization,* 7(3), pp. 11–14.

Duchêne, V., Padilla, P., van de Velde, E., Wastyn, A., Nuñez, L., Knotter, S., Magistrelli, G., Nieminen, M., Puukko, P., Eklund, P., Rilla, N., Deschyvere, M., Mäntylä, M., Kasztler, A., Leitner, K.-H., Schiebel, E., and Wepner, B. (2016) Identifying current and future application areas, existing industrial value chains and missing competences in the EU, in the area of additive manufacturing (3D-printing): Final Report. Brussels: European Union.

Eysenbach, G. (2006). "Citation Advantage of Open Access Articles". *PLoS Biology*, 4(5), e157.

Flath, C.M., Friesike, S., and Wirth, M. (2015). "Successfully Remixing Innovations: Evidence From 3D Printing", Proceedings of the 15th European Academy of Management Conference (EURAM), Warsaw.

Flath, C.M., Friesike, S., Wirth, M., and Thiesse, F. (2017). "Copy, Transform, Combine: Exploring the Remix as a Form of Innovation". *Journal of Information Technology*, 32(4), pp. 306–325.

Ford, S., Mortara, L., and Minshall, T. (2016). "The Emergence of Additive Manufacturing: Introduction to the Special Issue". *Technological Forecasting and Social Change*, 102, pp. 156–159.

Fordyce, R., Heemsbergen, L., Apperley, T., Arnold, M., Birtchnell, T., Luo, M., and Nansen, B. (2016). "Things, tags, topics: Thingiverse's object-centred network". *Communication Research and Practice*, 2(1), pp. 63–78.

Friesike, S., Flath, C.M., Wirth, M., and Thiesse, F. (2018). 'Creativity and productivity in product design for additive manufacturing: Mechanisms and platform outcomes of remixing'. *Journal of Operations Management*, (In Press).

Gausemeier, J., Wall, M., and Peter, S. (2013) *Thinking ahead the Future of Additive Manufacturing: Exploring the Research Landscape.* Paderborn: Heinz Nixdorf Institute.

Gebhardt, A. and Hötter, J.-S. (2016) *Additive Manufacturing: 3D Printing for Prototyping and Manufacturing.* Munich: Carl Hanser.

Gershenfeld, N.A. (2012). "How to Make Almost Anything: The Digital Fabrication Revolution". *Foreign Affairs*, 91(6), pp. 43–57.

Gruber, M., Harhoff, D., and Hoisl, K. (2013). "Knowledge Recombination Across Technological Boundaries: Scientists vs. Engineers". *Management Science*, 59(4), pp. 837–851.

Gu, Z., Gu, L., Eils, R., Schlesner, M., and Brors, B. (2014). "circlize implements and enhances circular visualization in R". *Bioinformatics*, 30(19), pp. 2811–2812.

Gunkel, D.J. (2016) *Of Remixology: Ethics and Aesthetics after Remix.* Cambridge: The MIT Press.

Guo, N. and Leu, M.C. (2013). "Additive manufacturing: Technology, applications and research needs". *Frontiers of Mechanical Engineering*, 8(3), pp. 215–243.

Haefliger, S., Krogh, G. von, and Spaeth, S. (2008). "Code Reuse in Open Source Software". *Management Science*, 54(1), pp. 180–193.

Hargadon, A. (2003) *How Breakthroughs Happen: The Surprising Truth About How Companies Innovate.* Boston: Harvard Business School Press.

Heckhausen, J. and Heckhausen, H. (eds.) (2018) *Motivation and Action.* 3rd edn. Cham: Springer International Publishing.

Hill, B.M. and Monroy-Hernández, A. (2013). "The Remixing Dilemma: The Trade-Off Between Generativity and Originality". *American Behavioral Scientist*, 57(5), pp. 643–663.

Hippel, E. von (1988) *The Sources of Innovation.* Oxford: Oxford University Press.

Hippel, E. von (2005) *Democratizing Innovation.* Cambridge: MIT Press.

Holweg, M. (2015). "The Limits of 3D Printing". *Harvard Business Review.* Available at: https://hbr.org/2015/06/the-limits-of-3d-printing (Accessed: 4 May 2019).

Huysman, M. and Wulf, V. (2006). "IT to support knowledge sharing in communities, towards a social capital analysis". *Journal of Information Technology,* 21(1), pp. 40–51.

Ihaka, R. and Gentleman, R. (1996). "R: A Language for Data Analysis and Graphics". *Journal of Computational and Graphical Statistics,* 5(3), pp. 299–314.

Jackson, B. (2018). "Thingiverse celebrates decade of 3D printed things and over 300 million downloads". *3D Printing Industry.* Available at: https://3dprintingindustry.com/news/thingiverse-celebrates-decade-of-3d-printed-things-and-over-300-million-downloads-142346/ (Accessed: 4 May 2019).

Jiang, R., Kleer, R., and Piller, F.T. (2017). "Predicting the future of additive manufacturing: A Delphi study on economic and societal implications of 3D printing for 2030". *Technological Forecasting and Social Change,* 117, pp. 84–97.

Kasparek, C. (1994). "Prus' Pharaoh: The Creation of a Historical Novel". *The Polish Review,* 39(1), pp. 45–50.

Knobel, M. and Lankshear, C. (2008). "Remix: The Art and Craft of Endless Hybridization". *Journal of Adolescent & Adult Literacy,* 52(1), pp. 22–33.

Koman, R. (2005). "Remixing Culture: An Interview with Lawrence Lessig." O"Reilly Policy DevCenter. Available at: http://www.oreillynet.com/pub/a/policy/2005/02/24/lessig.html (Accessed: 4 May 2019).

Kyriakou, H., Nickerson, J.V., and Sabnis, G. (2017). "Knowledge Reuse for Customization: Metamodels in an Open Design Community for 3D Printing". *MIS Quarterly,* 41(1), pp. 315–322.

Leimeister, J.M., Huber, M., Bretschneider, U., and Krcmar, H. (2009). "Leveraging Crowdsourcing: Activation-Supporting Components for IT-Based Ideas Competition". *Journal of Management Information Systems,* 26(1), pp. 197–224.

Lessig, L. (2008) *Remix: Making Art and Commerce Thrive in the Hybrid Economy.* New York: Penguin Press.

Li, J., Myant, C., and Wu, B. (2016) *The Current Landscape for Additive Manufacturing Research: A review to map the UK"s research activities in AM internationally and nationally.* London: Imperial College London.

Luchs, M.G., Swan, K.S., and Creusen, M.E.H. (2016). "Perspective: A Review of Marketing Research on Product Design with Directions for Future Research". *Journal of Product Innovation Management,* 33(3), pp. 320–341.

Lune, H. and Berg, B.L. (2017) *Qualitative Research Methods for the Social Sciences.* 9th edn. New York: Pearson.

Markillie, P. (2012). "The Third Industrial Revolution: Special Report". Manufacturing and Innovation. *The Economist,* 403(8781), pp. 1–14.

Markus, L.M. (2001). "Toward a Theory of Knowledge Reuse: Types of Knowledge Reuse Situations and Factors in Reuse Success". *Journal of Management Information Systems,* 18(1), pp. 57–93.

Metcalfe, J.S. (1998) *Evolutionary Economics and Creative Destruction.* London: Routledge.

Mitchell, B.T. and Subramani, M. R. (2010). "Knowledge Repositories and Knowledgeable Action", Proceedings of the 31st International Conference on Information Systems (ICIS), Saint Louis.

Müller, O., Junglas, I., Vom Brocke, J., and Debortoli, S. (2016). "Utilizing big data analytics for information systems research: challenges, promises and guidelines". *European Journal of Information Systems,* 25(4), pp. 289–302.

Müller-Wienbergen, F., Müller, O., Seidel, S., and Becker, J. (2011). "Leaving the Beaten Tracks in Creative Work: A Design Theory for Systems that Support Convergent and Divergent Thinking". *Journal of the Association for Information Systems,* 12(11), pp. 714–740.

Murray, F. and O"Mahony, S. (2007). "Exploring the Foundations of Cumulative Innovation: Implications for Organization Science". *Organization Science,* 18(6), pp. 1006–1021.

Nelson, R.R. and Winter, S.G. (1982). *An evolutionary theory of economic change.* Cambridge: Harvard University Press.

Oehlberg, L., Willett, W., and Mackay, W.E. (2015). "Patterns of Physical Design Remixing in Online Maker Communities", Proceedings of the 33rd Conference on Human Factors in Computing Systems (CHI), Seoul, pp. 639–648.

Özkil, A.G. (2017). "Collective design in 3D printing: A large scale empirical study of designs, designers and evolution". *Design Studies,* 51, pp. 66–89.

Paré, G. (2004). "Investigating Information Systems with Positivist Case Research". *Communications of the Association for Information Systems,* 13, pp. 233–264.

QSR International (2018) *NVivo: Qualitative Data Analysis Software* (Version 11). Melbourne: QSR International Pty Ltd.

R Core Team (2016) R: A Language and Environment for Statistical Computing. Viena: R Foundation for Statistical Computing. Available at: https://www.r-project.org/ (Accessed: 4 May 2019).

Richardson, M. (2012). "Designer/Maker: The Rise of Additive Manufacturing, Domestic-Scale Production and the Possible Implications for the Automotive Industry". *Computer-Aided Design and Applications,* PACE(2), pp. 33–48.

Rosenberg, N. (1982) *Inside the black box: Technology and economics.* Cambridge: Cambridge University Press.

Salter, A. and Alexy, O. (2014*) The Nature of Innovation. Oxford*: Oxford University Press.

Sambamurthy, V. and Subramani, M.R. (2005). "Special Issue on Information Technologies and Knowledge Management". *MIS Quarterly,* 29(2), pp. 1–7.

Sapsed, J. and Tschang, F.T. (2014). "Art is long, innovation is short: Lessons from the Renaissance and the digital age". *Technological Forecasting and Social Change,* 83, pp. 127–141.

Schumpeter, J.A. (1942) *Capitalism, Socialism and Democracy.* New York: Harper and Brothers.

Scotchmer, S. (1991). "Standing on the Shoulders of Giants: Cumulative Research and the Patent Law". *The Journal of Economic Perspectives,* 5(1), pp. 29–41.

Simonton, D.K. (2004) *Creativity in Science: Chance, Logic, Genius, and Zeitgeist.* Cambridge: Cambridge University Press.

Sojer, M. and Henkel, J. (2010). "Code Reuse in Open Source Software Development: Quantitative Evidence, Drivers, and Impediments". *Journal of the Association for Information Systems,* 11(12), pp. 868–901.

Stanko, M.A. (2016). "Toward a Theory of Remixing in Online Innovation Communities". *Information Systems Research,* 27(4), pp. 773–791.

Tanenbaum, J.G., Williams, A.M., Desjardins, A., and Tanenbaum, K. (2013). "Democratizing Technology: Pleasure, Utility and Expressiveness in DIY and Maker Practice", Proceedings of the 31st SIGCHI Conference on Human Factors in Computing Systems (CHI), Paris, pp. 2603–2612.

Thiesse, F., Wirth, M., Kemper, H.-G., Moisa, M., Morar, D., Lasi, H., Piller, F.T., Buxmann, P., Mortara, L., Ford, S., and Minshall, T. (2015). "Economic Implications of Additive Manufacturing and the Contribution of MIS". *Business & Information Systems Engineering,* 57(2), pp. 139–148.

Tuite, K. and Smith, A.M. (2012). "Emergent Remix Culture in an Anonymous Collaborative Art System", Proceedings of the 8th Artificial Intelligence and Interactive Digital Entertainment Conference (AAAI), Palo Alto, pp. 16–23.

Usher, A.P. (2011) *A History of Mechanical Inventions.* New York: Dover Publications.

Uzzi, B., Mukherjee, S., Stringer, M., and Jones, B. (2013). "Atypical Combinations and Scientific Impact". *Science,* 342(6157), pp. 468–472.

Vallés, J.L. (2014) Additive Manufacturing in FP7 and Horizon 2020: Report from the EC Workshop on Additive Manufacturing. Brussels: European Commission.

Van de Ven, A.H. (1986). "Central Problems in the Management of Innovation". *Management Science,* 32(5), pp. 590–607.

Van de Ven, A.H. (1999) *The Innovation Journey.* Oxford: Oxford University Press.

Weitzman, M.L. (1998). "Recombinant Growth". *Quarterly Journal of Economics,* 113(2), pp. 331–360.

West, J. and Kuk, G. (2016). "The complementarity of openness: How MakerBot leveraged Thingiverse in 3D printing". *Technological Forecasting and Social Change,* 102, pp. 169–181.

Wickham, H. (2009) *ggplot2: Elegant Graphics for Data Analysis.* (Use R). New York: Springer.

Wickham, H. and Francois, R. (2016) dplyr: A Grammar of Data Manipulation. Available at: https://cran.r-project.org/package=dplyr (Accessed: 4 May 2019).

Wickham, H. and Grolemund, G. (2016) *Data Science with R.* Farnham: O"Reilly.

Wirth, M. (2018) *Additive Fertigung: Technologie, Markt und Innovation.* Dissertation. University of Würzburg. Available at: https://nbn-resolving.org/urn:nbn:de:bvb:20-opus-155970 (Accessed: 4 May 2019).

Wirth, M., Friesike, S., Flath, C.M., and Thiesse, F. (2015). "Patterns of Remixes or Where Do Innovations Come from: Evidence from 3D Printing",

Proceedings of the 23rd European Conference on Information Systems (ECIS), Münster.

Wirth, M. and Thiesse, F. (2014). "Shapeways and the 3D Printing Revolution", Proceedings of the 22nd European Conference on Information Systems (ECIS), Tel Aviv.

Yew, J. and Monroy-Hernández, A. (2014). "Harnessing Serendipity: A Study of Accidental Creative Collaborations in Two Online Remixing Communities", Selected Papers of Internet Research 15: 15th Annual Meeting of the Association of Internet Researchers (AoIR), Daegu.

Chapter 14

# Sustainable Industrial Value Creation: An Analysis of Industry 4.0 with Special Regard to SMEs

Julian M. Müller

*Salzburg University of Applied Sciences, Austria*

**Abstract:** Industrial value creation is facing increased demands for increased sustainability. Industry 4.0 is expected to generate such potentials, but practice shows that to achieve those, several challenges need to be overcome. This is especially true for small and medium-sized enterprises, which play an important role for industrial value creation, but require strategies specifically tailored to their demands and frame conditions, which have scarcely been investigated. Based on this research gap, the dissertation identifies potentials and challenges of Industry 4.0 in the context of sustainability and delineates those for several company characteristics and industry sectors. Thereupon, the paper explores ways to innovate SMEs' business models, attempting to find economically feasible ways to generate ecological and social potentials with respect to the challenges uncovered. Last, these aspects are compared among German and Chinese SMEs, also providing one of the first comparisons between the concepts Industry 4.0 and Made in China 2025.

**Keywords:** Industry 4.0; Industrial Internet of Things; Digital Transformation; Small and Medium-Sized Enterprises; Sustainability; Triple Bottom Line, Business Model Innovation; Qualitative Research; Case Studies; Structural Equation Modelling

## 14.1. Introduction

The concept of Industry 4.0 experiences increased the interest in research and practice worldwide. Going back to its origin, the term Industry 4.0 was coined by the German federal government. It was designed as a response to changing and more challenging environmental conditions for the German industrial sector. These include, for example, shortening innovation skylines, augmenting competitive pressure, steadily increasing globalization and ever more individual and demanding customer demands (Arnold, Kiel and Voigt, 2016; Kagermann et al., 2013; Lasi et al., 2014).

Industry 4.0 is based on the Internet of Things, which is why comparable concepts are internationally also known as the Industrial Internet of Things. The concept has been followed by numerous programs worldwide. These include, among others, the "Industrial Internet Consortium" in the USA, or the program "Made in China 2025" within the "Internet Plus Initiative" in China (Kang et al., 2016).

An essential basis for Industry 4.0 is the interconnection of the real and virtual worlds via the Internet of Things, whereby Cyber-Physical-Systems are created, which are characterized in particular by the representation of the real world in the virtual world by the means of sensor technology and artificial intelligence. A further central characteristic of Industry 4.0 is the horizontal and vertical interconnection in real-time, i.e., across entire supply chains and across several organizational levels. (Kagermann et al., 2013; Lasi et al., 2014; Porter and Heppelmann, 2014). These characteristics of Industry 4.0, enabled by technological means, are expected to affect economic, ecological and social aspects of industrial value creation.

Accordingly, the Triple Bottom Line of sustainability represents a suitable instrument for analysis. The Triple Bottom Line of sustainability was originally developed as a result of the "Brundtland Report" of the United Nations. It reflects society's growing expectations to consider all three dimensions of sustainability: economy, ecology and social issues (Elkington, 1998; Norman, Macdonald and Arnold, 2004). A primary focus on profit maximization is, therefore, no longer acceptable for a contemporary industrial company (McWilliams et al., 2016). While sustainability in science and practice is usually understood from an ecological perspective, the consideration of all three dimensions of sustainability, especially its interactions, is essential to achieve potentials in all three dimensions (Littig and Griessler, 2005). Today, sustainable industrial value creation can be found in the United Nations' Sustainable Development Goal 12 - "Ensure sustainable consumption and production patterns".

While the primary goal of Industry 4.0 is to achieve potential benefits in all three dimensions of sustainability, industrial companies, especially in the implementation phase of Industry 4.0, face numerous challenges at the same time. These challenges can be found, again, in all three dimensions of the Triple Bottom Line of sustainability. As a result, many companies show a rather reluctant implementation of Industry 4.0.

From an economic point of view, operative potentials are to be achieved, i.e. process improvements through increasing process transparency, interconnection of production plants, products and people via the Internet of

Things (Porter and Heppelmann, 2014). Overall, this leads to higher efficiency, for example, through increased quality, reduced cycle and reaction times as well as optimized logistics processes. Similarly, benefits are to be achieved at the strategic level, in particular through new, data-based business models (Arnold, Kiel and Voigt, 2016). The constant adaptation of the business model to changing environmental conditions and new technologies is an essential measure to secure the future viability of a company (Chesborugh, 2010). At the ecological level, Industry 4.0 promises lower environmental impact and resource wastage, while from a social perspective, industrial jobs of the future should achieve reduced physical and psychological workload, leading to a higher employee satisfaction.

A special focus of this dissertation is on small and medium-sized enterprises (SMEs), which require a separate consideration in the context of Industry 4.0 for several reasons. This includes the enormous economic importance of SMEs, as they generate about 50 percent of Germany's value added. This contribution by SMEs, especially as suppliers, demands the integration of SMEs into Industry 4.0 for its successful implementation. Furthermore, the social perspective on SMEs should not be neglected, since they employ 60 percent of the workforce and achieve more than 80 percent of the apprentice training (Airaksinen et al., 2015). Hence, due to their economic and social importance, SMEs are particularly well suited for analysing sustainability in the context of Industry 4.0.

## 14.2. Background

Research in the context of Industry 4.0 that is related to non-technical fields, such as business management or social sciences, is lagging behind technical research disciplines (Arnold, Kiel and Voigt., 2016). However, already the first description of the concept Industry 4.0 by the German government and several industry associations described the implications of Industry 4.0 beyond technical developments. Among other aspects, Industry 4.0 was designed from the very beginning on to trigger new, data-driven business models, transform traditional industrial value creation and merge it with value creation logics of, for instance, the software industry. Further, organizational transformation with new hierarchical and organizational structures is described, for instance, allowing cross-disciplinary thinking. Another aspect includes the implications for innovation management, as horizontal and vertical interconnection leads to data transparency that allows a backflow of data from product usage to product development in real-time, allowing to shorten innovation cycles and enhancing customer satisfaction. From a social perspective, these changes were described to require a change of skills, mind-set and new workforce required in traditional industries, leading to a large demand for training and requalification (Kagermann et al., 2013).

Still, before this thesis was begun, the majority of scientific studies only mentioned such aspects indirectly, whereas media releases, articles in trade journals and reports from management consultancies reported with increasing interest on the topic. Further, many companies showed a reluctant or fearful attitude towards the concept of Industry 4.0. Despite the promised benefits, first barriers for implementation and partial inapplicability for traditional industries was described from managerial practice.

In response, this chapter is dedicated to generating a holistic picture on the phenomenon of Industry 4.0 from an academic perspective, combining managerial relevance with scientific rigor. In order to generate this holistic picture, and to draw from a scientifically established framework, the Triple Bottom Line of sustainability was chosen, as described in the introduction.

Several studies exist that consider Industry 4.0 from an economic, ecological, or social perspective. However, an integrative perspective on all three dimensions within the Triple Bottom Line of sustainability, especially regarding their interrelations across benefits and challenges in all three dimensions, is scarcely found in extant literature. However, extant scientific literature shows that especially the interrelations and combined perspective on all three dimensions of the Triple Bottom Line is essential to be able to balance challenges and benefits against one another in order to maximize the latter (Littig and Griessler, 2005).

Table 14.1 gives an overview of the literature that existed before the chapter regarding Industry 4.0 in the Triple Bottom Line of sustainability. As mentioned above, the majority of extant literature did not regard more than one dimension of the Triple Bottom Line, rarely examining two dimensions.

Further, despite their economic importance stated above, SMEs have been investigated much more scarcely in comparison to large enterprises, especially in academic literature. However, already the initial concept of Industry 4.0 of the German government had stressed out the importance to regard entire supply chains and especially smaller suppliers within the concept of Industry 4.0 in order to ensure its successful implementation (Kagermann et al., 2013).

**Table 14.1:** Extant literature dealing with sustainability aspects of Industry 4.0

| *TBL dimension* | *Brief overview of relevant aspects* | *Exemplary literature* |
|---|---|---|
| Economic | • Increased cost transparency<br>• Enhanced efficiency, flexibility, customization, and quality<br>• Shorter lead times<br>• New business models<br>• Large investments required<br>• Uncertain profitability<br>• Unclear customer demand | Amshoff et al. (2015); Arnold, Kiel, & Voigt (2016); Hofmann & Rüsch (2017); Kagermann, Wahlster, & Helbig (2013); Oesterreich & Teuteberg (2016); Peukert et al. (2015); Schuhmacher & Hummel (2016); Stock & Seliger (2016); Zhou et al. (2017) |
| Ecological | • Transparency of greenhouse gas emissions<br>• Increased resource and energy efficiency<br>• Reduction of waste<br>• Reduction of logistics processes, e.g., due to reshoring<br>• Reduction of wrong delivery and damaged goods | Gabriel & Pessel (2016); Herrmann et al. (2014); Müller, Dotzauer, & Voigt (2017); Qiu et al. (2015); Sarkis & Zhu (2017); Stock & Seliger (2016); Gabriel & Pessel (2016); Herrmann et al. (2014); Stock & Seliger (2016); Tesch, Brillinger, & Bilgeri (2017) |
| Social | • Fair wages, human learning, and employee motivation<br>• Unclear effect on job creation or reduction<br>• Expected reduction of simple tasks, whereas creative tasks might emerge<br>• Organizational transformation required<br>• Network, environment, and politics influence Industry 4.0 adoption | Gabriel & Pessel (2016); Herrmann et al. (2014); Stock & Seliger (2016); Tesch, Brillinger, & Bilgeri (2017) |

## 14.3. Research design

The dissertation is of cumulative nature, based on five research articles, that have been published individually in peer-reviewed journals. All five articles are based on empirical samples, while the empirical data is either of qualitative nature (articles 1, 3, and 4) or of quantitative nature (articles 2 and 5). Hence, the dissertation attempts to generate new insights and theory in an exploratory way, whilst separating and testing this in quantitative research designs. All research articles have the German industry sectors of mechanical and plant engineering, electrical and ICT engineering, and automotive industry as an empirical basis. Those three industry sectors are also those three named to be primarily affected by Industry 4.0 in Germany (Kagermann et al., 2013). Further, article 2 extends these industry sectors for chemical and plastics engineering and the steel industry, adding two traditional process industries to a sample that includes five of the major industrial sectors in Germany. Further, article 5 extends the German perspective by including quantitative data of Chinese SMEs and compares them with German SMEs.

The first article (Kiel et al., 2017) of this dissertation creates a holistic understanding of the benefits and challenges of Industry 4.0 in the context of sustainability. The concept of the Triple Bottom Line of sustainability serves as a basis for examining the economic, ecological and social potentials and challenges of Industry 4.0. Relating to the early stage of research, the paper uses a qualitative exploratory research design to gain a detailed understanding of the implications of Industry 4.0. It is based on 46 expert interviews with German company representatives.

Based on the model developed in the first article (Kiel et al., 2017), the second article (Müller, Kiel and Voigt, 2018) takes a closer look at the impact of potential benefits and challenges on the decision to implement Industry 4.0. Structural equation modelling serves to design and test six hypotheses in the developed research model, which is empirically validated by means of an online survey of 746 companies from five German industrial sectors.

On the basis of one of the key insights regarding the more operational than strategic orientation of SMEs with regard to Industry 4.0, the third article (Müller, 2019) examines the importance of strategic innovations through Industry 4.0, or more precisely, the role of business model innovations. The empirical basis of the third article is provided by qualitative study within 43 SMEs, of which more than half of the sample are CEOs.

The fourth article (Müller, Buliga and Voigt, 2018) of this dissertation examines more closely how Industry 4.0 drives innovation in the business models of manufacturing SMEs, as found in the third article (Müller, 2019). The fourth article presents the results of a qualitative study based on expert interviews with representatives of 68 German SMEs. Further, the article develops a stage-gate model of Industry 4.0-driven business model innovation in SMEs.

The fifth article (Müller and Voigt, 2018) analyses the "Made in China 2025" concept compared to Industry 4.0. The research model is based on the model of the potential benefits and challenges of Industry 4.0 from the perspective of sustainability, which was developed in the first article (Kiel et al., 2017). The empirical data basis of the article is an online survey of 329 SMEs, with 222 companies from Germany and 107 companies from China.

Table 14.2 gives an overview of the five articles, stating the empirical sample and method used.

**Table 14.2:** Overview of samples and methods used.

| *Research article* | *Sample* | *Method used* |
|---|---|---|
| Sustainable Industrial Value Creation: Benefits and Challenges of Industry 4.0 | 46 German industrial companies | Multiple case study, qualitative expert interviews |
| What drives the Implementation of Industry 4.0? The role of Opportunities and Challenges in the Context of Sustainability | 746 German industrial companies | Structural equation modelling, Quantitative survey |
| Business Model Innovation in Small and Medium-Sized Enterprises: Strategies for Industry 4.0 Providers and Users | 43 German industrial SMEs | Multiple case study, qualitative expert interviews |
| Fortune favours the prepared: How SMEs approach business model innovation in Industry 4.0 | 68 German industrial SMEs | Multiple case study, qualitative expert interviews |
| Sustainable Industrial Value Creation in SMEs: A Comparison between Industry 4.0 and Made in China 2025 | 222 German SMEs, 107 Chinese SMEs | Quantitative survey |

## 14.4. Conclusion

The purpose of this dissertation is to contribute to theoretical and partial knowledge on Industry 4.0 research regarding sustainable industrial value creation. In this course, the dissertation takes a closer look at implications of SMEs, that possess a special importance for the German industry and require research focused on them. In response, the dissertation encompasses five research articles.

The first article explores Industry 4.0-related potentials and challenges against the background of sustainable industrial value creation. Therefore, it integrates the expert knowledge of 46 company representatives concerned with Industry 4.0 via expert interviews. The first article reveals that Industry 4.0 qualifies for a future model of sustainable industrial value creation as it possesses potentials in all three dimensions of the Triple Bottom Line.

However, several challenges have to be overcome to implement Industry 4.0. Further, an Industry 4.0-specific Triple Bottom Line framework of sustainability is developed, as shown in Figure 14.1 below.

**Figure 14.1**: Framework of benefits and challenges of Industry 4.0 in the context of sustainability.

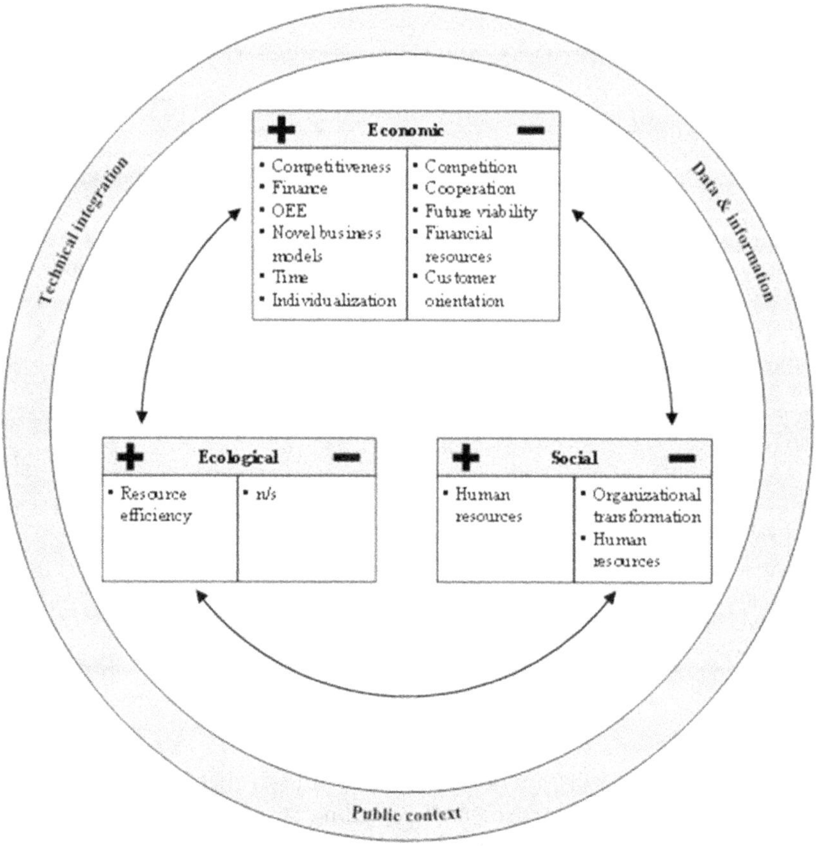


The second article investigates the relation of the potentials and challenges of Industry 4.0 with companies' decision to implement it. It differentiates between company sizes, industry sectors, and role as Industry 4.0 provider or user. The study confirms the significant influence of Industry 4.0-related potentials and challenges on companies' decision. In addition, it reveals interesting industry-specific differences, especially the rather operative orientation of SMEs for the implementation of Industry 4.0. The same applies to the process industries within this sample, chemical and plastics engineering and the steel industries. On the other hand, Industry 4.0

providers or enterprises taking the role of Industry 4.0 providers and users and the same time are rather strategically oriented towards Industry 4.0. Interestingly, the automotive industry is the only one that does not see the environmental benefits of Industry 4.0 as a driver for its implementation.

The third article delineates the role as Industry 4.0 provider and user in the context of SMEs. It shows that a majority of SMEs rather regard themselves as Industry 4.0 users, whereas Industry 4.0 providers are foremost experiencing changes in their business models through Industry 4.0. Thereupon, the paper further develops this important differentiation of Industry 4.0 providers and users, showing that especially SMEs need to grasp the strategic opportunities presented by Industry 4.0

The fourth article develops a stage-gate model of business model innovation through Industry 4.0 in SMEs. It shows that further aspects, extending the delineation of Industry 4.0 user or provider, such as internal motivation or external pressure as well as the digitization level determine to what extent business model innovations unfold. In this regard, the paper builds upon the findings of the second and third article, showing that distinct changes in the business model triggered by Industry 4.0 are foremost depending on the company characteristics and orientation towards Industry 4.0. Whereas value creation is mainly affected for Industry 4.0 users which are externally pressured to implement Industry 4.0, SMEs that are also internally motivated and additionally take a role as Industry 4.0 providers also change their value offer and value capture mechanisms.

The fifth article compares sustainability aspects of Industry 4.0 to the Chinese program "Made in China 2025" in the context of SMEs, showing that the German program is rather perceived to aim for the benefits of large enterprises. Also, potentials for environmental and economical improvements through the program "Made in China 2025" are rather perceived by Chinese SMEs than for German SMEs through "Industry 4.0". Chinese SMEs also expect larger hurdles to be taken as their digitization levels have not reached those of their German counterparts.

## 14.5. Implications and future research

### Theoretical Implications and future research

First, it is shown that Industry 4.0 is suitable as a future model for more sustainable industrial value creation, despite a number of challenges and, in particular, a wide range of potential benefits. In doing so, the existing triple bottom line of sustainability is expanded to include three Industry 4.0-

specific dimensions: Technical integration, data and information as well as the public context.

Second, it is shown that there is a stronger connection between potential benefits in terms of business models and the implementation of Industry 4.0 at large companies and Industry 4.0 providers, as well as in the following sectors: mechanical and plant engineering and electrical engineering. This is in contrast to SMEs and Industry 4.0 users, as well as process industries, such as the chemical and steel industries, which see operational potentials rather than drivers of the realization of Industry 4.0

Third, SMEs see themselves as users of Industry 4.0 technologies rather than as providers of Industry 4.0 solutions. Nevertheless, the smaller group of Industry 4.0 providers sees significantly larger changes in the respective business model. This finding can be used to justify the overall rather low importance of business model innovations of SMEs in the findings of the second article, as these are oriented more towards the usage of Industry 4.0 and thus more to the operational potential of Industry 4.0. For theory, it is shown that the distinction between provider and user perspective of a technology is very important when referring to business model innovations.

Fourth, it is shown that Industry 4.0 for SMEs predominantly comprises three dimensions: a high degree of digitization of processes, intelligent production and cross-company connectivity. Further, both the role of the company, as a user or provider of Industry 4.0, as well as its internal motivation or external pressure to implement it, determine the extent to which the resulting business model innovations unfold. Based on these findings, the chapter develops a maturity model of four stages of development of business model innovation through Industry 4.0 in SMEs.

As a central limitation of this study, it must be noted that Industry 4.0 implementation is still in its initial stages, which means that the findings must be closely validated, specified, and extended in this ongoing process. Comparably, extending and comparing the findings in other contexts, such as further countries or industry sectors, represents a fruitful research context. Further, the majority of the study's findings is based on self-reporting of managers within German and Chinese industrial enterprises. The extension of these findings by other research methods, such as longitudinal studies or the usage of secondary sources, is a further recommendation for future research.

## Managerial implications

The chapter describes economic potentials and challenges of Industry 4.0 relevant for practice, such as new and changing business models and derives adequate strategies in response. In particular, SMEs and specific industry sectors are separated within the analysis and given distinct recommendations. Also, social potentials and challenges, such as better and eased collaboration and innovation, but also fears regarding job losses are described in the chapter, as well as specific recommendations. Further, the chapter finds the necessary technical integration for the concept, which requires companies' efforts, for example, in terms of data exchange, standards and interfaces. Furthermore, aspects of data and information security are an essential cornerstone of successful implementation of Industry 4.0, while government and legislation must take even more account of legal and infrastructural aspects as expressed by the surveyed companies. These findings are further compared between Germany and China, giving specific recommendations for action. In short, the recommendations across all five articles can be subsumed as follows:

1. Developing a holistic understanding of sustainable industrial value creation. Without regarding all three dimensions of sustainability, especially their interconnection, Industry 4.0 will not be able to unfold its benefits in all three dimensions. Consequently, potentials and challenges of sustainable industrial value creation need to be balanced against each other.
2. Understanding economical potentials and challenges of Industry 4.0. Economic potentials can be achieved via strategic benefits, e.g. new, data-based business models, or operational benefits, e.g. time, quality and flexibility. Both are interconnected and need to be regarded at the same time. To achieve both, investments and organizational transformation processes are required, potentially threatening established business models. Therefore, short-term losses need to be balanced against long-term benefits of Industry 4.0.
3. Understanding ecological potentials and challenges of Industry 4.0. Reduction of energy consumption, waste production and logistics processes are achievable but require a high level of inter-company interconnectivity to unfold its benefits. So far, ecological challenges are not well understood, e.g. energy consumption of data transmission or consequences of largely individualized production that cannot be reused as easily as today.
4. Understanding social potentials and challenges of Industry 4.0. More employee-suitable workplaces with new, more creative and less monotonous and physically challenging tasks are achievable, also through new employee support systems. Those can help to better integrate elderly employees, refugees, or disabled workers. However, job losses, especially for manual labor, but also for planning and

coordinative tasks are expected, as well as employee resistance against the changes expected.

5. Business model innovation towards Industry 4.0. Business models require to be designed accordingly to what companies want to achieve, building on their existing strengths but extending them with those required for Industry 4.0. Especially for SMEs, the focus on a single or predominant business model requires them to carefully, but courageously developing their business models.
6. Understanding the role as users or providers of Industry 4.0. Whereas using Industry 4.0 foremost develops operational benefits, serving as Industry 4.0-providers enables companies to better unfold the potentials of Industry 4.0. Especially SMEs are encouraged to consider their positioning towards Industry 4.0.
7. Developing internal motivation and understanding own positioning towards Industry 4.0. Developing internal motivation towards Industry 4.0 rather than sole external pressure helps companies to unfold Industry 4.0 business models better. Accordingly, companies should better understand, question and develop their strategy and positioning towards Industry 4.0.
8. Supply-chain collaboration for Industry 4.0. Without supply chain interconnection, a large proportion of Industry 4.0 potentials will not be able to fully unfold. Therefore, entire supply chains are required to work together towards Industry 4.0 implementation, mastering challenges such as standardization and data interchange interfaces. Also, for large enterprises, integration of their suppliers, of which many are SMEs, is a vital task.
9. Developing a cross-company mindset for Industry 4.0. Thinking within company boundaries will not help Industry 4.0 to unfold its benefits, as it requires cross-company data exchange. Therefore, new, more open and collaborative mindsets need to be developed towards the integration of Industry 4.0.
10. Designing existing programs towards the requirements of SMEs. So far, Industry 4.0 remains an intimidating concept for many SMEs, therefore preventing its implementation. As outlined before, SMEs are required to be integrated within industrial supply chains in order to make Industry 4.0 a success. Therefore, concerns such as resource limitation, a different mindset, fear of transparency and low compound effects achievable need to be addressed for future Industry 4.0 programs. In response, large companies and industry

associations are required to share the benefits of Industry 4.0 with their SME partners.

11. Ensuring data and legal security. Government and legal institutions are required to develop several aspects better to the concerns uttered by company representatives. Foremost, data security needs to be improved by technical and legal means. Further, the question of data ownership requires an adequate response to ensure legal certainty for Industry 4.0.

To face the rapid process of digital transformation that Industry 4.0 is even expected to exacerbate in the future and with a competition that is increasing worldwide, industrial manufacturers and especially SMEs in Germany need to overcome current challenges that might be intimidating for them, therefore so far still hampering or even preventing Industry 4.0 implementation. This dissertation intends to illustrate a holistic picture on the opportunities of sustainable industrial value creation through Industry 4.0, especially regarding the unique requirements of SMEs. It therefore attempts to address the quote of Louis Pasteur, "Fortune favors the prepared", enabling industrial manufacturers to better prepare for a sustainable industrial value creation in Industry 4.0.

## References

Airaksinen, A., Luomaranta, H., Alajääskö, P., & Roodhuijzen, A. (2015). Statistics on small and medium-sized enterprises: Dependent and independent SMEs and large enterprises. *http://ec.europa.eu/eurostat/statistics-explained/index.php/Statistics_on_small_and_medium-sized_ enterprises.*

Amshoff, B., Dülme, C., Echterfeld, J., & Gausemeier, J. (2015) *Business model patterns for disruptive technologies.* International Journal of Innovation Management 19(3): 1540002.

Arnold, C., Kiel, D. & Voigt, K.-I. (2016). "How the Industrial Internet of Things Changes Business Models in Different Manufacturing Industries." *International Journal of Innovation Management,* 20(8): 1640015-1 – 1640015-25.

Chesbrough, H. (2010). "Business Model Innovation: Opportunities and Barriers." *Long Range Planning,* 43(2/3): 354–363.

Elkington, J. (1998). "Partnerships from cannibals with forks: The triple bottom line of 21st-century business." *Environmental Quality Management,* 8(1): 37-51.

Gabriel, M., & Pessel, E. (2016) "Industry 4.0 and sustainability impacts: critical discussion of sustainability aspects with a special focus on future of work and ecological consequences." Annals of Faculty Engineering Hunedoara – *International Journal of Engineering* 1(16): 131-136.

Herrmann, C., Schmidt, C., Kurle, D., Blume, S., & Thiede, S. (2014) "Sustainability in manufacturing and factories of the future." *International*

*Journal of Precision Engineering and Manufacturing - Green Technology* 1(4): 283-292.

Hofmann, E., & Rüsch, M. (2017) "Industry 4.0 and the current status as well as future prospects on logistics." *Computers in Industry* 89: 23-34.

Kagermann, H., Wahlster, W., & Helbig, J. (2013) *Recommendations for implementing the strategic initiative Industrie 4.0 – Final report of the Industrie 4.0 Working Group.* Frankfurt am Main: Communication Promoters Group of the Industry-Science Research Alliance, acatech.

Kang, H.S., Lee, J.Y., Choi, S., Kim, H., Park, J.H., & Son, J.Y. (2016) "Smart manufacturing: Past research, present findings, and future directions." *International Journal of Precision Engineering and Manufacturing-Green Technology* 3(1): 111-128.

Kiel, D., Müller, J. M., Arnold, C., & Voigt, K. I. (2017). "Sustainable industrial value creation: Benefits and challenges of industry 4.0." *International journal of innovation management, 21*(08), 1740015.

Lasi, H., Fettke, P., Kemper, H.-G., Feld, T., & Hoffmann, M. (2014) "Industry 4.0." *Business & Information Systems Engineering* 6(4): 239-242.

Littig, B., & Griessler, E. (2005). Social sustainability. "A catchword between political pragmatism and social theory." *International Journal of Sustainable Development,* 8(1/2): 65-78.

McWilliams, A., Parhankangas, A., Coupet, J., Welch, E., & Barnum, D. T. (2016). "Strategic Decision Making for the Triple Bottom Line." *Business Strategy and the Environment,* 25(3): 193-204.

Müller, J. M. (2019). "Business model innovation in small-and medium-sized enterprises: Strategies for industry 4.0 providers and users." *Journal of Manufacturing Technology Management,* in press, available online.

Müller, J. M., Buliga, O., & Voigt, K. I. (2018). "Fortune favors the prepared: How SMEs approach business model innovations in Industry 4.0." *Technological Forecasting and Social Change,* 132: 2-17.

Müller, J. M., Kiel, D., & Voigt, K. I. (2018). "What drives the implementation of Industry 4.0? The role of opportunities and challenges in the context of sustainability." *Sustainability,* 10(1): 247.

Müller, J. M., & Voigt, K. I. (2018). "Sustainable Industrial Value Creation in SMEs: A Comparison between Industry 4.0 and Made in China 2025." *International Journal of Precision Engineering and Manufacturing-Green Technology,* 5(5): 659-670.

Müller, J., Dotzauer, V., & Voigt, K.-I. (2017) *Industry 4.0 and its Impact on Reshoring Decisions of German Manufacturing Enterprises.* In C. Bode, R. Bogaschewsky, M. Eßig, R. Lasch, & W. Stölzle (Eds.), Supply Management Research - Advanced Studies in Supply Management (pp. 165-179). Wiesbaden: Springer Gabler.

Norman, W., MacDonald, C., & Arnold, D. G. (2004). Getting to the Bottom of "Triple Bottom Line". *Business Ethics Quarterly,* 14(2): 243-262.

Oesterreich, T.D., & Teuteberg, F. (2016) "Understanding the implications of digitisation and automation in the context of Industry 4.0: A triangulation approach and elements of a research agenda for the construction industry." *Computers in Industry* 83: 121–139.

Peukert, B., Benecke, S., Clavell, J., Neugebauer, S., Nissen, N.F., Uhlmann, E., & et al. (2015) *Addressing Sustainability and Flexibility in Manufacturing Via Smart Modular Machine Tool Frames to Support Sustainable Value Creation.* Procedia CIRP 29: 514-519.

Porter, M.E., & Heppelmann, J.E. (2014). "How Smart Connected Products Are Transforming Competition." *Harvard Business Review,* 92(11): 64-88.

Qiu, X., Luo, H., Xu, G., Zhong, R., & Huang, G.Q. (2015) "Physical assets and service sharing for IoT-enabled Supply Hub in Industrial Park (SHIP)." *International Journal of Production Economics* 159: 4-15.

Sarkis, J., & Zhu, Q. (2017) "Environmental sustainability and production: taking the road less travelled." *International Journal of Production Research,* 56(1-2): 743-759.

Schuhmacher, J., & Hummel, V. (2016) *Decentralized Control of Logistic Processes in Cyber-physical Production Systems at the Example of ESB Logistics Learning Factory.* Procedia CIRP 54: 19-24.

Stock, T., & Seliger, G. (2016) *Opportunities of Sustainable Manufacturing in Industry 4.0.* Procedia CIRP 40: 536-541.

Tesch, J.F., Brillinger, A. S., & Bilgeri, D. (2017) "Internet of Things Business Model Innovation and the Stage-Gate Process: An Exploratory Analysis." *International Journal of Innovation Management* 21(5): 1740002.

Zhou, W., Piramuthu, S., Chu, F., & Chu, C. (2017) "RFID-enabled flexible warehousing." *Decision Support Systems* 98: 99-112.

Chapter 15

# Innovation and the Role of Problem Formulation: Capitalizing on the Potential of Collective Intellect for Value Creation

Marta Morais-Storz

*University of South-Eastern Norway, Norway*

**Abstract:** The emphasis on improving decision-making and problem solving within management literature points to the prevailing assumption that the context for which a decision is needed is self-evident and that the problems to be solved are well formulated. This may certainly be the case in a context characterised by stability or when problems are of a routine or operational kind. In a context characterized by volatility, uncertainly, complexity, and ambiguity (VUCA), however, and specifically within the context on innovation and the novelty that it entails, both the decision space as well as the actual boundaries and contents of the problem to be solved do not present themselves neatly delineated and ready for decision making or problem solving. Rather, the decision space and the problem to be solved must be formulated. Although there is research that proclaims the importance of problem formulation, it remains fragmented and lacking in empirical testing. This chapter is based on the dissertation of the same title that addresses the phenomena of problem formulation, and sheds light on how problem formulation unfolds, and on what characterizes the phenomena. In addition, the findings of the dissertation demonstrate how problem formulation—when conceptualized specifically as a strategic behavioural construct of top management teams—can be usefully gauged and demonstrated to have an important significance to organizational innovation outcomes.

**Keywords:** innovation; problem formulation; sensemaking; strategic resilience, organizational metamorphosis, unlearning; psychological safety; teams; leadership; top management teams.

## 15.1. Introduction

The significance of innovation lies in the practical value of satisfying society's unmet needs and in the visceral delight of transcending desires. Innovation defines organizational success, but most importantly, it continually re-defines and shapes the world we live in. Innovation is the result of how we solve problems, but also of the problems we choose to solve. Although some problems have seemingly obvious solutions—innovative or not—most problems of great importance have so many dimensions (technological, functional, ethical, political, environmental, aesthetic, et cetera) that no obvious solution exists. People must nevertheless formulate these problems in such a way as to guide action—however preliminary—to begin to solve them or to develop a greater understanding of their dimensions. How this is done (i.e. how problems are formulated) is consequential to the innovativeness of solutions and the value to society that those solutions create. In spite of this, management literature and arguably, practice, primarily emphasizes increasing the success rate, efficiency, and process of decision making and problem solving, subsuming problem formulation within these processes or taking for granted the representation of the decision space or problem as given.

The fundamental research question of the dissertation is: "How does problem formulation engender innovation, and what processes lead to formulating problems such that innovative solutions thrive?" A basic premise underlying this research question is that how we interpret the stimuli that drive action—how we formulate problems, opportunities, unmet needs or desires—determines the actions that we take, and that the actions that we take today shape our future and define who we are in that future. This is as true for an individual as it is for an organization or for society in general. Our interpretations, however, have limitations due to various biases and constraints that arise from assumptions that are shaped by both experience and lore, and tend to give primacy to the status quo. All knowledge is therefore derived from and based on these assumptions, that although are certainly useful when it comes to solving well-defined problems of an unambiguous nature, they can be hindrances in the context of novelty. In this dissertation, problem formulation is conceptualized as a team level mechanism to overcome these hindrances. By studying various facets of this phenomena, empirically and conceptually, this dissertation aims to (1) clarify how and why it unfolds, (2) make explicit what it entails relative to specific boundary conditions, and (3) measure its significance to innovative outcomes.

The dissertation is composed of five studies each of which explore a facet of the phenomena of problem formulation. The primary implication for practice, is that in a context of turbulence, complexity, and uncertainty, problem formulation (characterized by forward-looking, open and dialectic dialogue, where assumptions are surfaced, challenged, and revised) must be a deliberate practice. As such, management must not only nurture the sort of climate that is conducive to doing so, but also invest in efforts that it undoubtedly entails. The broader connections that emerged along the research journey of this dissertation also signal implications beyond the boundaries of the firm. Because the problems we chose to solve foreshadow our actions (how we solve those problems or what solutions we find for them), they inherently contribute to shaping our future. In addition, because our knowledge is imperfect (Popper, 2009) —we don't know what we don't know and what we do know may be difficult to put into words—"a process by which knowledge is constantly communicated and acquired" (Hayek, 1945, p. 530) is needed.

Problem formulation—as a process that is characterized by forward-looking, open and dialectic dialogue, where assumptions are surfaced, challenged, and revised—may hold the promise of hedging the fallibility of our knowledge (Miller & Tsang, 2011). In addition, by asserting the importance of a forward-looking perspective in problem formulation, a broader connection is made to resilience. Specifically, strategic resilience, as an emergent and dynamic characteristic of organizations, is manifest by the way organizations—and its members—formulate who or what they wish to become and the actions they take consequent to that endeavor. The point of the matter is that nurturing the processes that can engender innovation has repercussions beyond the short-term profit maximization or the competitive advantage of a focal firm. Rather, nurturing the processes that can engender innovation, has repercussions for value creation in the long-haul that can be captured not only by the focal firm and its members, but also by the communities in which they operate.

## 15.2. Background

Finding a solution to a problem is gratifying, and solutions that are deemed successful and innovative are directly attributed to the process of problem solving which serves as an unambiguous causal agent of performance. It is no wonder then that focus on improving problem solving (Newell & Simon, 1972) and solution search (Cohen, March, & Olsen, 1972) reigns strong in the management of innovation and strategy. This focus is certainly important, but in an effort to gain the satisfaction that comes from what is considered a successful resolution to a problem, people jump to solutions (Enders, Koenig, & Barsoux, 2016) as though the problems confronting them are unequivocally well defined. Problems, however, are inherently characterized by multidimensionality that stems from individual differences of interpretation (based on beliefs, values, and aspirations) of what constitutes a problem and what does not (Dillon, 1982). Therefore, problems require formulation, and when it comes to the management of innovation and strategy, how problems are formulated is consequential to the innovativeness of solutions and the value that they impart on society (Baer, Dirks, & Nickerson, 2013; Lyles & Mitroff, 1980).

The notion that the important problems of the world, and that the problems worth solving—that will create value—must be formulated, such that the formulation will drive action and search that will increase the odds of devising or finding an innovative solution, is not outlandish or foreign (Baer et al., 2013; Nickerson, Yen, & Mahoney, 2012). Organizations, teams, and individuals, however, struggle to embrace this notion, and in the process not only limit innovation but also repeatedly (and inadvertently) commit type three errors—i.e., they solve the wrong problem correctly (Lyles, 1981; Mitroff & Silvers, 2010). They struggle to embrace this notion not only because of the gratification and performance measurability of problem solving and solution finding, but also because of bounded rationality (Simon, 1945/1997) and the societally pathological primacy of the "fixed" performance-driven mindsets (Dweck, 2006). Both bounded rationality and the primacy of performance mindsets can lead to a simplified understanding of the true nature of problems. Because uncertainty and complexity can be paralyzing, given our bounded rationality, we attempt to "decompose" problems that may be non-decomposable (Simon, 1962), and in the process find solutions to the limited dimensions of the problem with which we are most familiar, without malice or ignorance, circumventing the complex, multifarious, and dynamic nature of important problems to the detriment of innovation.

Real-world problems that require innovative solutions are messy, value-laden, subject to interpretation, involve various stakeholders with various belief systems and motivations, and have many dimensions (technological, functional, ethical, political, environmental, aesthetic, et cetera). In addition, the outcomes of the solutions to those problems are beyond what anyone can predict, so formulating them is fraught with uncertainty. The incessant need to eradicate uncertainty (Mitroff & Silvers, 2010), however, has straightjacketed society and our thinking, and muzzled the beauty that is also inherent in complexity. In a quest for efficiency and control, by conceptualizing problems as given or well-defined, innovative practices may have lost touch with mechanisms that allow fruitful transgressions from predetermined trajectories and are a paradox to the very indeterminate nature of innovation.

As part of the dissertation upon which this chapter is based, an extensive literature review (Morais-Storz, 2019) on the topic of problem formulation reveals that although there is a recent up-tick in the literature concerning problem formulation, it remains fragmented over more than half a decade with research that espouses its significance but which has many different points of departure. For instance, there is literature that considers problem formulation as a dependent variable measured by the quality or quantity of problem statements generated (Buyukdamgaci, 2003; Nadler, Smith, & Frey, 1989; Volkema, 1983), and there are studies that consider problem formulation as an independent variable that is conceptualized as an ability (Reiter-Palmon, Mumford, Boes, & Runco, 1997; Reiter-Palmon, Mumford, & Threlfall, 1998) or skill (Mumford, Baughman, Victoria Threlfall, Supinski, & Costanza, 1996). In addition, the literature spans various fields (management strategy, certainly, but also operations, creativity, and education) using different terms (such as problem finding, problem definition, problem identification, and problem construction to name a few) and also with different levels of analysis. Among the studies that consider problem formulation at the individual level of analysis, problem formulation is conceptualized as an individual's attribute or ability (Basadur & Basadur, 2011; Csikszentmihalyi & Getzels, 1971; Okuda, Runco, & Berger, 1991), as a capability (Fontenot, 1993; Nadler et al., 1989; Volkema, 1983), as a cognitive construct (Cowan, 1990; Pounds, 1969; Smith, 1989), or as a behavioural construct (Foss, Frederiksen, & Rullani, 2015; Lyles & Mitroff, 1980; Nutt, 1993). Studies that consider problem formulation at the organizational level of analysis are few and ultimately tend to highlight the importance of communication, interaction, and coordination among individuals in formulating problems such that complexity can be reduced (McGuiness, 1990), a shared organizational vision can be created (Björkdahl & Linder, 2015), and how problems can be framed as opportunities for the organization (MacDuffie, 1997). When it comes to problem formulation at the team level of analysis the importance of closing representational gaps (Frishammar, Dahlskog, Krumlinde, & Yazgan, 2016) is highlighted, as is the importance of language (Volkema, 2009), the dialectic (Mitroff & Kilmann, 1977), and sensemaking (Gralla, Goentzel, & Fine, 2016) in the process of collective problem formulation.

In spite of the many strides within the literature on problem formulation, there are significant research gaps. To start, a large portion of the empirical studies have experimental research designs, and there is a dearth of empirical research designs that study the phenomena within real-world organizational settings. In addition, while problem formulation can be usefully studied at the individual, team, or organizational levels of analysis, more important still is a delineation in the research that outlines why a particular level of analysis is important when considering specific boundary conditions. Finally, there is a need to articulate what actually characterizes problem formulation in those specific boundary conditions, and how that characterization can be translated to a useful instrument that is determinant of specific organizational outcomes, such as innovation. The studies contained in the dissertation upon which this chapter is based contribute to bridging these gaps. First the boundary conditions are delineated by situating problem formulation as a key mechanism of innovation best achieve collectively (in teams), and second, a team level scale is developed that can be useful for gauging team behaviours—specifically that of top-management-teams—and which was tested and shown to influence organizational outcomes (innovativeness).

## 15.3. Research design

Studying the various facets of the phenomena of problem formulation entailed a multifarious research design that was organized along five different research papers. The first paper of this dissertation comprises a literature review (Morais-Storz, 2019) with the aim to understand how others have studied the phenomena of problem formulation and to determine what their research has to say about the role of problem formulation in organizational performance and innovativeness. The findings of this literature review highlight the relevance of the phenomena of problem formulation (along with various associated terms) in diverse fields, such as creativity, education, operations management, and of course, strategic management and innovation, and reveal the strides that have been made in articulating a useful theory for its application as well as the gaps. Although lauded in the literature, the review showed that the empirical research on problem formulation is underdeveloped and represents a research wellspring with great potential.

Driven by the assumption that a shift in action requires a shift in problem representation (or in the interpretation of a stimulus), and that the most forceful trigger to such a shift is crisis or failure, the second paper (Morais-Storz, Nguyen, & Sætre, 2017) of this dissertation sought to answer the question of "How do problem representations come to be changed in the face of failure?" with the specific aim to understand how problem formulation unfolds. This paper entails a qualitative case-research methodology based primarily on team-member interviews. Data comprised four case studies of innovation projects in three Norwegian organizations. These case studies were based on twenty-five in-depth interviews and archival data that included product catalogues, internal documents, presentations, and company websites. The findings of this paper reveal that in the face of failure, problem representations come to be changed by process of problem formulation that is characterized by sensemaking that is both retrospective and prospective. In addition, the findings suggest that leadership behaviors that encourage change as well as the clarity of the initial problem representation determined the team's ability to engage in prospective sensemaking which is key to problem re-formulation that ultimately precedes success post-failure.

The importance of letting go of outdated or inadequate problem representations in order to formulate new ones that could help shift trajectories and actions, motivated the research question of "How can unlearning drive organizational metamorphosis toward strategic resilience without the pain and demoralization of crisis?" that is the focus of the third paper (Morais-Storz & Nguyen, 2017). This paper considers how organizations shape their mission (who they are and want to become) and builds on the understanding that in order to learn—i.e. revise assumptions—unlearning is needed. In this conceptual paper, it is proposed that problem formulation—considered at the top-management-team level as a deliberate process where assumptions are challenged and revised—is a key mechanism to the dynamic cycle of organizational learning and unlearning that is necessary for the proactive metamorphosis which thwarts organizational death and increases the odds of resilience.

The fourth paper builds on the previous study by articulating what is meant by strategic resilience in a context of turbulence, complexity, and uncertainty (Morais-Storz, Stoud Platou, & Berild Norheim, 2018). Given this context, in this conceptual paper, it is proposed that strategic resilience is most usefully conceptualized as an emergent and dynamic characteristic of organizations that can be defined in terms of the rate and consistency in which innovation leads to value creating strategic metamorphoses. Problem formulation is conceptualized as a key mechanism of innovation that engenders metamorphosis, and belief systems and antecedents that can either hinder or bolster it are proposed.

Whereas paper 1 informed understanding of how the phenomena of problem formulation has been studied to date and the gaps that remain to further its understanding for the purpose of deploying it usefully in organizations and teams, and paper 2 provided empirical insights about how problem formulation unfolds and about how it is or is not successfully deployed post failure, papers 3 and 4 served as thought trials focused on the organizational level of analysis that helped shape the stance towards what is suggested in paper 5 (Morais-Storz, Sætre, & Edmondson, 2018) to be the nature of strategic problem formulation and its role to organizational innovativeness. As such, the fifth paper of this dissertation asks "What is the role of strategic problem formulation in organizational innovativeness?" and in order to answer this question, a strategic problem formulation scale is developed and validated. This paper entails both qualitative and quantitative methods in the development and validation of the scale. The scale development portion of this study revealed three dimensions of problem formulation that are particularly important in the context of strategic problems, namely, comprehensiveness, active dialogue, and strategic intent, and the items developed and used in the validation of the scale reflect this tri-partite dimensionality.

The hypothesized relationships tested as part of this study comprised psychological safety (Edmondson, 1999) as the independent variable, strategic problem formulation as the mediating variable, and organizational innovativeness (Ruvio, Shoham, Vigoda-Gadot, & Schwabsky, 2014) as the dependent variable, where the unit of analysis is the top management team, and the level of analysis is the organization. The sample consisted of 309 Norwegian industry top-management teams. The findings of this study provide further support for the importance of psychological safety to innovation, but also reveal that a conducive context alone is not enough for innovation, because strategic problem formulation—and the behaviours it entails—provide crucial mediation. More to the point, this study sheds light on the practical usefulness of problem formulation at the strategic level that can be manipulated (Cook, Campbell, & Shadish, 2002) such that it influences organizational outcomes.

## 15.4. Conclusion

The primary implication of the findings contained in this dissertation is that how we formulate problems holds the promise of increasing the odds of success by engendering innovative solutions. In addition, in in a context of volatility, uncertainty, complexity, and ambiguity, problem formulation (characterized by forward-looking, open and dialectic dialogue, where assumptions are surfaced, challenged, and revised) must be a deliberate practice. The emphasis on problem solving and the penchant for jumping to solutions makes a deliberate process of problem formulation a hard sell. Problem formulation—and specifically strategic problem formulation which pertains to devising a representation for who the company wants to be and what problems it will choose to solve—is effortful and costly. The studies contained within this dissertation, and in particular paper 5 (Morais-Storz, Sætre, et al., 2018), suggest and demonstrate that when it comes to innovative outcomes, it is worth the effort.

In addition to empirically demonstrating (paper 2 and 5) the benefit of problem formulation, the findings of this dissertation suggest that the behaviours attributed to strategic problem formulation matter to innovative outcomes. In particular, comprehensiveness in communication, active dialogue, and a future-oriented outlook in formulating the decision space and problems to be solved, are defining of the process of problem formulation in successful teams. The implication is that teams (and specifically top-management-teams) must attempt to be exhaustive (Fredrickson, 1984; Fredrickson & Mitchell, 1984) in considering diverse perspectives (Baer et al., 2013) such that various dimensions and potential stakeholders are addressed. The implication is also that problem formulation requires a context of psychological safety (Edmondson, 1999) where team members can actively engage in debate (Hewing, 2014; Mitroff & Emshoff, 1979) and be able to expose to collective reflection and critique individually held assumptions (Lyles, 1981; Schwenk & Thomas, 1983). Lastly, because strategic problem formulation figures prominently "in determining the future direction of the organization" (Lyles, 1981, p. 74), it must be characterized by a forward-looking and future-oriented lens that considers how the problems formulated today can confer competitive advantage tomorrow (Heiman, Nickerson, & Zenger, 2009).

## 15.5. Implications and future research

This dissertation contributes to the emergent research perspectives that highlight the importance of problem formulation (Heiman et al., 2009; Nickerson, Silverman, & Zenger, 2007; Nickerson et al., 2012) to value creation, demonstrating via empirical evidence, in particular, that problem formulation is key to success post failure—paper 2—(Morais-Storz et al., 2017), and that strategic problem formulation is key to variance in organizational level performance outcomes—paper 5—(Morais-Storz, Sætre, et al., 2018). Additionally, through conceptual analysis—papers 3 and 4 (Morais-Storz & Nguyen, 2017; Morais-Storz, Stoud Platou, et al., 2018)—this dissertation makes the link between problem formulation and the broader outcome of resilience, suggesting that it is mediated by innovation and metamorphoses. Making this link to resilience—innovation and metamorphoses—implicates the role of change and "unlearning" (Starbuck, 2017; Tsang & Zahra, 2008), the letting go of routines, assumptions, and beliefs that are no longer adequate or valid in the changing circumstances within which the organization finds itself. By extension, this link highlights the importance of a "growth mindset" (Dweck, 2006), and suggests that learning is not simply triggered reactively by crises, but that it can be developed proactively in anticipation of inevitable change.

While the findings of this dissertation suggest that psychological safety is an antecedent of the behaviours conducive to problem formulation, future research should explore other possible antecedents—both the barriers and enablers. For example, while research has suggested an inverted U-shape relationship between slack and innovation in organizations, it is possible that that relationship is mediated by problem formulation, in the sense that some resource slack is needed for teams to adequately engage in strategic problem formulation. Because the empirical setting of the studies contained in this dissertation is limited to Norway where the industry is marked by flat organizational structures, future research is encouraged to expand the research on strategic problem formulation in other contexts. This will facilitate further construct validity and reliability of the proposed strategic problem formulation scale of this dissertation (paper 5). Lastly, future research that is longitudinal in design is needed to go beyond the snapshot understanding of the phenomena of problem formulation that is possible with cross-sectional data, and demonstrate how problem formulation plays out in teams over time and demonstrate its consequences relative to the long-term performance of organizations.

## References

Baer, M., Dirks, K. T., & Nickerson, J. A. (2013). "Microfoundations of strategic problem formulation." *Strategic Management Journal, 34*(2), 197-214.

Basadur, M., & Basadur, T. (2011). "Where Are the Generators?" *Psychology of Aesthetics, Creativity, and the Arts, 5*(1), 29-42.

Björkdahl, J., & Linder, M. (2015). "Formulating problems for commercializing new technologies: The case of environmental innovation." *Scandinavian Journal of Management, 31*(1), 14-24.

Buyukdamgaci, G. (2003). "Process of organizational problem definition: how to evaluate and how to improve." *Omega-International Journal of Management Science, 31*(4), 327-338.

Cohen, M. D., March, J. G., & Olsen, J. P. (1972). "A Garbage Can Model of Organizational Choice." *Administrative Science Quarterly, 17*(1), 1-25.

Cook, T. D., Campbell, D. T., & Shadish, W. (2002). *Experimental and quasi-experimental designs for generalized causal inference.* Boston: Houghton Mifflin.

Cowan, D. A. (1990). "Developing a Classification Structure of Organizational Problems: An Empirical Investigation." *The Academy of Management Journal, 33*(2), 366-390.

Csikszentmihalyi, M., & Getzels, J. W. (1971). "Discovery-oriented behavior and the originality of creative products: A study with artists." *Journal of Personality and Social Psychology, 19*(1), 47-52.

Dillon, J. T. (1982). "Problem Finding and Solving." *Journal of Creative Behavior, 16*(2), 97-111.

Dweck, C. S. (2006). *Mindset: The New Psychology of Success.* (Random House, Inc.. Kindle Edition.).

Edmondson, A. C. (1999). "Psychological Safety and Learning Behavior in Work Teams." *Administrative Science Quarterly, 44*(2).

Enders, A., Koenig, A., & Barsoux, J.-L. (2016). "Stop Jumping to Solutions." *MIT Sloan Management Review, 57*(4), 62-70.

Fontenot, N. A. (1993). "Effects of training in creativity and creative problem finding upon business people." *Journal of Social Psychology, 133*(1), 11-22.

Foss, N. j., Frederiksen, L., & Rullani, F. (2015). "Problem-formulation and problem-solving in self-organized communities: How modes of communication shape project behaviors in the free open-source software community." *Strategic Management Journal, 37*(13), 2589-2610.

Fredrickson, J. W. (1984). "The Comprehensiveness of Strategic Decision Processes: Extension, Observations, Future Directions." *The Academy of Management Journal, 27*(3), 445-466.

Fredrickson, J. W., & Mitchell, T. R. (1984). "Strategic Decision Processes: Comprehensiveness and Performance in an Industry with an Unstable Environment." *The Academy of Management Journal, 27*(2), 399-423.

Frishammar, J., Dahlskog, E., Krumlinde, C., & Yazgan, K. (2016). "The Front End of Radical Innovation: A Case Study of Idea and Concept Development at Prime Group." *Creativity and Innovation Management, 25*(2), 179-198.

Gralla, E., Goentzel, J., & Fine, C. (2016). "Problem Formulation and Solution Mechanisms: A Behavioral Study of Humanitarian Transportation Planning." *Production and Operations Management, 25*(1), 22-35.

Hayek, F. A. (1945). "The use of knowledge in society." *The American Economic Review, 35*(4), 519 -530.

Heiman, B., Nickerson, J. A., & Zenger, T. R. (2009). "Governing Knowledge Creation: A Problem-Finding and Problem-Solving Perspective." In N. J. Foss & S. Michailova (Eds.), *Knowledge Governance: Processes and Perspectives* (pp. 25-46). London: Oxford University Press.

Hewing, M. (2014). "The playful ingenuity of potential users in collaboration: Enriched compensation and improvisation." In *Collaboration with Potential Users for Discontinuous Innovation: Experimental Research on User Creativity* (pp. 103-149).

Lyles, M. A. (1981). "Formulating strategic problems: Empirical analysis and model development." *Strategic Management Journal, 2*(1), 61-75.

Lyles, M. A., & Mitroff, I. I. (1980). "Organizational Problem Formulation: An Empirical Study." *Administrative Science Quarterly, 25*(1), 102-119.

MacDuffie, J. P. (1997). "Road to 'root cause': shop-floor problem-solving at three auto assembly plants." *Management Science, 43*(4), 479-502.

McGuiness, N. (1990). "New product idea activities in large technology based firms." *Journal of Product Innovation Management, 7*(3), 173-185.

Miller, K. D., & Tsang, E. W. K. (2011). "Testing management theories: critical realist philosophy and research methods." *Strategic Management Journal, 32*(2), 139-158.

Mitroff, I. I., & Emshoff, J. R. (1979). "On Strategic Assumption-Making: A Dialectical Approach to Policy and Planning." *The Academy of Management Review, 4*(1), 1-12.

Mitroff, I. I., & Kilmann, R. H. (1977). "Teaching Managers to Do Policy Analysis: The Case of Corporate Bribery." *California Management Review, 20*(1), 47-54.

Mitroff, I. I., & Silvers, A. (2010). *Dirty rotten strategies: How we trick ourselves and others into solving the wrong problems precisely.* Stanford, CA: Stanford University Press.

Morais-Storz, M. (2019). "Problem formulation and its role in innovation and organizational performance: a literature review." *working paper.*

Morais-Storz, M., & Nguyen, N. (2017). "The role of unlearning in metamorphosis and strategic resilience." *The Learning Organization, 24*(2), 93-106.

Morais-Storz, M., Nguyen, N., & Sætre, A. S. (2017). "Success post failure: The role of sensemaking in problem representation re-formulation." *Working paper (in-review).*

Morais-Storz, M., Sætre, A. S., & Edmondson, A. C. (2018). “Unpacking Strategic Problem Formulation in Top Management Teams.” *Working-paper.*

Morais-Storz, M., Stoud Platou, R., & Berild Norheim, K. (2018). “Innovation and metamorphosis towards strategic resilience.” *International Journal of Entrepreneurial Behavior & Research, 24*(7), 1181-1199.

Mumford, M. D., Baughman, W. A., Victoria Threlfall, K., Supinski, E. P., & Costanza, D. P. (1996). “Process-based measures of creative problem-solving skills: I. Problem construction.” *Creativity Research Journal, 9*(1), 63-76.

Nadler, G., Smith, J. M., & Frey, C. E. (1989). “Research needs regarding formulation of the initial design problem.” *Design Studies, 10*(3), 151-154.

Newell, A., & Simon, H. A. (1972). *Human problem solving.* Englewood Cliffs, NJ: Prentice-Hall.

Nickerson, J. A., Silverman, B. S., & Zenger, T. R. (2007). “The ‘problem’ of creating and capturing value.” *Strategic Organization, 5*(3), 211-225.

Nickerson, J. A., Yen, C. J., & Mahoney, J. T. (2012). “Exploring the Problem-Finding and Problem-Solving Approach for Designing Organizations.” *Academy of Management Perspectives, 26*(1), 52-72.

Nutt, P. C. (1993). “The Formulation Processes and Tactics Used in Organizational Decision Making.” *Organization Science, 4*(2), 226-251.

Okuda, S. M., Runco, M. A., & Berger, D. E. (1991). “Creativity and the finding and solving of real-world problems.” *Journal of Psychoeducational Assessment, 9*(1), 45-53.

Popper, K. (2009). *All life is problem solving.* New York, NY: Digital Printing.

Pounds, W. F. (1969). “The Process of Problem Finding.” *Industrial Management Review, 11*(1), 1-19.

Reiter-Palmon, R., Mumford, M. D., Boes, J. O., & Runco, M. A. (1997). “Problem construction and creativity: The role of ability, cue consistency, and active processing.” *Creativity Research Journal, 10*(1), 9-23.

Reiter-Palmon, R., Mumford, M. D., & Threlfall, K. V. (1998). “Solving everyday problems creatively: The role of problem construction and personality type.” *Creativity Research Journal, 11*(3), 187-197.

Ruvio, A. A., Shoham, A., Vigoda-Gadot, E., & Schwabsky, N. (2014). “Organizational Innovativeness: Construct Development and Cross-Cultural Validation.” *Journal of Product Innovation Management, 31*(5), 1004-1022.

Schwenk, C. R., & Thomas, H. (1983). “Formulating the mess: The role of decision aids in problem formulation.” *Omega, 11*(3), 239-252.

Simon, H. A. (1962). “The architecture of complexity.” *Proceedings of the American Philosophical Society, 106*(6), 467-482.

Simon, H. A. (1997). *Administrative Behavior* (Fourth ed.). New York, NY: Free Press.

Smith, G. F. (1989). “Managerial problem identification.” *Omega, 17*(1), 27-36.

Starbuck, W. H. (2017). “Organizational learning and unlearning.” *The Learning Organization, 24*(1), 30-38.

Tsang, E. W. K., & Zahra, S. A. (2008). “Organizational unlearning.” *Human Relations, 61*(10), 1435-1462.

Volkema, R. J. (1983). "Problem Formulation in Planning and Design." *Management Science, 29*(6), 639-652.

Volkema, R. J. (2009). "Natural language and the art and science of problem/opportunity formulation: a transportation planning case analysis." *Journal of the Operational Research Society, 60*(10), 1360-1372.

Chapter 16

# Exploring the Effects of Organisational Culture on Innovation: A Mixed-Methods Study of Multinational Subsidiaries in the Irish ICT Sector

Frauke Wolf

*Trinity College Dublin, Ireland*

**Abstract:** This research explores how organisational culture affects innovation in subsidiaries of multinational corporations (MNCs) in the Irish information and communications technology (ICT) sector. This research seeks to conceptualise a supportive organisational culture in a subsidiary as an antecedent to innovation at the subsidiary level. A sequential explanatory mixed methods research design was employed, consisting of a quantitative survey followed by semi-structured interviews with top management in selected subsidiaries in the Irish ICT sector. The findings indicate that organisational culture represents a significant influence on innovation in subsidiaries. The level of subsidiary innovation was also found to be affected by organisational systems and processes designed to support innovation, other organisational determinants, such as management support, and the headquarters subsidiary relationship.

**Keywords:** Innovation; Organisational Culture; Subsidiaries; Multinationals; Ireland; ICT Sector; Mixed Methods; Survey; Interviews.

## 16.1. Introduction

This research explores how organisational culture affects innovation in subsidiaries of multinational corporations (MNCs) in the Irish information and communications technology (ICT) sector. Much recent discourse has highlighted the supporting role of organisational culture in regard to stimulating innovation, which has culminated in the emergence of the concept of innovation-supportive culture (Jassawalla and Sashittal, 2002). An innovation-supportive culture is indicated by initiative-taking, creativity, risk-taking, mutual trust, early involvement, receptivity to change, autonomy, collaboration, and feedback-seeking (Jassawalla and Sashittal, 2002). Whereas it is recognised that organisational culture has an impact on the level of innovation in an organisation and can either support or hinder innovation implementation (Ahmed, 1998; Jassawalla and Sashittal, 2002), little is known about this association in the context of the multinational subsidiary. According to Birkinshaw et al. (1998), an entrepreneurial culture in subsidiaries supports subsidiary initiative and in turn supports innovation. A strand of literature focusing on entrepreneurial subsidiaries based on research conducted on Scottish and other UK MNC subsidiaries is emerging (see Boojihawon et al., 2007).

A number of previous studies have reported that organisational culture is important in regard to innovation (Amabile et al., 1996; Angle, 2000; Jassawalla and Sashittal, 2002; Kanter, 1984, 1988; O'Reilly et al., 1991; van der Panne et al., 2003). This importance stems from organisational culture's instrumental role in guiding behaviour and the potential support or inhibition of innovation (Ahmed, 1998). In fact, organisational culture has been found to influence innovation in a number of ways: Firstly, through the process of socialisation and through basic values, assumptions and beliefs that become a guide for preferred behaviours; Secondly, by emphasising behaviours indicative of an innovation-supportive culture, such as creativity, risk-taking, freedom, teamwork, communication, and encouragement of trust and respect (Dobni, 2008); Thirdly, by providing a coordination function (Martins and Terblanche, 2003). This coordination function can offer a competitive advantage and present a sense-making mechanism regarding acceptable behaviour and social system stability. Finally, based on the arguments laid out above, organisational culture can be considered an antecedent of innovation. Thus, organisational culture at the subsidiary level can be thought of as an antecedent of subsidiary innovation. This study aims to answer calls for an investigation of innovation-supportive culture at the subsidiary level (Birkinshaw, 1997; Birkinshaw et al., 1998). Further, this study addresses some of the criticism that previous innovativeness research has been subject to. Previous research in this area has either focused on a single dimension of organisational culture or a single form of innovation (see Dobni, 2008). This study utilises a multidimensional construct of innovation-supportive organisational culture and explores the effects of organisational culture on four different forms of innovation.

Knowledge and understanding of the organisational culture dimensions that affect innovation at the subsidiary level may provide additional insight into the construct of innovation-supportive culture as well as into the unique subsidiary-related factors that may affect this relationship. This becomes especially important in the context of Ireland, which is considered a highly globalised economy that has also been characterised as the "most MNC-dependent economy in the EU" (Gunnigle et al., 2005). Ireland has reached this position due to a focus on attracting Foreign Direct Investment (FDI) which has been fundamental to its economic policy for several decades (Collings et al., 2008). The Industrial Development Agency (IDA) placed a strong emphasis on the ICT sector as one of the focus areas for investment promotion (Department of Jobs, Enterprise and Innovation, 2014), which explains the strong presence of ICT firms in Ireland. The ICT sector plays a central role in the world economy, the EU economy and the EU's economic recovery, as confirmed by its pervasive impact, its inherent R&D magnitude and intensity, its innovation performance and global dynamics (Turlea et al., 2010). Thus, Ireland and its ICT sector present a compelling context in which to investigate the influence of organisational culture on innovation in multinational subsidiaries. This focus has led to the development of the following research questions for this study.

For the first, quantitative phase of this study the guiding research question was:

What dimensions of organisational culture predict the number of innovations implemented in multinational subsidiaries in the Irish ICT sector?

The hypotheses and sub-hypotheses tested in Phase One were:

*$H1_0$: The more the organisational culture emphasises specific dimensions of an innovative culture, the higher the presence of innovation.*

*$H2_0$: The relationship of innovation to organisational culture differs for specific forms of innovation.*

*$H2_a$: Organisational culture has an influence on product innovation.*

*$H2_b$: Organisational culture has an influence on process innovation.*

*$H2_c$: Organisational culture has an influence on marketing innovation.*

*$H2_d$: Organisational culture has an influence on organisational innovation.*

*$H3_0$: Organisational culture has an influence on innovation generation.*

For the second, qualitative phase of this study, the overarching research questions were:

What are subsidiary management's perceptions of innovation-supportive organisational culture dimensions?

What influences the relationship between organisational culture and innovation in multinational subsidiaries in the Irish ICT sector?

The questions for the second phase of the study were formulated after the completion of the first, quantitative phase of this study and were grounded in the results of the statistical tests that were undertaken in that phase.

## 16.2. Background

Until recently, innovation had mainly been considered as a process or a sequence of activities and factors that may impact innovation, such as an organisational culture for innovation, had only been acknowledged to some degree (Meissner and Kotsemir, 2016). This demonstrated a strong tendency in the innovation management literature to view innovation as manageable by an innovation process that can be structured to a certain extent (Meissner and Sprenger, 2010). This trend resulted in an increased number of attempts to employ linear innovation processes – either derived from literature or from practice. Examples of this approach are innovation process models such as the Cooper Stage-Gate-Model (Cooper, 1990), the Funnel Model (Terwiesch and Ulrich, 2009), or the Open Innovation Process Model (Chesbrough, 2006). Whereas this approach presents easy to follow models of the innovation process, it does not provide a way of dealing with innovation dynamics that are not captured or regulated by a process model. These models make little to no attempt to consider the social determinants of the innovation process. Models such as the Schein Culture Model (Schein, 2009), the Sackmann Iceberg Model (Sackmann, 1991), or the Want Corporate Culture Hierarchy (Want, 2003) explain the relevance of implicit and not easily observable influences on innovation within organisations. Tacit knowledge held by organisational members is expressed in behaviours and the organisational culture (Nonaka and Takeuchi, 1995). Organisational members' beliefs and assumptions about innovation can have a substantial influence on the social processing of innovation projects. So, even when it is not explicitly considered, organisational culture can have a strong influence on the innovation process (Meissner and Sprenger, 2010).

An understanding of the relationship between organisational culture and innovation has become central for MNCs and their subsidiaries as an increased pressure to innovate means that MNCs are increasingly dependent on their subsidiaries, where much of the innovative capabilities reside (Lind and Kang, 2011). If a subsidiary is actively involved in the innovation process, the MNC can leverage these innovations on a global basis, which can serve to enhance the global competitiveness of the firm (Keupp and Gassmann, 2009; Venaik et al., 2005). Innovative subsidiaries then become a potentially important source of competitive advantage for the MNC (Frost, 2001).

Even though several studies have been undertaken to examine the link between organisational culture and innovation (e.g. Amabile et al., 1996; Damanpour, 1991; Lumpkin and Dess, 1996), the concept of an innovation-supportive culture is relatively new to the innovation literature. While a general definition of an innovation-supportive culture does not exist, a convergence of organisational culture dimensions that have been identified as supporting innovation can be noted. These dimensions of organisational culture are autonomy and teamwork, support for change, risk-taking, trust and openness, and constructive conflict. While these organisational culture dimensions have consistently been identified as being supportive of innovation, previous studies into the relationship between organisational culture and innovation are somewhat fragmented. Innovativeness research to date has largely been of an uni-dimensional nature, focusing on either one dimension of organisational culture and its effect on innovation (e.g. De Dreu, 2006; Hoegl and Gemuenden, 2001) or on a specific form or magnitude of innovation (e.g. Khazanchi et al., 2007; Tellis et al., 2009). However, due to the complex nature of innovation, a more multidimensional view is called for and a number of multidimensional constructs and frameworks have been introduced in more recent years (Crossan and Apaydin, 2010; Dobni, 2008; Prajogo and McDermott, 2011). While the above studies deliver valuable insights into the linkages between organisational culture and innovation, they leave some key research questions unanswered. This study, therefore, set out to apply a multidimensional research model derived from the reviewed literature. This multidimensional approach combined the aspects of organisational culture and innovation with a specific emphasis on five dimensions of organisational culture, incorporating the four major forms of innovation.

## 16.3. Research design

Owing to the topic being investigated, a mixed methods research design was deemed most appropriate. A sequential explanatory mixed methods research design was adopted for this study, consisting of a first, quantitative phase followed by a second, qualitative phase. This research design allows for the organisational culture dimensions to be tested with a large sample in the quantitative phase and a more in-depth exploration of cases to be undertaken during the qualitative phase. In the first, quantitative phase of the study, the research question centred on how five selected organisational culture dimensions served as predictors of innovation in multinational subsidiaries. Three hypotheses and their corresponding sub-hypotheses were tested using univariate and multivariate analysis methods. In the second, qualitative phase, four interviews were undertaken to allow a deeper insight into the results from the statistical tests. The quantitative and qualitative methods were connected during the intermediate phase of the research process. The selection of participants for the interview as well as the development of the interview guide for the qualitative data collection was based on the results of the statistical tests undertaken in the first, quantitative phase. The findings of the two phases were also further integrated into the discussion of the study outcomes.

**Quantitative Phase**

In the first, quantitative phase, data was collected using a self-administered web-based survey. The design of the survey instrument was based on several instruments pre-existing in the literature. All survey questions utilised a 5-point Likert scale. Three hypotheses and their respective sub-hypotheses were tested to examine the relationships and differences between the different forms of innovation, and participants' perceptions of their organisational culture with a focus on five specific dimensions. The hierarchical regression analyses identified a number of organisational culture dimensions that significantly impacted the total number of innovations as well as the number of product, process, organisational, and marketing innovations. Based on the results of the first, quantitative phase, an interview guide was developed and participants for the qualitative in-depth study were selected. To aid the selection of participants for the qualitative phase, results from the first phase were segmented and respondent subsidiaries were classified into three different categories (low, medium, and high), depending on the total number of innovations implemented.

**Qualitative Phase**

In the second, qualitative phase, data was collected using in-depth semi-structured interviews. The selection of the four interview participants was grounded in the results from the first phase (two from the low total innovation category, one from the medium total innovation category and one from the high total innovation category, reflecting the proportionate distribution of the number of total innovations within the subsidiary sample). Additional documentary information was collated from company records and from newspapers and government reports. Qualitative data for the study consisted of transcribed interviews which were analysed with a thematic analysis approach using MAXQDA software. The five organisational culture dimensions were largely supported by the perceptions of an innovation-supportive culture displayed in the interviews. Three factors affected the relationship between organisational culture and innovation and are reflected in the themes that emerged from the qualitative analysis: 1) innovation-supportive organisational systems and processes, 2) other organisational determinants, and 3) the headquarters subsidiary relationship.

Based on the findings from the quantitative and qualitative phase of this study, a preliminary model of innovation-supportive culture in multinational subsidiaries was developed, which includes factors internal and external to the subsidiary that affect an innovation-supportive culture.

## 16.4. Conclusion

The findings indicate that the five organisational culture dimensions investigated in this study, autonomy and teamwork, risk-taking, support for change, trust and openness, and constructive conflict, differentially affected innovation in the subsidiary. The organisational culture dimensions support for change, risk-taking, and trust and openness had a significant impact on the total number of innovations. Support for change and trust and openness also had significant predictive power on the number of product innovations implemented. Only one of the five organisational culture dimensions, risk-taking, had a positive impact on the number of process innovations implemented. For marketing innovation, only the control variable, subsidiary age, had significant predictive power. For organisational innovation, none of the five organisational culture dimensions had significant predictive power. Overall, organisational culture was found to represent a significant influence on innovation in subsidiaries. The relationship between organisational culture and innovation in subsidiaries, as well as the level of subsidiary innovation, is influenced by three key factors. These are 1) organisational systems and processes designed to support innovation, 2) other organisational determinants, such as the organisational structure and management support, and 3) the headquarters subsidiary relationship.

Based on the findings from the quantitative and qualitative phases of this study, the preliminary model of innovation-supportive culture in multinational subsidiaries was developed (Figure 16.1). This model represents a first attempt at understanding the internal and external factors that support or impede an innovation-supportive culture in multinational subsidiaries in the Irish ICT sector.

Considering the factors internal to the subsidiary first, the solid boxes in Figure 16.1 represent the core concepts of organisational culture and innovation and the solid arrow line represents the effects of the five dimensions of organisational culture on the level of innovation in subsidiaries. Organisational culture comprises the dimensions of autonomy and teamwork, support for change, risk-taking, trust and openness, and constructive conflict. The broken box outlines represent four factors internal to the subsidiary that arose in the quantitative phase of the study: organizational structure, subsidiary initiative, subsidiary mandate and subsidiary autonomy. Broken arrow lines indicate the effects these were found to have on the relationship between organisational culture and innovation as well as the level of innovation at the subsidiary.

**Figure 16.1:** Model of Innovation-Supportive Culture in Subsidiaries

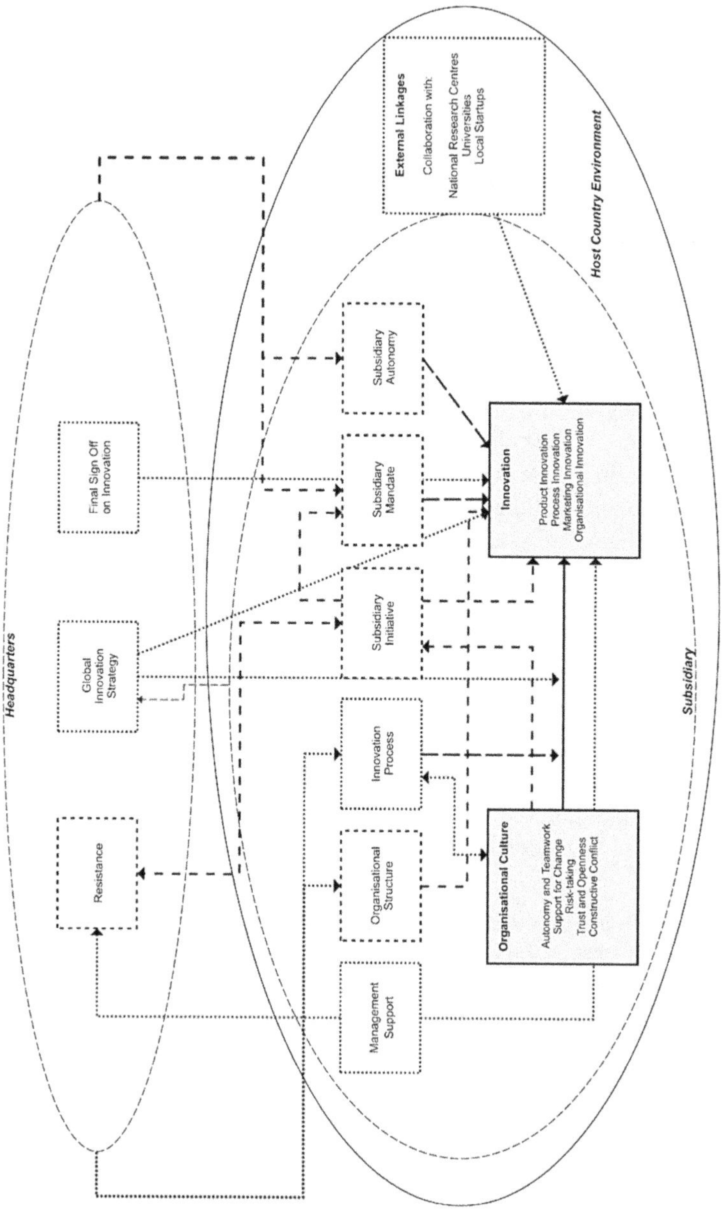

Additional factors internal to the subsidiary, such as management support and the nature of the innovation process, were added to the model following the qualitative phase, having been found to influence the relationship between organisational culture and innovation in the subsidiary as well as the total level of subsidiary innovation. Dotted outlines highlight these factors in the model and dotted arrow lines represent the effects of these factors on the relationship between organisational culture and innovation as well as the level of innovation at the subsidiary.

As the subsidiary forms part of the overall MNC network, headquarters also presents an influence on the subsidiary's innovation dynamics. Headquarters resistance emerged as a result of the quantitative phase of the research and is therefore represented by broken outlines and its effects are depicted by a broken arrow line. Two additional factors, the formulation of a global innovation strategy and the final sign-off on innovation, were added following the qualitative phase. These factors are shown in dotted outlines and their influences are represented by dotted arrow lines.

Having considered the influences internal to the subsidiary and the headquarters subsidiary relationship, the influences of the host country environment were added to the model following the qualitative phase of this study. A subsidiary operates within the host country environment and several linkages with this environment influence the level of subsidiary innovation. Subsidiaries in the study generally engaged in collaboration with institutions in the local environment. These ranged from national research centres and universities to local start-ups. The collaborations were undertaken to expand the subsidiaries' knowledge and capabilities, often with a view to ultimately extending the subsidiary mandate.

The factors laid out in stages in the preceding sections were combined into a full model of innovation-supportive culture in subsidiaries (Figure 16.1). This model is a first attempt at understanding the internal and external factors that support or impede an innovation-supportive culture in multinational subsidiaries in the Irish ICT sector. This study was limited to a specific sector and included a limited number of organisational culture dimensions. Additional research is required to validate and extend these findings to develop a reliable model of innovation-supportive culture in multinational subsidiaries.

## 16.5. Implications and future research

### Theoretical and methodological implications

This study contributes to the somewhat underdeveloped area of innovation-supportive culture in multinational subsidiaries. Whereas it is generally accepted that organisational culture impacts the level of innovation in an organisation and can either support or hinder the implementation of innovations (Ahmed, 1998; Jassawalla and Sashittal, 2002), little is known about this relationship in the context of the multinational subsidiary. An enhanced understanding of the organisational culture dimensions that affect innovation at the subsidiary level may provide deeper insights into the construct of innovation-supportive culture as well as the unique subsidiary-related factors that may affect the organisational culture-innovation relationship.

The findings from this study make several contributions to the current literature. First, from an international business perspective, this study addresses the dearth of research on entrepreneurship in the multinational subsidiary (Birkinshaw, 1997; Birkinshaw et al., 2005), with a focus on innovation-supportive culture in subsidiaries. This study has shown that a subsidiary's organisational culture represents an important influence on the level of innovation undertaken in the subsidiary and has identified key contextual elements of this relationship. This work extends the concept of an innovation-supportive culture to the level of the subsidiary. Second, the multidimensional approach adopted in this study presents an important contribution to the mainly uni-dimensional domain of innovativeness research. This uni-dimensionality has been one of the main criticisms of prior innovation studies (Dobni, 2008; Read, 2000). This study has taken a finer-grained approach to investigating the relationship between organisational culture and innovation by employing a multidimensional approach that determined the effect of five organisational culture dimensions on four different forms of innovation. This approach has shown that multiple organisational culture dimensions simultaneously affect innovation and that the effect of organisational culture on innovation depends on the form of innovation being studied. By doing so, this study has indicated the need for future research to consider multiple organisational culture dimensions and/or multiple forms of innovation. In the absence of a theoretical framework of innovation-supportive culture in subsidiaries, this work has provided such a model following the integration of the quantitative and qualitative findings. The model includes factors internal and external to the subsidiary that affect the relationship between organisational culture and innovation. This model represents the main theoretical contribution of this study and sheds light on the importance of an innovation-supportive culture in subsidiaries whilst also illustrating the complexities involved.

Additionally, the present study yielded valuable results owing to the mixed methods research design. By combining quantitative and qualitative approaches (Creswell, 2009; Teddlie and Tashakkori, 2009), this study sheds new light on the construct of innovation-supportive culture in multinational subsidiaries. Firstly, the predictive power of selected organisational culture dimensions affecting innovation at the subsidiary level was identified. Secondly, participants' views of dimensions of an innovation-supportive organisational culture as well as influences on the relationship between organisational culture and innovation were explored. The set of factors that was gathered by combining qualitative and quantitative methods was more comprehensive and reached a deeper level of culture than either approach on its own would likely have achieved. A mixed-methods approach can therefore be an appropriate tool to determine and discover the diverse interrelations and dynamics of an innovation-supportive culture in a subsidiary.

**Implications for practice**

This research has several practical applications. Firstly, it highlights the importance of an innovation-supportive culture in subsidiaries in the Irish ICT sector. An understanding of this concept is valuable to subsidiary managers contemplating how to support innovation. Secondly, knowing the predictive power of selected organisational culture dimensions to innovation as well as understanding the contextual factors involved may help subsidiary managers in developing processes to enhance innovation. Thirdly, understanding the fact that the effects of the five organisational culture dimensions differ for the four forms of innovation may assist subsidiary managers with supporting specific forms of innovation. Fourthly, subsidiary managers can utilise the questionnaire employed in this study to measure the existing innovation culture in the organisation. Fifthly, the construct can be used for evaluation purposes. An organisation's initial level of innovation-supportive culture could be measured and its efforts to improve its culture could then be tracked. Finally, the multidimensional construct could be used diagnostically. For example, if an organisation scores poorly on the risk-taking dimension, further investigation may uncover specific areas for improvement. Or if a business unit or team scores well on a defined dimension, efforts could be mapped, replicated, and introduced to other business units or teams in the organisation.

## Directions for future research

This study adds to a growing body of research on entrepreneurial subsidiaries (see Boojihawon et al., 2007; Dimitratos et al., 2009) and points to some interesting insights into the relationship between organisational culture and innovation at the subsidiary level. A future study conducted at both corporate and subsidiary level could help establish whether differences exist between the innovation-supportive culture at headquarters and at the subsidiary level. The results of this line of research may provide additional evidence to suggest whether structural or power concerns in the MNC have a dampening effect on the organisational culture. The scope of this study was limited to IDA client companies. Further research should be carried out to establish whether the effects found in this population would differ substantially from the wider MNC subsidiary population in Ireland.

This study has been undertaken in the Irish context. Different national settings may be host to different types of subsidiaries. Depending on the strategic importance of the host country, subsidiaries may take on a different role in the MNC network. Future research replicating this study across numerous sectors, instead of limiting it to the ICT sector, would be useful. This would allow establishing potential differences between sectors.

This study's findings demonstrate that carrying out further empirical work in relation to innovation-supportive culture in subsidiaries can help advance our understanding of this phenomenon as well as the contextual factors that affect it.

The present study has shown the richness of data that can be gathered using a mixed-methods approach and as such could serve as an example as to the advantages of adopting a mixed-methods approach for innovation research (as advocated by Anderson et al., 2004) as well as organisational culture research (as recommended by Yauch and Steudel, 2003). This study could, therefore, form a basis for further research in these areas.

## References

Ahmed, P.K. (1998), "Culture and Climate for Innovation", *European Journal of Innovation Management*, Vol. 1 No. 1, pp. 30–43.

Amabile, T.M., Conti, R., Coon, H., Lazenby, J. and Herron, M. (1996), "Assessing the Work Environment for Creativity", *Academy of Management Journal*, Vol. 39 No. 5, pp. 1154–1184.

Anderson, N., De Dreu, C.K.W. and Nijstad, B.A. (2004), "The routinization of innovation research: a constructively critical review of the state-of-the-science", *Journal of Organizational Behavior*, Vol. 25 No. 2, pp. 147–173.

Angle, H.L. (2000), "Psychology and Organizational Innovation", in Van de Ven, A.H., Angle, H.L. and Poole, M.S. (Eds.), *Research on the Management of Innovation: The Minnesota Studies,* Harper and Row, New York, pp. 135–170.

Birkinshaw, J. (1997), "Entrepreneurship in Multinational Corporations: The Characteristics of Subsidiary Initiatives", *Strategic Management Journal,* Vol. 18 No. 3, pp. 207–229.

Birkinshaw, J., Hood, N. and Jonsson, S. (1998), "Building Firm-Specific Advantages in Multinational Corporations: The Role of Subsidiary Initiative", *Strategic Management Journal,* Vol. 19, pp. 221–241.

Birkinshaw, J., Hood, N. and Young, S. (2005), "Subsidiary entrepreneurship, internal and external competitive forces, and subsidiary performance", *International Business Review,* Vol. 14 No. 2, pp. 227–248.

Boojihawon, D.K., Dimitratos, P. and Young, S. (2007), "Characteristics and influences of multinational subsidiary entrepreneurial culture: The case of the advertising sector", *International Business Review,* Vol. 16 No. 5, pp. 549–572.

Chesbrough, H.W. (2006), *Open Innovation: The New Imperative for Creating and Profiting from Technology,* Harvard Business Press, Boston.

Collings, D.G., Gunnigle, P. and Morley, M.J. (2008), "Between Boston and Berlin: American MNCs and the Shifting Contours of Industrial Relations in Ireland", *International Journal of Human Resource Management,* Vol. 19 No. 2, pp. 242–263.

Cooper, R.G. (1990), "Stage-Gate Systems: A New Tool for Managing New Products", *Business Horizons,* Vol. 33 No. 3, pp. 44–54.

Creswell, J.W. (2009), *Research Design: Qualitative, Quantitative, and Mixed Methods Approaches,* Sage, London.

Crossan, M.M. and Apaydin, M. (2010), "A Multi-Dimensional Framework of Organizational Innovation: A Systematic Review of the Literature", *Journal of Management Studies,* Vol. 47 No. 6, pp. 1154–1191.

Damanpour, F. (1991), "Organizational Innovation: A Meta-Analysis of Effects of Determinants and Moderators", *The Academy of Management Journal,* Vol. 34 No. 3, pp. 555–590.

Department of Jobs, Enterprise and Innovation. (2014), *Policy Statement on Foreign Direct Investment in Ireland.*

Dimitratos, P., Liouka, I., Ross, D. and Young, S. (2009), "The multinational enterprise and subsidiary evolution: Scotland since 1945", *Business History,* Vol. 51 No. 3, pp. 401–425.

Dobni, C.B. (2008), "Measuring innovation culture in organizations: The development of a generalized innovation culture construct using exploratory factor analysis", *European Journal of Innovation Management,* Vol. 11 No. 4, pp. 539–559.

De Dreu, C.K.W. (2006), "When Too Little or Too Much Hurts: Evidence for a Curvilinear Relationship Between Task Conflict and Innovation in Teams", *Journal of Management,* Vol. 32 No. 1, pp. 83–107.

Frost, T.S. (2001), "The Geographic Sources of Foreign Subsidiaries' Innovations", *Strategic Management Journal,* Vol. 22 No. 2, pp. 101–123.

Gunnigle, P., Collings, D.G. and Morley, M. (2005), "Exploring the Dynamics of Industrial Relations in US Multinationals: Evidence from the Republic of Ireland", *Industrial Relations Journal*, Vol. 36 No. 3, pp. 241–256.

Hoegl, M. and Gemuenden, H.G. (2001), "Teamwork Quality and the Success of Innovative Projects: A Theoretical Concept and Empirical Evidence", *Organization Science*, Vol. 12 No. 4, pp. 435–449.

Jassawalla, A.R. and Sashittal, H.C. (2002), "Cultures that support product-innovation processes", *The Academy of Management Executive*, Vol. 16 No. 3, pp. 42–54.

Kanter, R.M. (1984), *The Change Masters*, Allen & Unwin, London.

Kanter, R.M. (1988), "When a Thousand Flowers Bloom: Structural, Collective and Social Conditions for Innovation in Organizations", in Staw, B. and Cummings, L. (Eds.), *Research in Organizational Behavior*, Vol. 10, JAI Press, Greenwich, pp. 169–211.

Keupp, M.M. and Gassmann, O. (2009), "International innovation and strategic initiatives: A research agenda", *Research in International Business and Finance*, Vol. 23 No. 2, pp. 193–205.

Khazanchi, S., Lewis, M.W. and Boyer, K.K. (2007), "Innovation-supportive culture: The impact of organizational values on process innovation", *Journal of Operations Management*, Vol. 25 No. 4, pp. 871–884.

Lind, C.H. and Kang, O.H. (2011), "Subsidiary Entrepreneurship and Headquarters Involvement During Innovation Development: Dual Paths to Subsidiary Performance", in Verbeke, A., Tavares-Lehmann, A.T. and van Tulder, R. (Eds.), *Entrepreneurship in the Global Firm*, Emerald Group Publishing Limited, Bingley, pp. 139–166.

Lumpkin, G.T. and Dess, G.G. (1996), "Clarifying the Entrepreneurial Orientation Construct and Linking It to Performance", *The Academy of Management Review*, Vol. 21 No. 1, pp. 135–172.

Martins, E. and Terblanche, F. (2003), "Building organisational culture that stimulates creativity and innovation", *European Journal of Innovation Management*, Vol. 6 No. 1, pp. 64–74.

Meissner, D. and Kotsemir, M. (2016), "Conceptualizing the innovation process towards the 'active innovation paradigm'—trends and outlook", *Journal of Innovation and Entrepreneurship*, Vol. 5 No. 1, p. 14.

Meissner, J. and Sprenger, M. (2010), "Mixing Methods in Innovation Research: Studying the Process-Culture-Link in Innovation Management", *Forum: Qualitative Social Research*, Vol. 11 No. 3, pp. 1–14.

Nonaka, I. and Takeuchi, H. (1995), *The Knowledge-Creating Company: How Japanese Companies Create the Dynamics of Innovation*, Oxford University Press.

O'Reilly, C., Chatman, J. and Caldwell, D.F. (1991), "People and Organizational Culture: A Profile Comparison Approach to Assessing Person-Organization Fit", *Academy of Management Journal*, Vol. 34 No. 3, pp. 487–516.

van der Panne, G., van Beers, C. and Kleinknecht, A. (2003), "Success and Failure of Innovation: A Literature Review", *International Journal of Innovation Management*, Vol. 7 No. 3, pp. 309–338.

Prajogo, D.I. and McDermott, C.M. (2011), "The relationship between multidimensional organizational culture and performance", *International Journal of Operations & Production Management*, Vol. 31 No. 7, pp. 712–735.

Read, A. (2000), "Determinants of Successful Organisational Innovation: A Review of Current Research", *Journal of Management Practice*, Vol. 3 No. 1, pp. 95–119.

Sackmann, S.A. (1991), "Uncovering Culture in Organizations", *The Journal of Applied Behavioral Science*, Vol. 27 No. 3, pp. 295–317.

Schein, E.H. (2009), *The Corporate Culture Survival Guide*, Jossey-Bass, San Francisco.

Teddlie, C. and Tashakkori, A. (2009), *Foundations of Mixed Methods Research: Integrating Quantitative and Qualitative Approaches in the Social and Behavioural Sciences*, Sage, London.

Tellis, G.J., Prabhu, J.C. and Chandy, R.K. (2009), "Radical Innovation Across Nations: The Preeminence of Corporate Culture", *Journal of Marketing*, Vol. 73 No. 1, pp. 3–23.

Terwiesch, C. and Ulrich, K.T. (2009), *Innovation Tournaments: Creating and Selecting Exceptional Opportunities*, Harvard Business Press, Boston.

Turlea, G., Nepelski, D., de Prato, G., Lindmark, S., de Panizza, A., Picci, L., Desruelle, P., et al. (2010), *The 2010 Report on R&D in ICT in the European Union*, Publications Office of the European Union, Luxembourg.

Venaik, S., Midgley, D.F. and Zeitlin, J. (2005), "Dual paths to performance: the impact of global pressures on MNC subsidiary conduct and performance", *Journal of International Business Studies*, Vol. 36 No. 6, pp. 655–675.

Want, J. (2003), "Corporate Culture - Illuminating the Black Hole", *The Journal of Business Strategy*, Vol. 24 No. 4, pp. 14–21.

Yauch, C. and Steudel, H. (2003), "Complementary Use of Qualitative and Quantitative Cultural Assessment Methods", *Organizational Research Methods*, Vol. 6 No. 4, pp. 465–481.

Chapter 17

# Facilitating university-industry collaboration with a multi-level stakeholder perspective

Ekaterina Albats

*LUT University, Finland*

**Abstract:** University-industry collaboration has been widely acknowledged as a vital source of innovation. Despite a rather long history, a number of barriers in such collaboration remain, and the ways to overcome those stay unexplored. The research field particularly calls for studying the ways to facilitate university-industry collaboration and connect the key stakeholders of the Triple Helix – university, industry, government – and intermediaries, which all have very diverse nature. Applying a blend of such research streams as Institutional Theory, Knowledge-based view of the firm, Human Capital theory, open innovation, Triple Helix model and Stakeholder Theory – as an overarching framework, this study proposes several mechanisms for facilitating university-industry relationships at the various levels of analysis. An abductive approach and a combination of a survey among Europe-based companies, a series of case studies from Europe and the US allow developing a holistic theoretical framework along with multiple theoretical and practical implications.

**Keywords:** university–industry collaboration, stakeholder, multi-level, Triple Helix, innovation, open innovation, human capital, intermediary

## 17.1. Introduction

Collaboration with universities has become a widely recognized source of corporate innovation (Perkmann, Neely and Walsh, 2011). The phenomenon of university-industry collaboration (UIC), though, is very complex; along with many opportunities, it implies multiple challenges. To start unpacking the UIC phenomenon, let's first take a look at its multiple forms (Alexander and Martin, 2013; Galán-Muros and Plewa, 2016).

*First,* universities and companies collaborate in *education*: when universities design and shape a curriculum together with companies and invite business representatives to train their students, also when students are co-trained at the companies or, the other way around, when companies' employees take lifelong learning programs at the universities. This type of collaboration, thus, assures a timely training of human capital to meet the rapidly changing needs of the economic environment (Wilson, 2012) – as successfully achieved e.g. in the case of University Colleges Leuven-Limburg in Belgium (Wilmots *et al.*, 2016) or by the ME310 course program at Stanford University, USA (Stenholm *et al.*, 2018).

*Second*, universities and companies collaborate in *research*: they undertake joint R&D projects and arrange professional motilities between the two. The value of university-originated breakthrough for corporate innovation is recognized for already quite a while (Laursen and Salter, 2006; Perkmann and Walsh, 2007). Among the first documented cases, MIT's research Laboratory of Applied Chemistry, for example, had a research contract with an industrial partner already in 1927 (Kenney, 1987).

*Finally*, university-industry collaboration also takes a form of *valorisation*: when university R&D results are being commercialized – through the means of intellectual property rights (IPR) transfer, academic or student entrepreneurship (D'Este and Patel, 2007; Galán-Muros and Plewa, 2016). Among the world benchmarks in this UIC form are schools that produce the most of startup founders – like Stanford, University of California, Berkeley, MIT in the US (Wolfe, 2018) or the University of Twente in The Netherlands (Feenstra and Hofste, 2016).

Despite its rather long history, multiple success stories and continuous efforts of practitioners, researchers, policymakers and intermediary organizations, university-industry collaboration as a phenomenon still face a number of barriers. Simultaneously, a number of research gaps exist in the scientific body of knowledge on university-industry collaboration (Agrawal, 2001; Galán-Muros and Plewa, 2016). As the phenomenological issues are closely intervened with the related research problems in the university-industry collaboration context (Santoro, 2000), the former ones are introduced first and the later ones follow.

If looking at the university-industry collaboration as a process (Brown and Svenson, 1998; Perkmann, Neely and Walsh, 2011), there is a number of problems in university-industry relations from the stage of its initiation. First, universities and companies are very different by their nature and primary motives: universities are oriented towards scientific advancements and educating students, while companies are organically oriented towards profit-making (Parker, 1992; Siegel *et al.*, 2003). That keeps these diverse types of partners distant from each other. Both universities and companies may often encounter difficulties in finding an appropriate UIC partner and lack awareness of what such partnership could offer. All of that result in a '*connection barrier*' (Galán-Muros and Plewa, 2016). Furthermore, as any type of collaboration, but specifically as a collaboration between very *heterogeneous partners*, university-industry partnerships require funding, demand organizational, and coordination costs. A *lack of funding*, thus, becomes a barrier of university-industry collaboration in itself (Galán-Muros and Plewa, 2016). *Differences in organizational cultures, organizational structures and practices* form additional obstacles in university-industry relations, and thus, limit the probability and potential value of university-industry collaboration for innovation.

Many researchers have studied the abovementioned problems of university-industry collaboration, aiming to shed light on these issues and find ways to facilitate university-industry collaboration. Each study, however, tends to take *a solely single actor' perspective* towards studying university-industry collaboration in a 'Triple Helix' (university-industry-government) setting (Etzkowitz and Leydesdorff, 2000). Particularly, they tend to take either a university' perspective (Miller *et al.*, 2018); a firm' perspective (Laursen and Salter, 2006; Perkmann, Neely and Walsh, 2011) an intermediary' perspective (Howells, 2006; Alexander and Martin, 2013) or a governmental perspective (Rossi and Rosli, 2015).

One may bring in a fair argument in support of a single actor focus in UIC research – it allows clarity as significantly simplifies the research process in comparison with the case when a multi-actor perspective is applied and thus, multiple and quite diverse (Parker, 1992) perspectives should be taken into account. However, in studying such a complex phenomenon as UIC, were exactly multiple and very heterogeneous actors are engaged into inter-organizational relations, application of a multi-stakeholder lens is necessary to grasp a holistic picture towards UIC (Albats, 2018). In this respect, the recent works on university–industry collaboration tend to apply a Stakeholder Theory (Freeman, 1984) increasingly more (Phillips, Freeman and Wicks, 2003; Freeman *et al.*, 2010) to grasp the perspective of heterogeneous stakeholders (Carlos *et al.*, 2015; Mcadam, Miller and Mcadam, 2016). Furthermore, recent research also highlights the importance of a cross-level analysis of inter-organizational relations – from individual, through organizational, inter-organizational towards ecosystem levels (Bogers *et al.*, 2017).

Therefore, the managerial recipes of facilitating university-industry collaboration are scares, and a theoretical framework, which would include a multi-level and a multi-stakeholder perspective for studying a phenomenon of UIC – an engagement of particularly heterogeneous stakeholders – is missing so far (Albats, 2018). Thus, the research question tackled in this chapter is: *How to facilitate university-industry collaboration, taking into account the perspectives of the stakeholders involved in/influencing the collaboration at the multiple levels?*

## 17.2. Background

The phenomenon of university-industry collaboration and consequently the research on this phenomenon has started to develop quite intensively since the introduction of the Bayh-Dole Act in the United States in 1980. Thanks to the Bayh-Dole Act, the US universities and individual researchers received a right to pursue ownership of their inventions developed with federal funding. The Bayh-Dole Act had many follow-up initiatives in other countries, which enabled universities from other regions to retain the intellectual property arising from publically funded research. That, in turn, boosted technology transfer initiatives, increased the number of inventions disclosed, licences issued and royalties generated (Aldridge and Audretsch, 2011). Despite these positive outcomes, the Bayh-Dole Act and similar legislation changes in other countries also stressed the ethical issues of '*academic capitalism*'(Renault, 2006). Nevertheless, the Bayh-Dole Act and acts alike became drivers for university (also students and researchers) patenting and licencing processes and hence, kicked-off the next forty years of intensively developing university-industry collaboration research, where each decade has provided numerous insights to our current understanding of this phenomenon (Grimaldi *et al.*, 2011; Mahdad, 2016). Figure 1 below outlines the key studies on the topic against the timeline of the last forty years (adopted from Mahdad 2016).

**Figure 17.1**: The last forty years of university-industry collaboration research (adopted from Mahdad, 2016) – taking a multi-level stakeholder perspective (Albats, 2018)

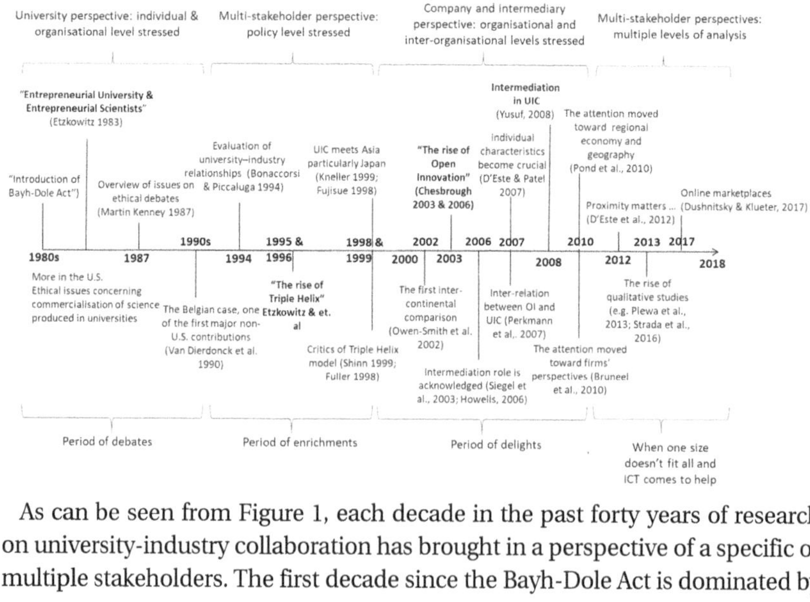


As can be seen from Figure 1, each decade in the past forty years of research on university-industry collaboration has brought in a perspective of a specific or multiple stakeholders. The first decade since the Bayh-Dole Act is dominated by studies, which take a solely *university' perspective* and then study the phenomenon of an *entrepreneurial' university* (Etzkowitz, 1983). Which is natural, as the essence of the university has faced a serious shift. As any academic debate, a discussion on entrepreneurial university soon faces the first criticism on ethical issues behind the concept of an entrepreneurial university (Kenney, 1987). Overall, in the 80s the debate stayed mostly on a perspective of a university and at its organizational level of analysis.

The research during the following decade of the 90s brought in the first non-U.S. focused studies (Van Dierdonck, Debackere and Engelen, 1990), the discussions on evaluating UIC performance and the role of *government* as an orchestrator of university-industry relations. These considerations, in turn, helped to develop a Triple Helix concept (Etzkowitz and Leydesdorff, 1995) – a model of university-industry-government relations. This model became one of the concepts, which started to assist in advancing our understanding of UIC as a multi-stakeholder phenomenon. Despite its wide recognition though, the Triple Helix model inevitably faces some criticism already in the late 90s (Fuller, 1998). Overall, the decade of the 90s enriches the body of knowledge on UIC with a *multi-stakeholder perspective* and highlights the *level of policy-making* in university-industry relationships.

The next decade of the 2000s brings some progress in bridging the UIC research field with other research streams. Particularly, the role of the university as a source of corporate innovation becomes more and more acknowledged and accepted (Laursen and Salter, 2004). That not only boosts the studies of UIC from a *company perspective,* but also bridges the UIC research fields with a newly introduced concept of open innovation (Chesbrough, 2003; Perkmann and Walsh, 2007). Furthermore, the research continuously progresses in analyzing the UIC from various levels of analysis and the role of individual-level characteristics in contrast to organizational level starts to receive particular attention (D'Este and Patel, 2007). The study of Hitt et al. (2007) becomes a particular highlight in bridging multiple level of analysis in the field of human capital – another source of corporate innovation being nurtured at the universities. Additional research 'bridge' from the 2000s was a stream of research on innovation *intermediaries* (university-based and independent Technology Transfer Offices (TTOs), innovation centres, etc.) (Howells, 2006) – another actor in a multi-stakeholder UIC (Yusuf, 2008). Overall, the decade of the 2000s in UIC research, among other contributions, brings the point of view of corporates and intermediaries, while still mainly at organizational or inter-organizational levels.

Finally, the latest decade of UIC research brought some evidence of *one size not fitting all* (Mahdad, 2016). Particularly, the UIC researchers focus has started to go both wider and deeper. The levels of research analysis become more and more diverse from policy and ecosystem levels (Kim, Kim and Yang, 2012; Radziwon, 2017), through inter-organizational and organizational level (D'Este, Guy and Iammarino, 2012) to individual level of *academic engagement* (Perkmann *et al.*, 2013) and micro-level contextual studies (Abreu and Grinevich, 2013; Plewa *et al.*, 2013; Mahdad, 2016). Overall, along with many opportunities opened, the importance of a multi-level stakeholder perspective in UIC research highlighted, the last decade of UIC research has revealed multiple challenges in university-industry relations and consequently, multiple research gaps across different stakeholder perspectives and different levels of analysis (Galán-Muros and Plewa, 2016).

First, from the *university' (academia')* perspective there has been a confusion in the literature in conceptualizing the terms of an '*academic entrepreneur*' and '*entrepreneurial academic*' having their relevance mainly at individual and organizational levels of analysis (Nyeko and Sing, 2015). This gap invites to bridge the constructs of Institutional Theory and The Theory of Entrepreneurship (Wadhwani *et al.*, 2017). Second, from the *company*' perspective and similarly across individual and organizational level there is a lack of knowledge and understanding on what types of human capital is required to establish and run university collaborations as the novel concept of 'open innovation' still 'neglects the human side' (Gassmann, Enkel and Chesbrough, 2010; Hosseini *et al.*, 2017). Furthermore, on the inter-organizational level, there exists a confusion in conceptualizing open innovation, as perceptions of it vary within and between academic and business communities (Gulati, 2007; Vrande and Man, 2011). Third, although the role of intermediation in UIC has been studied, the novel forms of those, particularly digital types of intermediaries remain unstudied in UIC context (Dushnitsky and Klueter, 2017). Finally, while the evaluation of UIC has been studied for long, our understanding of the role of contextual settings and multi-stakeholder perspective in this regard remain limited (Rossi and Rosli, 2015).

## 17.3. Research design

Given a multi-level and multi-stakeholder approach and the focal focus of this research towards a highly context-dependent phenomenon of university-industry collaboration, this research work relies on a complex research design.

First, in terms of the research strategy, this research is following an abductive approach (Bryman and Bell, 2015). The theoretical developments in the field of university-industry collaboration have an established agenda (Perkmann *et al.*, 2013), which is to be used for further theory testing as per the deductive approach. However, as discussed earlier in this chapter, a great variety of issues in the field remain unsolved. A combination of these factors requires constantly balancing between the theoretical developments at the actual phenomenon and simultaneously grasping the perceptions from multiple participants of the UIC process.

**Table 17.1**: Overview of the research methods used for the study

| *Research sub-goals: 'To…'* | *Research method* | *Data Sources & Data Collection Technique(s)* | *Data Analysis* |
|---|---|---|---|
| Systematically review literature on academic entrepreneurs and entrepreneurial academics, identify the key patterns and research gaps | Systematic literature review | Peer-reviewed articles published over the past 25 years in 17 journals leading in the fields of higher education, entrepreneurship and innovation. 5-stage process: key words search, journal search, scanning and selecting, data extraction according to proforma developed, papers analysis. | Open coding and template analysis |
| Identify components of company's human capital required for university collaboration. | Survey &10 case studies | Secondary data: managers' profiles, information on companies' collaborative activities from companies' websites and online press releases. | Quantitative: analysis of means<br>Qualitative: Open coding and member check technique |
| Compare business and academic perspective towards open innovation concept | Survey | Primary data: Survey of over 500 Europe-based companies; 11 interviews with company managers responsible for university collaborations | Binary logistic regression |
| Identify novel forms, role and functions of online intermediation platforms in UIC | 5 case studies & participant observation | Survey of 251 European companies | Open coding and member check technique |
| Identify the common & context-specific UIC KPIs | 3 case studies | Secondary data: press releases, websites and platform users' public feedback on 15 UIC online platforms | Interpretative content analysis and member check technique |

Source: Albats, 2018

Second, given the multiple research gaps spotted across different stakeholders and levels of analysis, this chapter is based on research, which combines several research methods. To set up a robust theoretical ground, the research started with a systematic literature review. Following the goals of validating the current theory developments against the business practices and solving the issue of conceptual ambiguity around open innovation – compare and analyse the differences in academia and industry perceptions – a survey strategy was utilized. Survey strategy is particularly helpful in studying multi-stakeholder phenomena as it assists in "*gathering comparable information across a wide range of different social groups*" (Aldridge and Levine, 2001, p. 28). To achieve the required context richness in studying human capital required for UIC, emerging forms of digital intermediaries and context-specific forms of UIC assessment, a multiple case study was chosen as a research method. The main benefit of multiple case study as a research strategy is that it provides in-depth information on the topic and supplies the researcher with individuals' perspectives in various contexts – which is necessary for studying a multi-stakeholder phenomenon of UIC. A multiple case study method also enables cross-case and cross-context comparison (Yin, 2011).

Finally, aiming for high validity, trustworthiness, reliability and strong evidence, two kinds of triangulation (Bryman and Bell, 2015) were applied. Triangulation of the data sources and methods is reflected in combining primary sources (survey; interviews; participant observation) and secondary sources as well as quantitative and qualitative data collection and analysis techniques respectively – see Table 1. Theory triangulation implies using several theoretical perspectives to interpret the data (Patton, 2002). This study combines the lenses of the Institutional Theory, Knowledge-based view of the firm and open innovation concept, Triple-to-Quintuple Helixes and Human Capital Theory towards studying the phenomenon of UIC through the overarching prism of Stakeholder Theory.

## 17.4. Conclusion

Application of a Stakeholder Theory (Freeman, 1984) towards studying UIC enables consideration of each of the key heterogeneous actors in UIC – their values, believes, priorities, problems, approaches towards collaboration process and its assessment. Considerations of first, each of the stakeholder alone and then, comparison of their perceptions assisted in identifying the ways to facilitate UIC. Particularly, the facilitation strategies proposed further would require efforts from each of the stakeholders, but given the stakeholder approach applied, those strategies would be compatible with the needs and priorities of each of the stakeholders and are supposed to assist in bridging the polar views of stakeholders in UIC (Parker, 1992).

**University perspective**

From a *university management perspective*, if a certain university' management team aims to facilitate UIC, they would need to:

- acknowledge the diversity among research staff in their industry engagement channels and motivations;
- develop the incentives, time management and performance evaluation systems, which would acknowledge less formal knowledge transfer channels used by the research staff in industry engagements as well as the impact achieved;
- support the emergence of (or purposively hire) the role model individuals of two types. First, the *entrepreneurial academic – "adopts an entrepreneurial outlook and who readily seeks engagement with industrial partners, often through the less formal modes of engagement, to further their research objectives").* And second, *academic entrepreneur – "undertakes technology commercialisation, using formal modes of engagement, that capitalise on specific market opportunities")* (Alexander, Miller and Fielding, 2015; Miller *et al.*, 2018, p. 8).

This strategy according to the research findings is supposed to support a portfolio principle in developing the university human capital for industry engagements and contribute the transformation of the traditional education and research institution towards an entrepreneurial university (Albats, 2018; Miller *et al.*, 2018).

**Industry perspective**

From the companies' perspective, the research results suggest that company human capital appear one of the most vital assets in managing university relations. Thus, development of the specific components of the company human capital (either in a single manager, in a team or across the organization) required for university collaboration becomes itself a mechanism to facilitate the existing university relationships and encourage the future ones to emerge. Those components of the human capital required specifically for university relationships constitute five dimensions: skills, abilities, knowledge, experience and personal characteristics. Furthermore, most of the required characteristics bring the biggest value when those are acquired through the individual' experience rather than through studying as due to the gaps in the perceptions. University collaboration may require even more inter-personal attrition than in any company-to-company relationships (Albats, Bogers and Podmetina, 2016; Albats, 2018).

## Comparing university and industry perspectives

When comparing university (academia) and industry (business) perceptions towards open innovation concept, used widely by management scholars to study exactly the company external relationships for innovation, a significant mismatch has been identified (Albats, 2018; Teplov, Albats and Podmetina, 2018). This issue calls for careful considerations from the side of theory developers when disseminating the theoretical implications and constructs towards the business community. From the side of management researchers, it also requires continuous validation of their research results with the studied groups. The way to minimize the conceptual ambiguities and advance the common language building between academia and business communities is to organize and take part in the joint thematic events (e.g. conferences, seminars, workshops, joint teaching and supervision).

## Intermediary perspective

The research results indicate a growing demand for online intermediation (Albats, Fiegenbaum and Alexander, 2016). However, although the usage of online intermediaries in the company-to-company relationships appears a globally recognized phenomenon, in the company-to-university context, these tools remain simply less known (Dushnitsky and Klueter, 2017) although provide a great value in addressing information asymmetries and solving the connection problem of UIC (Galán-Muros and Plewa, 2016). The way to enhance online facilitation of UIC would be efforts towards disseminating such type of instruments on organizational, industrial and policy levels as a secure and efficient connector, knowledge (IPR) transfer tool or education supporter.

Finally, in facilitating UIC evaluation of UIC success from the multi-stakeholder perspective (university, industry, government, society) at the inter-organizational level is particularly necessary (Albats, 2018; Albats, Fiegenbaum and Cunningham, 2018). Here two aspects appear particularly important. First, the collaborations need to be carefully monitored by all the stakeholders beyond solely outputs of collaboration – from the initiation stage across the entire process towards outputs and impacts (Albats, Fiegenbaum and Cunningham, 2018). Furthermore, as contextual settings significantly change the importance of particular assessment metrics, the evaluation system is required to be adaptable to these contextual settings – involve expert evaluations whenever relevant, provide freedom in picking the relevant metrics and suggesting additional ones (Albats, 2018; Albats, Fiegenbaum and Cunningham, 2018).

## 17.5. Implications and future research

### Implications

This chapter has several implications for researchers, practitioners and policymakers.

For the researchers, this work, first of all, confirms the importance of a multiple stakeholder perspective and particularly the application of Stakeholder Theory principles towards studying university-industry collaboration phenomenon. The limits of a classical Stakeholder Theory have been acknowledged (Freeman, 2010), while the advanced applications of it in the context of university-industry collaboration took their start just recently (Mcadam *et al.*, 2012), and this research has demonstrated the limitations of a single-stakeholder approach. Second, this work contributes to clarifying the concepts of *entrepreneurial academic, academic entrepreneur* (Miller *et al.*, 2018) and *open innovation* (Teplov, Albats and Podmetina, 2018). That assists in bridging the gap between management research (academia) and real business life problems (business) (Gulati, 2007; Vrande and Man, 2011). Finally, while applying various theoretical lenses (open innovation, Human Capital Theory, Economic Theory of Intermediation, Triple, Quadruple and Quintuple Helixes) – this work affirms the existence of persistent barriers between academia and industry (Galán-Muros and Plewa, 2016) on several levels – individual, organizational, institutional and inter-organizational. Following the Stakeholder Theory principles (Freeman, 1984; Freeman *et al.*, 2010), this study offers a holistic – multi-stakeholder, multi-level and theoretically-rich – framework for further studying of the X-Helix collaborative relationships and networks across stakeholders perspectives and across multiple levels of analysis (Figure 2). The proposed framework invites scholars to debates and further advancement of university-industry collaboration research.

Second, for companies' managers, one of the key messages is that collaboration with universities has become vital for company competitiveness. However, the research results suggest that experience of collaboration with the university may appear dramatically different compared with other innovation partners (e.g. clients or suppliers), due to the differences in the basic rationale, goals and operational processes applied by business and universities. One of the key enablers of a rather smooth collaboration with universities is a company human capital (a combination of characteristics along such dimensions as skills, abilities, knowledge, experience and personality), which is capable to acknowledge these principle differences and assist in bridging the mentalities (Albats, Bogers and Podmetina, 2016; Albats, 2018).

**Figure 17.2**: Framing the theoretical landscape for studying university-industry collaboration on organizational and inter-organizational levels (Albats, 2018). Concept level – circles; theory level –rectangle & rhombus.

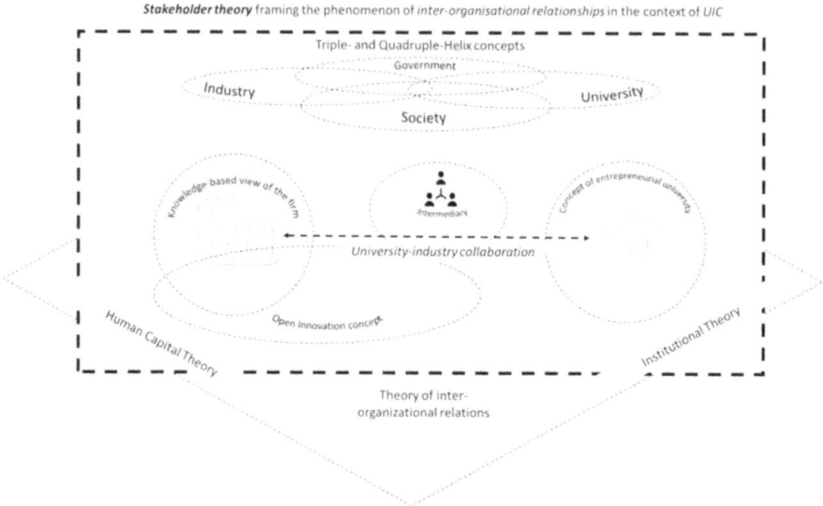


Finally, there is also a few messages for the policymakers. First, in terms of the evaluation of university-industry collaboration there is a need to develop an instrument for collaborating parties evaluations on a systematic base and across the entire process: from partner selection through all the in-process activities towards outputs and impact assessment (Albats, Fiegenbaum and Cunningham, 2018). Provision of such instruments tailored to the needs and perspectives of each of the key stakeholders (universities and companies) would not only enhance the evaluation process per se, but also would assist in stakeholder reflections on their collaborative experience and make the evaluation practice rather proactive than reactive. Furthermore, following the critics shared by Rossi and Rosli (2015), the evaluation system should include the context-specific metrics (depending on the region, sector, type of collaboration, parties' goals, etc.) and a possibility to express case-specific UIC results by each of the collaborating parties. That may not only assist in the current evaluations but also help in the future KPIs development. Lastly, to assist in bridging the mentalities more events joining in universities and companies would need to be developed and organized in a way that parties can come prepared (e.g. using digital match-making instruments) and thus, motivated for engagement and every participant may benefit from the face-to-face interaction.

## Limitations and future research

This research has a number of limitations, and each of those leaves avenues for future research.

First, despite a multi-stakeholder and multi-level approaches being applied, this research carries out the analysis at the particular levels per each of the stakeholders: for university as a stakeholder – at the individual level; for company and intermediary – at the organizational level; and only for the UIC evaluation it applies and inter-organizational level of analysis. Thus, a multi-level lens for studying UIC and a cross-level comparison are needed.

Second, although multiple cross-theory bridges have been built, considerations of other relevant theories and strengthening the ties between those are needed. The additional literature streams to bring into such a framework would be, for instance, entrepreneurship literature, strategic management literature, social and relational capital streams, literature on economic intermediation, literature on ethics and policy-making. The links to be built between and across these literature streams would further enhance multi-disciplinary approach towards analyzing UIC and generally developing the management research (Gupta, Tesluk and Taylor, 2007; Bogers *et al.*, 2017).

Finally, in terms of empirical evidence, this thesis is primarily focused towards analysing UIC in Europe as well as benchmarking it with the best practices in the USA – a pioneer in stimulating UIC on a policy level (Bayh-Dole Act of 1980). However, as it was affirmed also by the results of this research – contextual settings appear critically important in studying UIC. Thus, further exploration and analysis of UIC in other regions – best practices, challenges and facilitation mechanisms – is particularly important in building a holistic understanding of the UIC phenomenon and further development of its facilitation mechanisms.

## References

Abreu, M. and Grinevich, V. (2013) 'The nature of academic entrepreneurship in the UK: Widening the focus on entrepreneurial activities', *Research Policy*, 42(2), pp. 408–422. doi: 10.1016/j.respol.2012.10.005.

Agrawal, A. (2001) 'University-to-industry knowledge transfer: literature review and unanswered questions', *International Journal of Management Reviews*, 3(4), pp. 285–302. doi: 10.1111/1468-2370.00069.

Albats, E. (2018) *Facilitating university-industry collaboration with a multilevel stakeholder perspective.* Lappeenranta University of Technology.

Albats, E., Bogers, M. and Podmetina, D. (2016) 'Companies' human capital required for collaboration: toward a focus on university relations', in *university-industry interaction conference.* Amsterdam, pp. 1–25.

Albats, E., Fiegenbaum, I. and Alexander, A. (2016) 'Innovation intermediaries in university-industry collaboration: analysis of the online platforms', in *The XXVII ISPIM Innovation Conference – Blending Tomorrow's Innovation Vintage*. Porto, Portugal.

Albats, E., Fiegenbaum, I. and Cunningham, J. A. (2018) 'A micro level study of university industry collaborative lifecycle key performance indicators', *Journal of Technology Transfer*, 43(2), pp. 389–431. doi: 10.1007/s10961-017-9555-2.

Aldridge, A. and Levine, K. (2001) *Surveying the social world: Principles and practice in survey research*. Edited by A. Bryman. Buckingham, Philadelphia: McGraw-Hill Education.

Aldridge, T. T. and Audretsch, D. (2011) 'The Bayh-Dole Act and scientist entrepreneurship', *Research Policy*. Elsevier B.V., 40(8), pp. 1058–1067. doi: 10.1016/j.respol.2011.04.006.

Alexander, A. T. and Martin, D. P. (2013) 'Intermediaries for open innovation: A competence-based comparison of knowledge transfer offices practices', *Technological Forecasting and Social Change*, 80(1), pp. 38–49. doi: 10.1016/j.techfore.2012.07.013.

Alexander, A. T., Miller, K. and Fielding, S. (2015) 'Open for Business: Universities, Entrepreneurial Academics and Open Innovation', *International Journal of Innovation Management*, 16(6), p. 1540013.

Bogers, M. *et al.* (2017) 'The open innovation research landscape: established perspectives and emerging themes across different levels of analysis', *Industry and Innovation*, 24(1), pp. 8–40. doi: 10.1080/13662716.2016.1240068.

Brown, M. G. and Svenson, R. a. (1998) 'Measuring R & D Productivity', *Research-Technology Management*, 41(6), pp. 30–35.

Bryman, A. and Bell, E. (2015) *Business research methods*. Fourth. New York: Oxford University Press, USA.

Carlos, A. *et al.* (2015) 'Project Stakeholder Management : A Case Study of a Brazilian Science Park', *Journal of technology management & innovation*, 10(1), pp. 39–49.

Chesbrough, H. W. (2003) *Open innovation: the new imperative for creating and profiting from technology*. Harvard Business School Press. Available at: http://ictlogy.net/bibliography/reports/projects.php?idp=2546 (Accessed: 2 July 2017).

D'Este, P., Guy, F. and Iammarino, S. (2012) 'Shaping the formation of university-industry research collaborations: what type of proximity does really matter?', *Journal of Economic Geography*, 13(4), pp. 537–558. doi: 10.1093/jeg/lbs010.

D'Este, P. and Patel, P. (2007) 'University-industry linkages in the UK: What are the factors underlying the variety of interactions with industry?', *Research Policy*, 36(9), pp. 1295–1313. doi: 10.1016/j.respol.2007.05.002.

Van Dierdonck, R., Debackere, K. and Engelen, B. (1990) 'University-industry relationships: How does the Belgian academic community feel about it?', *Research Policy*, 19(6), pp. 551–566. Available at:

http://www.scopus.com/inward/record.url?eid=2-s2.0-0001628143&partnerID=tZOtx3y1.

Dushnitsky, G. and Klueter, T. (2017) 'Which industries are served by online marketplaces for technology?', *Research Policy*. Elsevier B.V., 46(3), pp. 651–666. doi: 10.1016/j.respol.2017.01.011.

Etzkowitz, H. (1983) 'Entrepreneurial Scientists and Entrepreneurial Universities in American Academic Science', *Minerva*, 21(2–3), pp. 198–233.

Etzkowitz, H. and Leydesdorff, L. (1995) 'The Triple Helix University-industry-government relations: A laboratory for knowledge based economic development', *EASST Review*, 14(1), pp. 14–19.

Etzkowitz, H. and Leydesdorff, L. (2000) 'The dynamics of innovation: from National Systems and "Mode 2" to a Triple Helix of university–industry–government relations', *Research Policy*, 29(2), pp. 109–123. doi: 10.1016/S0048-7333(99)00055-4.

Feenstra, J. and Hofste, M. (2016) 'University of Twente: becoming the most entrepreneurial university of the Netherlands', in Meerman, A. and Kliewe, T. (eds) *Good practice seriece 2016. Fostering university-industry relationships, entrepreneurial universities and collaborative innovation.* University-industry innovation network, p. 137.

Freeman, E. R. (1984) *Strategic management: A stakeholder approach*. First edit. Harpercollins College Div.

Freeman, R. E. *et al.* (2010) *Stakeholder Theory: The State of the Art*. Cambridge University Press.

Freeman, R. E. (2010) *Strategic Management: A Stakeholder Approach*. Cambridge University Press (Pitman Series in Business and Public Policy). Available at: https://books.google.fi/books?id=NpmA_qEiOpkC.

Fuller, S. (1998) 'A Myth of the Modes: A Critique of the New Production of Knowledge'. Helsinki: Finnish Society for Science Studies.

Galán-Muros, V. and Plewa, C. (2016) 'What drives and inhibits university-business cooperation in Europe? A comprehensive assessement', *R&D Management*, 46(2), pp. 369–382. doi: 10.1111/radm.12180.

Gassmann, O., Enkel, E. and Chesbrough, H. (2010) 'The future of open innovation', *R&D Management*, pp. 213–221. doi: 10.1111/j.1467-9310.2010.00605.x.

Grimaldi, R. *et al.* (2011) '30 years after Bayh–Dole: Reassessing academic entrepreneurship', *Research Policy*, 40(8), pp. 1045–1057. doi: 10.1016/j.respol.2011.04.005.

Gulati, R. (2007) 'Tent poles, tribalism, and boundary spanning: The rigor-relevance debate in management research.', *Academy of Management Journal*, 50(4), pp. 775–782.

Gupta, A. K., Tesluk, P. E. and Taylor, M. S. (2007) 'Innovation At and Across Multiple Levels of Analysis', *Organization Science*, 18(6), pp. 885–897. doi: 10.1287/orsc.1070.0337.

Hitt, M. A. *et al.* (2007) 'Building theoretical and empirical bridges across levels: Multilevel research in management', *Academy of Management Journal*, 50(6), pp. 1385–1399.

Hosseini, S. *et al.* (2017) 'What does it take to implement open innovation? Towards an integrated capability framework', *Business Process Management Journal*, 23(1), pp. 87–107. doi: 10.1108/BPMJ-03-2016-0066.

Howells, J. (2006) 'Intermediation and the role of intermediaries in innovation', *Research Policy*, 35(5), pp. 715–728. doi: 10.1016/j.respol.2006.03.005.

Kenney, M. (1987) 'The ethical dilemmas of university-industry collaborations', *Journal of Business Ethics*, 6(2), pp. 127–135.

Kim, Y., Kim, W. and Yang, T. (2012) 'The effect of the triple helix system and habitat on regional entrepreneurship: Empirical evidence from the U.S.', *Research Policy*, 41(1), pp. 154–166. doi: 10.1016/j.respol.2011.08.003.

Laursen, K. and Salter, A. (2004) 'Searching high and low: what types of firms use universities as a source of innovation?', *Research Policy*, 33(8), pp. 1201–1215. doi: 10.1016/j.respol.2004.07.004.

Laursen, K. and Salter, A. (2006) 'Open for innovation: The role of openness in explaining innovation performance among U.K. manufacturing firms', *Strategic Management Journal*, 27(2), pp. 131–150. doi: 10.1002/smj.507.

Mahdad, M. (2016) *The Micro-dynamics of University-Industry Collaboration: The case of Telecom Italia Joint Open Labs.* Sant'Anna School of Advanced Studies.

Mcadam, M., Miller, K. and Mcadam, R. (2016) 'Situated regional university incubation: A multi-level stakeholder perspective', *Technovation*. Elsevier, 50–51, pp. 69–78. doi: 10.1016/j.technovation.2015.09.002.

Mcadam, R. *et al.* (2012) 'The development of University Technology Transfer stakeholder relationships at a regional level : Lessons for the future', *Technovation*. Elsevier, 32(1), pp. 57–67. doi: 10.1016/j.technovation.2011.08.001.

Miller, K. *et al.* (2018) 'Entrepreneurial academics and academic entrepreneurs: A systematic literature review', *International Journal of Technology Management*, 77(1–3). doi: 10.1504/IJTM.2018.091710.

Nyeko, K. E. and Sing, N. K. (2015) 'Academic Entrepreneurs and Entrepreneurial Academics: Are They the Same', *International Journal of Social Science and Humanity*, 5(12), pp. 1050–1055. doi: 10.7763/IJSSH.2015.V5.603.

Parker, L. E. (1992) *Industry - university collaboration in developed and developing countries.* Washington, D.C. Available at: http://documents.worldbank.org/curated/en/675261468740666204/Industry-university-collaboration-in-developed-and-developing-countries.

Patton, M. Q. (2002) *Qualitative research and evaluation methods, Qualitative Inquiry.* doi: 10.2307/330063.

Perkmann, M. *et al.* (2013) 'Academic engagement and commercialisation: A review of the literature on university-industry relations', *Research Policy.* Elsevier B.V., 42(2), pp. 423–442. doi: 10.1016/j.respol.2012.09.007.

Perkmann, M., Neely, A. and Walsh, K. (2011) 'How should firms evaluate success in university-industry alliances? A performance measurement system', *R&D Management*, 41(2), pp. 202–216. doi: 10.1111/j.1467-9310.2011.00637.x.

Perkmann, M. and Walsh, K. (2007) 'University–industry relationships and open innovation: Towards a research agenda', *International Journal of Management Reviews*, 9(4), pp. 259–280. doi: 10.1111/j.1468-2370.2007.00225.x.

Phillips, R., Freeman, R. E. and Wicks, A. C. (2003) 'What Stakeholder Theory Is Not', *Business Ethics Quarterly*, 13(4), pp. 479–502. doi: 10.2307/3857968.

Plewa, C. *et al.* (2013) 'The evolution of university–industry linkages—A framework', *Journal of Engineering and Technology Management*. Elsevier B.V., 30(1), pp. 21–44. doi: 10.1016/j.jengtecman.2012.11.005.

Radziwon, A. (2017) *Exploring inter-organizational collaboration for innovation in a regional ecosystem.* University of Southern Denmark.

Renault, C. S. (2006) 'Academic capitalism and university incentives for faculty entrepreneurship', *Journal of Technology Transfer*, 31(2), pp. 227–239.

Rossi, F. and Rosli, A. (2015) 'Indicators of university–industry knowledge transfer performance and their implications for universities: evidence from the United Kingdom', *Studies in Higher Education*, 40(10), pp. 1970–1991. doi: 10.1080/03075079.2014.914914.

Santoro, M. D. (2000) 'Success breeds succes: The linkage between relationship intensity and tangible outcomes in industry-university collaborative ventures', *The Journal of High Technology Management Research*, 11(2), pp. 255–273. doi: 10.1016/S1047-8310(00)00032-8.

Siegel, D. *et al.* (2003) 'Commercial knowledge transfers from universities to firms: improving the effectiveness of university–industry collaboration', *The Journal of High Technology Management Research*, 14(1), pp. 111–133. doi: 10.1016/S1047-8310(03)00007-5.

Stenholm, D. *et al.* (2018) 'Fail Early, Fail Often: Exploring Stanford's Me310 Course As a Basis To Improve Innovation Outpost Efficacy', *INTERNATIONAL DESIGN CONFERENCE*, pp. 2505–2516. doi: doi.org/10.21278/idc.2018.0503.

Teplov, R., Albats, E. and Podmetina, D. (2018) 'What Does Open Innovation Mean? Business Versus Academic Perceptions', *International Journal of Innovation Management*. doi: 10.1142/S1363919619500026.

Vrande, V. Van De and Man, A. De (2011) 'A response to "' Is open innovation a field of study or a communication barrier to theory development ?'"', *Technovation*. Elsevier, 31(4), pp. 185–186. doi: 10.1016/j.technovation.2011.01.002.

Wadhwani, R. D. *et al.* (2017) 'Academic entrepreneurship and institutional change in historical perspective', *Management & Organizational History*. Routledge, 12(3), pp. 175–198. doi: 10.1080/17449359.2017.1359903.

Wilmots, B. *et al.* (2016) 'Improving the relevance of higher education by working with real life cases: the pop-up stories', in Meerman, A. and Kliewe, T. (eds) *Good practice seriece 2016. Fostering university-industry relationships, entrepreneurial universities and collaborative innovation.* University-industry innovation network, p. 137.

Wilson, S. T. (2012) *A Review of Business – University Collaboration.*

Wolfe, S. (2018) *The top 25 colleges that produce the most startup founders, Business Insider.* Available at: https://nordic.businessinsider.com/top-colleges-for-startup-founders-pitchbook-2018-9?r=US&IR=T.

Yin, R. K. (2011) *Applications of case study research.* Sage.

Yusuf, S. (2008) 'Intermediating knowledge exchange between universities and businesses', *Research Policy,* 37(8), pp. 1167–1174. doi: 10.1016/j.respol.2008.04.011.

# Index

## T



## V

www.ingramcontent.com/pod-product-compliance
Lightning Source LLC
LaVergne TN
LVHW010721210926
848485LV00007B/1414/J